THE UNCANNY AVENGERS

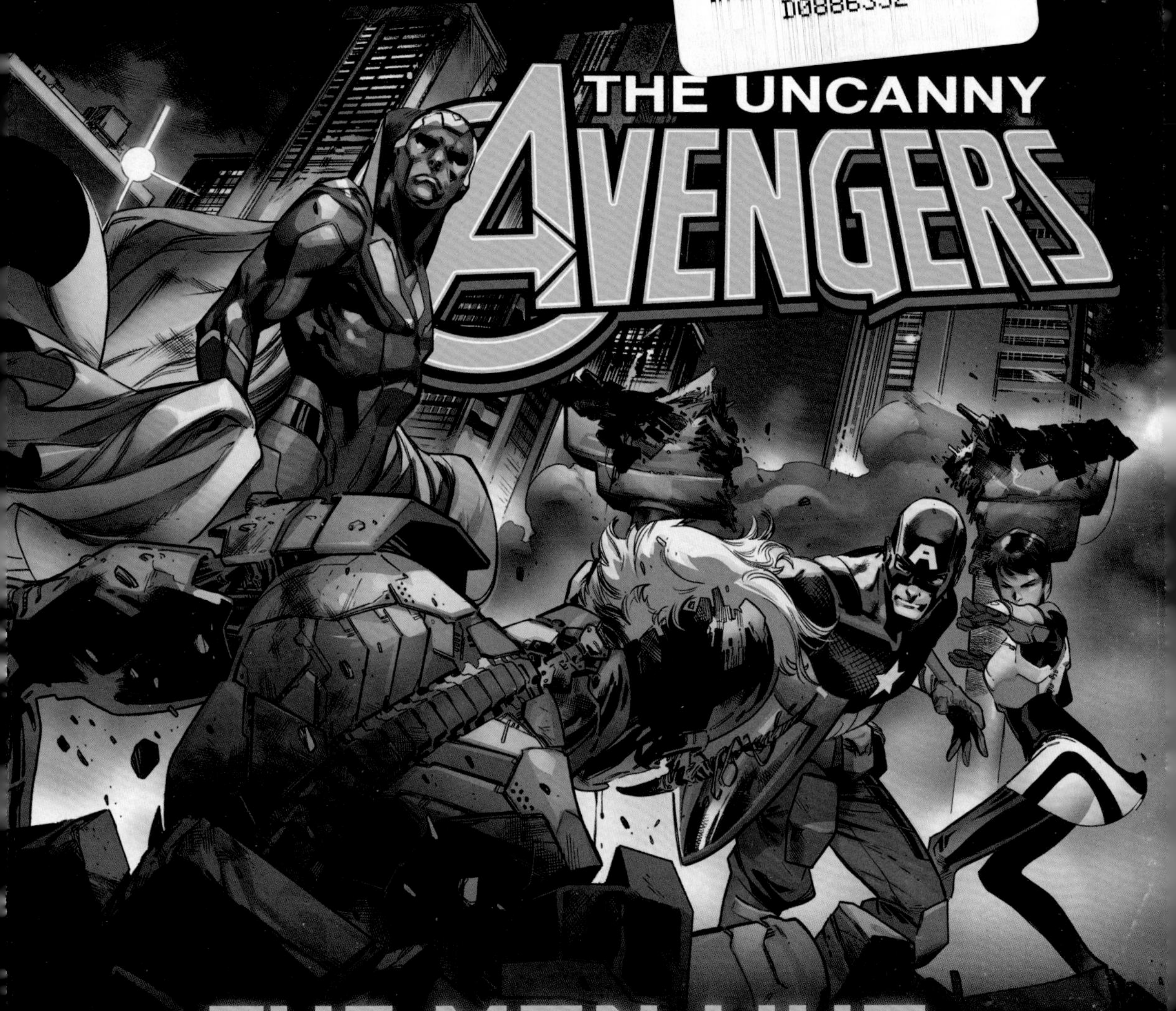

THE MAN WHO FELL TO EARTH

THE UNCANNY AVENGERS
THE MAN WHO FELL TO EARTH

GERRY DUGGAN
WRITER

#7-8

PENCILER: **RYAN STEGMAN**

INKERS: **MARK MORALES, GUILLERMO ORTEGO** &
DAVE MEIKIS WITH **RYAN STEGMAN**

COLORISTS: **RICHARD ISANOVE** WITH **MATT YACKEY**

COVER ART: **RYAN STEGMAN** & **RICHARD ISANOVE**

#9-12

ARTIST: **PEPE LARRAZ**

COLOR ARTIST: **DAVID CURIEL**

COVER ART: **MARK BAGLEY, DREW HENNESSY** & **RICHARD ISANOVE** (#9)
AND **RYAN STEGMAN** & **RICHARD ISANOVE** (#10-12)

VC's **CLAYTON COWLES**
LETTERER

ALANNA SMITH
ASSISTANT EDITOR

TOM BREVOORT WITH
DANIEL KETCHUM
EDITORS

AVENGERS CREATED BY **STAN LEE** & **JACK KIRBY**

COLLECTION EDITOR: **JENNIFER GRÜNWALD**
ASSOCIATE EDITOR: **SARAH BRUNSTAD**
EDITOR, SPECIAL PROJECTS: **MARK D. BEAZLEY**

VP, PRODUCTION & SPECIAL PROJECTS: **JEFF YOUNGQUIST**
SVP PRINT, SALES & MARKETING: **DAVID GABRIEL**
BOOK DESIGNER: **ADAM DEL RE**

EDITOR IN CHIEF: **AXEL ALONSO**
CHIEF CREATIVE OFFICER: **JOE QUESADA**
PUBLISHER: **DAN BUCKLEY**
EXECUTIVE PRODUCER: **ALAN FINE**

UNCANNY AVENGERS: UNITY VOL. 2 — THE MAN WHO FELL TO EARTH. Contains material originally published in magazine form as UNCANNY AVENGERS #7-12. First printing 2016. ISBN# 978-0-7851-9616-7. Published by MARVEL WORLDWIDE, INC., a subsidiary of MARVEL ENTERTAINMENT, LLC. OFFICE OF PUBLICATION: 135 West 50th Street, New York, NY 10020. Copyright © 2016 MARVEL No similarity between any of the names, characters, persons, and/or institutions in this magazine with those of any living or dead person or institution is intended, and any such similarity which may exist is purely coincidental. **Printed in Canada.** ALAN FINE, President, Marvel Entertainment; DAN BUCKLEY, President, TV, Publishing & Brand Management; JOE QUESADA, Chief Creative Officer; TOM BREVOORT, SVP of Publishing; DAVID BOGART, SVP of Business Affairs & Operations, Publishing & Partnership; C.B. CEBULSKI, VP of Brand Management & Development, Asia; DAVID GABRIEL, SVP of Sales & Marketing, Publishing; JEFF YOUNGQUIST, VP of Production & Special Projects; DAN CARR, Executive Director of Publishing Technology; ALEX MORALES, Director of Publishing Operations; SUSAN CRESPI, Production Manager; STAN LEE, Chairman Emeritus. For information regarding advertising in Marvel Comics or on Marvel.com, please contact Vit DeBellis, Integrated Sales Manager, at vdebellis@marvel.com. For Marvel subscription inquiries, please call 888-511-5480. **Manufactured between 7/22/2016 and 8/29/2016 by SOLISCO PRINTERS, SCOTT, QC, CANADA.**

10 9 8 7 6 5 4 3 2 1

TO ENCOURAGE PEACE AFTER THE WAR BETWEEN THE AVENGERS AND THE X-MEN, THE ORIGINAL CAPTAIN AMERICA, STEVE ROGERS, BROUGHT TOGETHER MEMBERS OF BOTH TEAMS TO FORM **THE AVENGERS UNITY SQUAD**. NOW, TO PROMOTE COOPERATION IN THE FACE OF RISING TENSIONS, THE UNITY SQUAD HAS EXPANDED TO INCLUDE A NEW FACTION: INHUMANS.

SIX MONTHS AGO, A MYSTERIOUS HACKER KNOWN AS **THE WHISPERER** LEAKED FILES EXPOSING A TOP SECRET S.H.I.E.L.D. SECURITY PROGRAM, CODENAMED **KOBIK**, WHICH WOULD ALLOW AUTHORITIES TO USE COSMIC CUBE FRAGMENTS TO MAKE CHANGES IN THE FABRIC OF REALITY WITHOUT PUBLIC KNOWLEDGE. AT THE TIME, MARIA HILL CLAIMED THE PROGRAM WAS SHUT DOWN AND THE FRAGMENTS DESTROYED, BUT UNITY SQUAD LEADER STEVE ROGERS RECENTLY LEARNED OTHERWISE...

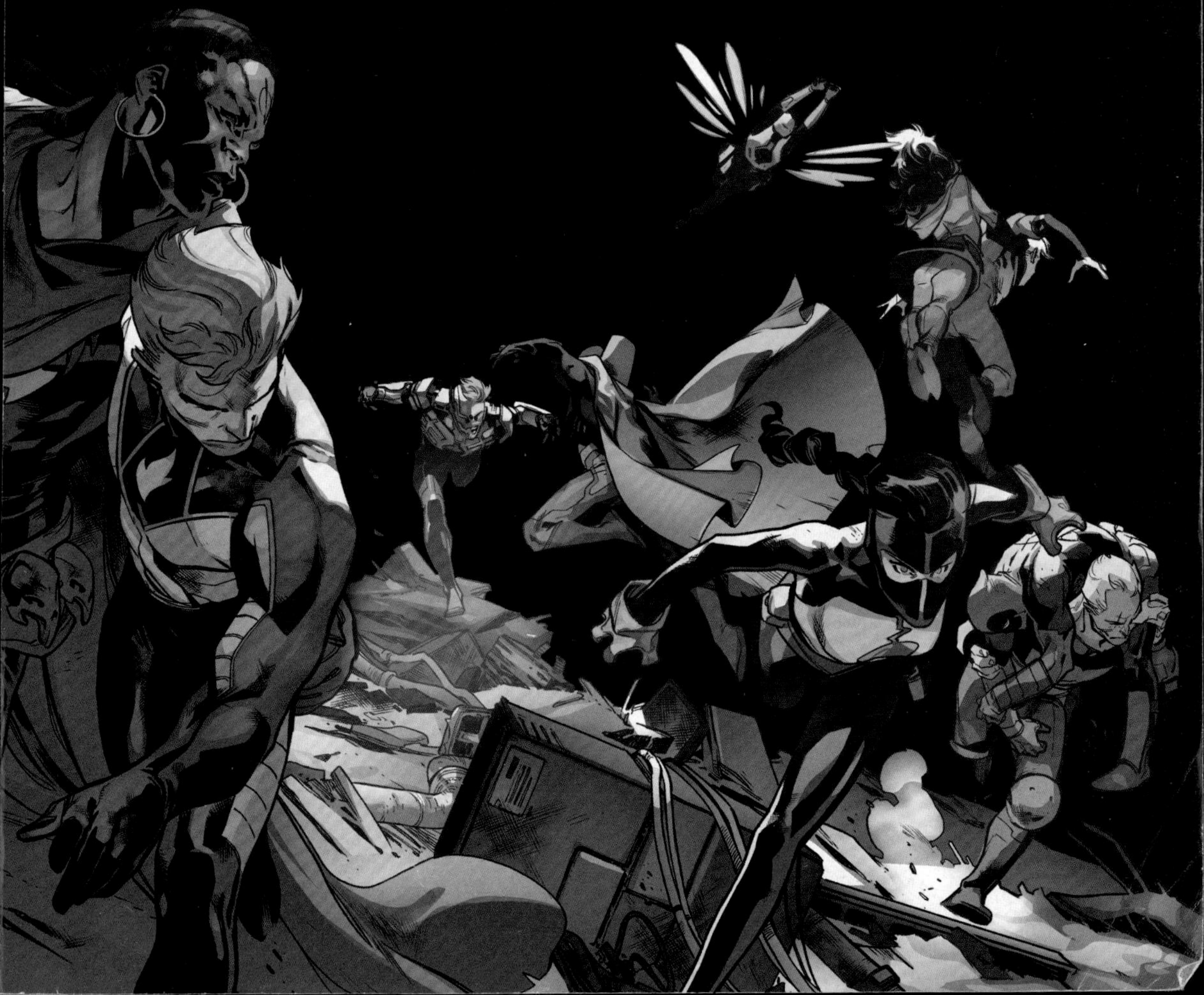

7

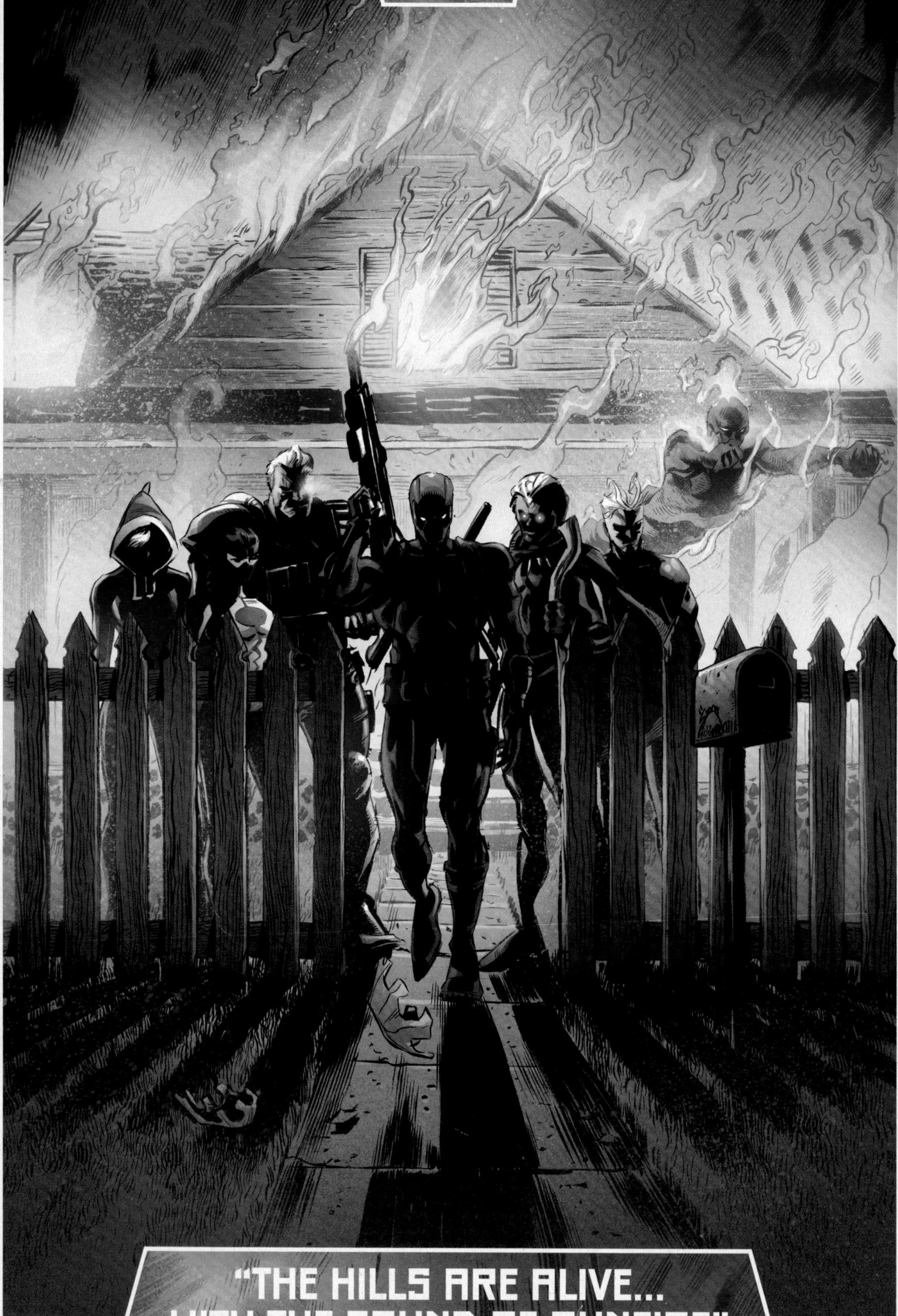

"THE HILLS ARE ALIVE... WITH THE SOUND OF GUNFIRE"

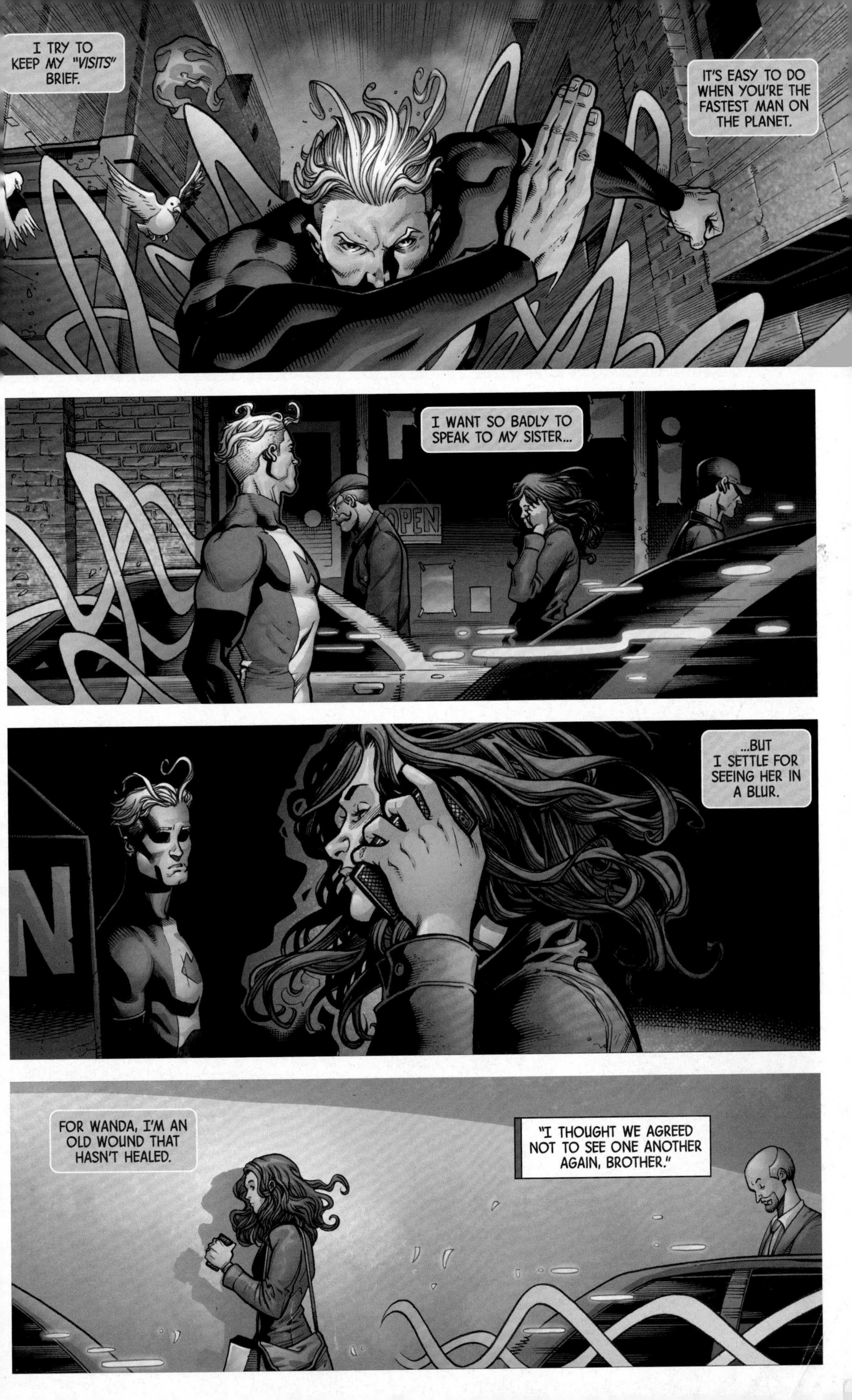

I TRY TO KEEP MY "VISITS" BRIEF.
IT'S EASY TO DO WHEN YOU'RE THE FASTEST MAN ON THE PLANET.
I WANT SO BADLY TO SPEAK TO MY SISTER...
OPEN
...BUT I SETTLE FOR SEEING HER IN A BLUR.
FOR WANDA, I'M AN OLD WOUND THAT HASN'T HEALED.
"I THOUGHT WE AGREED NOT TO SEE ONE ANOTHER AGAIN, BROTHER."

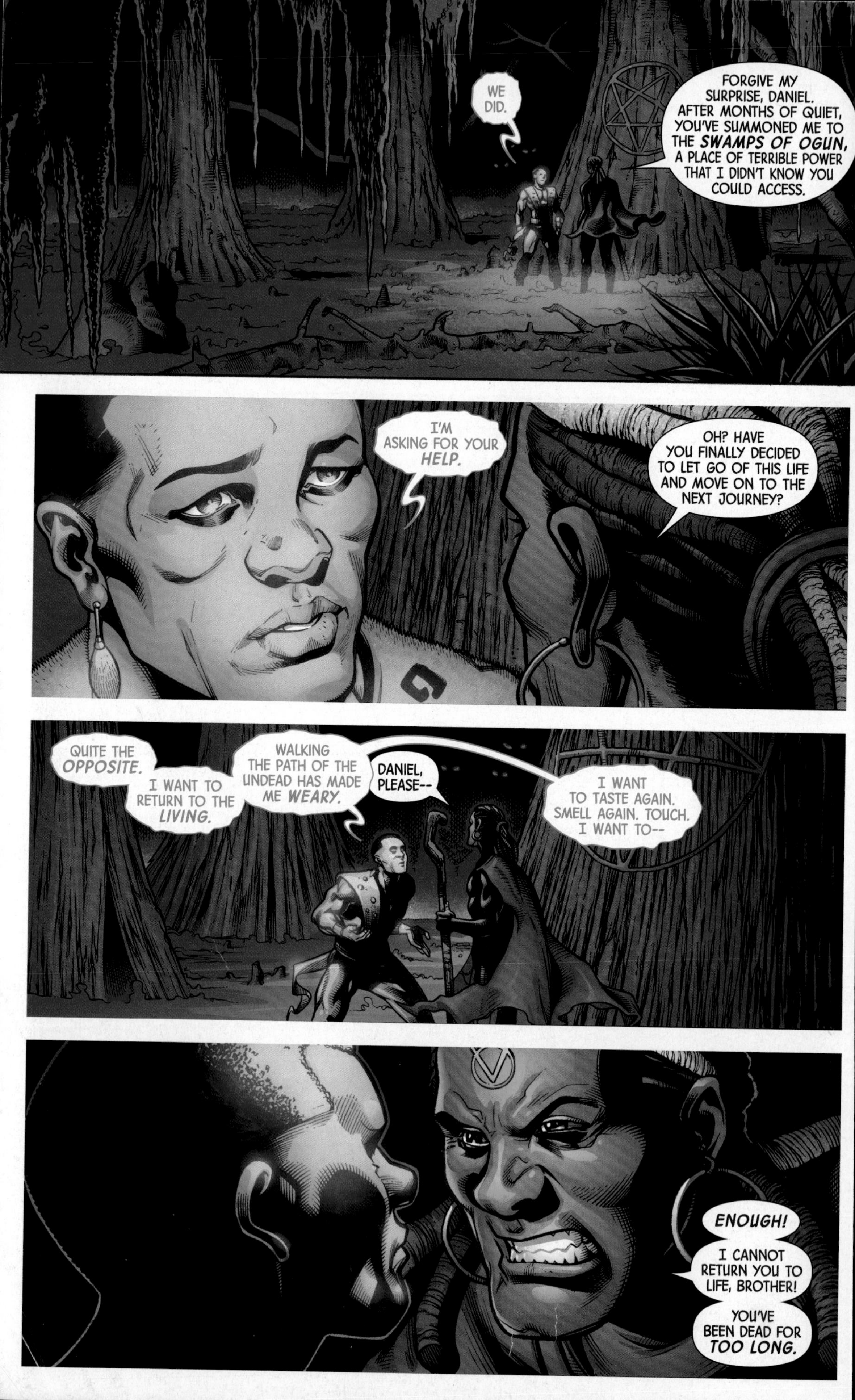

WE DID.
FORGIVE MY SURPRISE, DANIEL. AFTER MONTHS OF QUIET, YOU'VE SUMMONED ME TO THE SWAMPS OF OGUN, A PLACE OF TERRIBLE POWER THAT I DIDN'T KNOW YOU COULD ACCESS.
I'M ASKING FOR YOUR HELP.
OH? HAVE YOU FINALLY DECIDED TO LET GO OF THIS LIFE AND MOVE ON TO THE NEXT JOURNEY?
QUITE THE OPPOSITE.
I WANT TO RETURN TO THE LIVING.
WALKING THE PATH OF THE UNDEAD HAS MADE ME WEARY.
DANIEL, PLEASE--
I WANT TO TASTE AGAIN. SMELL AGAIN. TOUCH. I WANT TO--
ENOUGH!
I CANNOT RETURN YOU TO LIFE, BROTHER!
YOU'VE BEEN DEAD FOR TOO LONG.

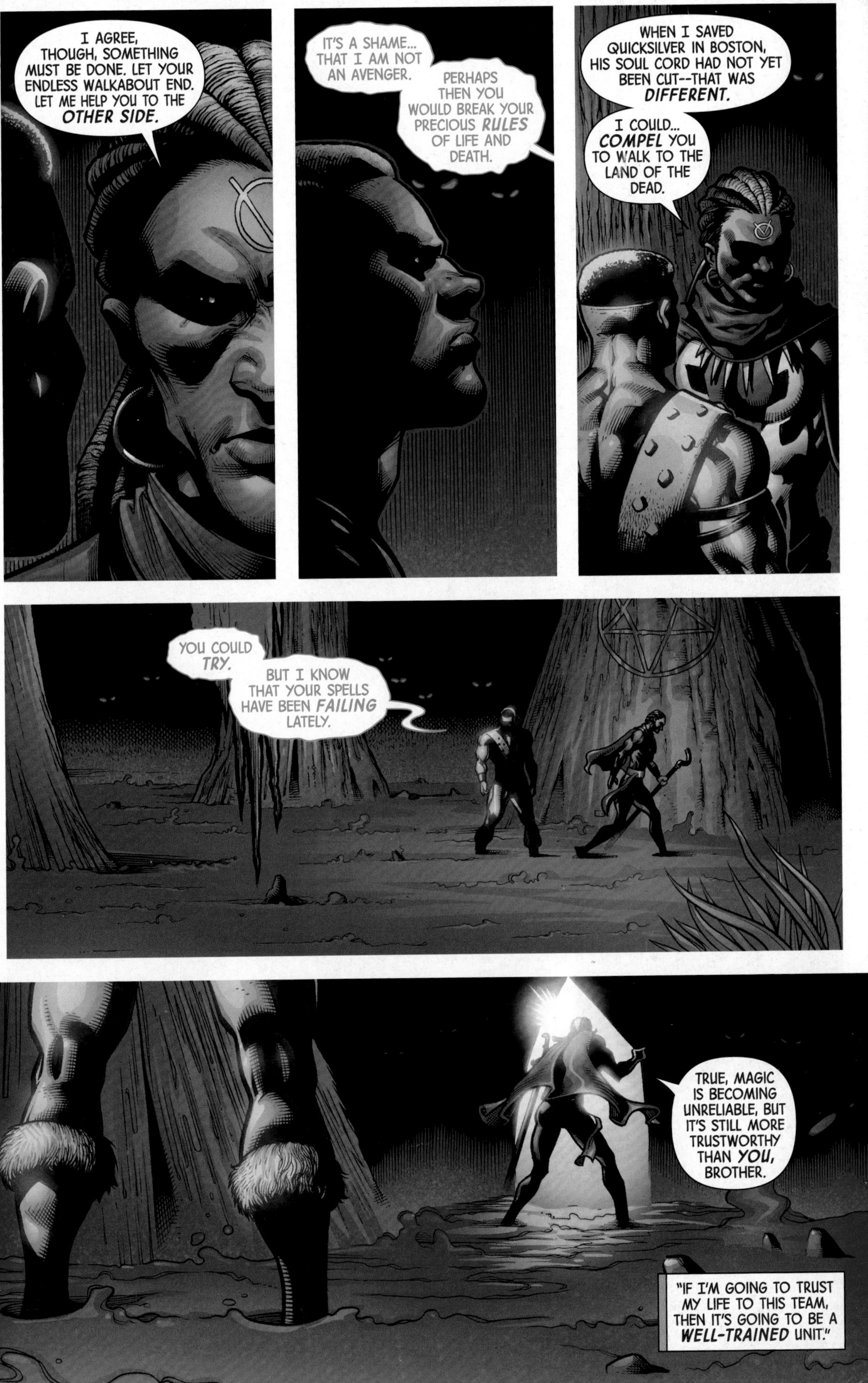
I AGREE, THOUGH, SOMETHING MUST BE DONE. LET YOUR ENDLESS WALKABOUT END. LET ME HELP YOU TO THE OTHER SIDE.
IT'S A SHAME... THAT I AM NOT AN AVENGER.
PERHAPS THEN YOU WOULD BREAK YOUR PRECIOUS RULES OF LIFE AND DEATH.
WHEN I SAVED QUICKSILVER IN BOSTON, HIS SOUL CORD HAD NOT YET BEEN CUT--THAT WAS DIFFERENT.
I COULD... COMPEL YOU TO WALK TO THE LAND OF THE DEAD.
YOU COULD TRY.
BUT I KNOW THAT YOUR SPELLS HAVE BEEN FAILING LATELY.
TRUE, MAGIC IS BECOMING UNRELIABLE, BUT IT'S STILL MORE TRUSTWORTHY THAN YOU, BROTHER.
"IF I'M GOING TO TRUST MY LIFE TO THIS TEAM, THEN IT'S GOING TO BE A WELL-TRAINED UNIT."

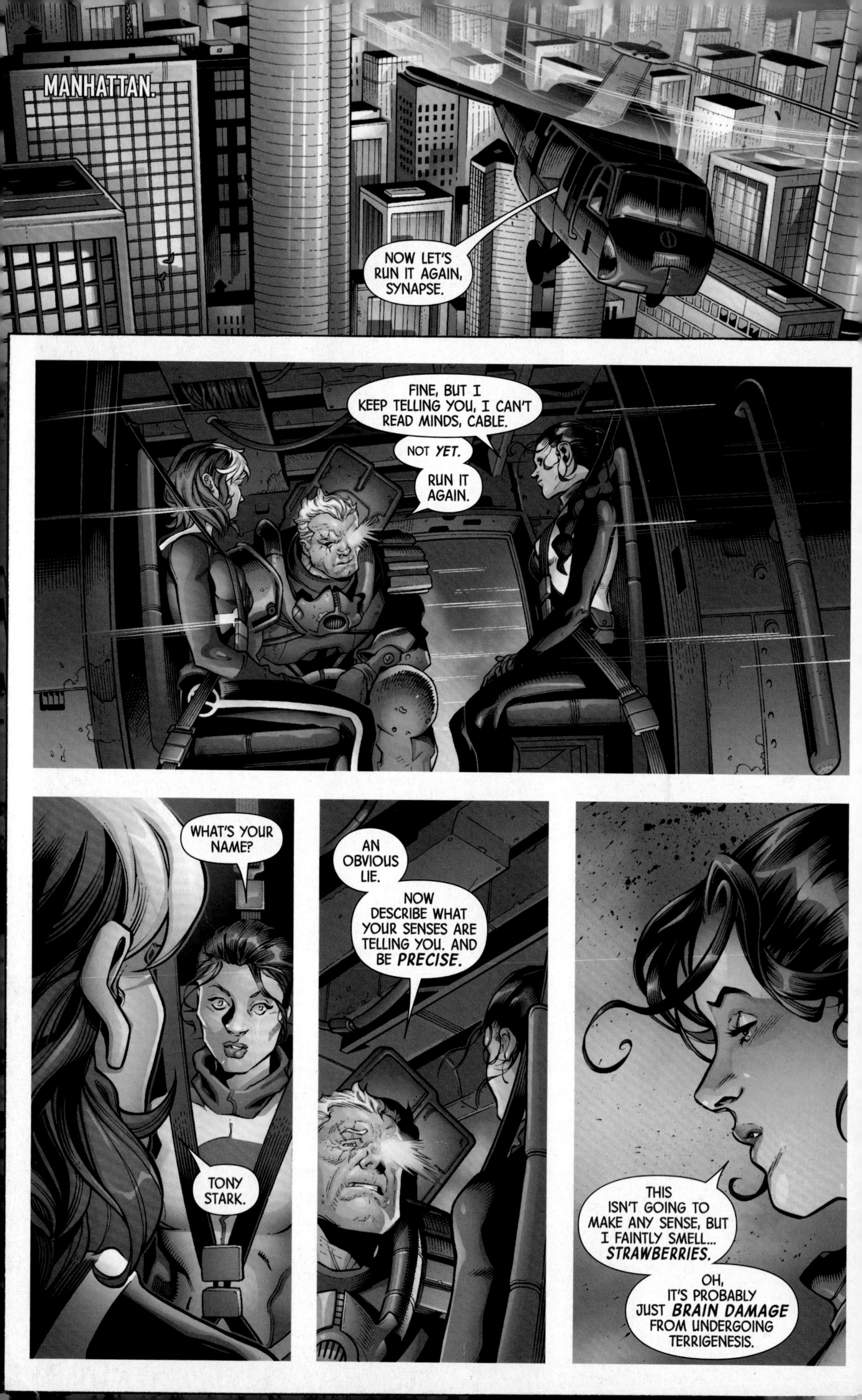
MANHATTAN.
NOW LET'S RUN IT AGAIN, SYNAPSE.
FINE, BUT I KEEP TELLING YOU, I CAN'T READ MINDS, CABLE.
NOT *YET.*
RUN IT AGAIN.
WHAT'S YOUR NAME?
TONY STARK.
AN OBVIOUS LIE.
NOW DESCRIBE WHAT YOUR SENSES ARE TELLING YOU. AND BE *PRECISE.*
THIS ISN'T GOING TO MAKE ANY SENSE, BUT I FAINTLY SMELL... *STRAWBERRIES.*
OH, IT'S PROBABLY JUST *BRAIN DAMAGE* FROM UNDERGOING TERRIGENESIS.

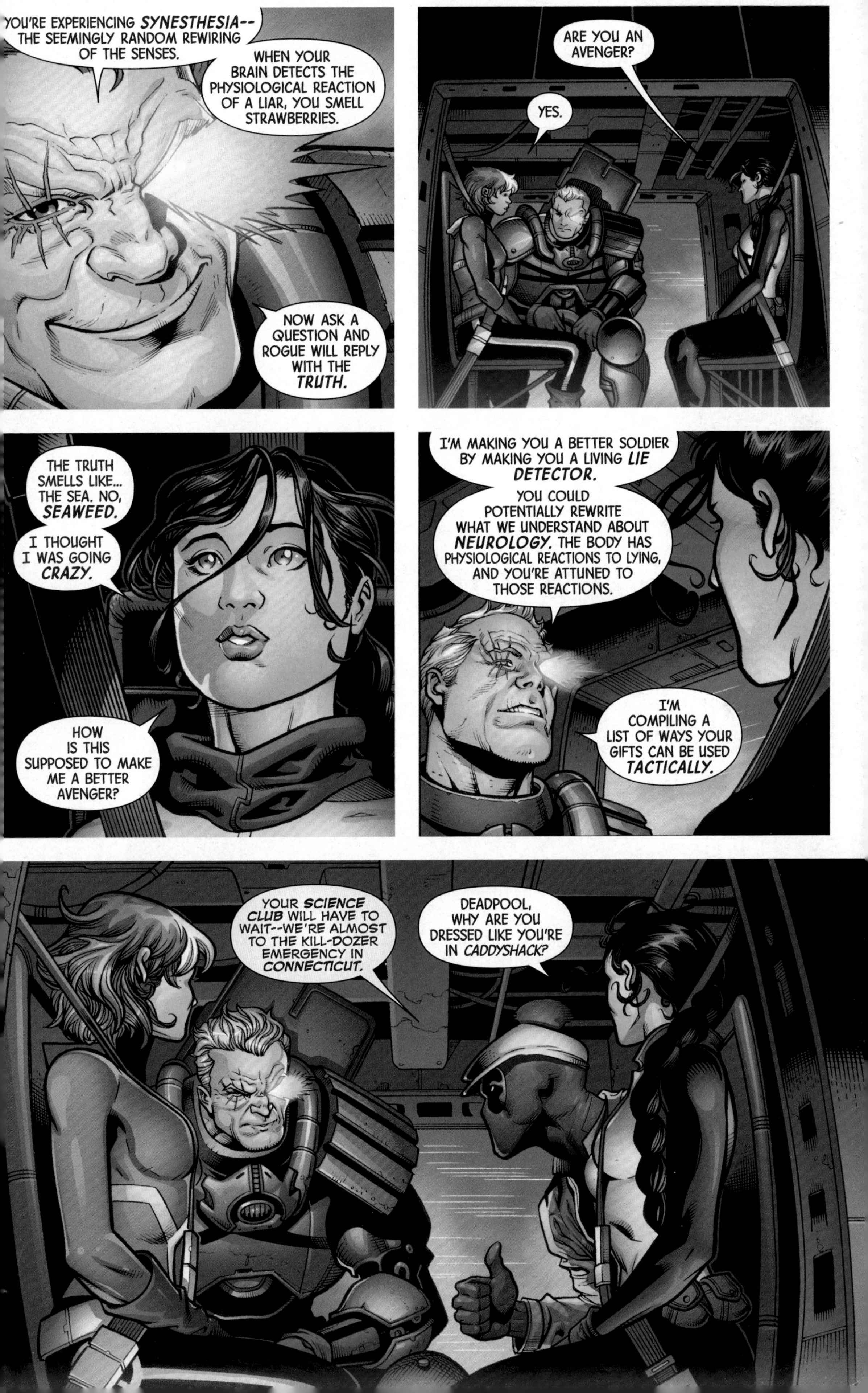
YOU'RE EXPERIENCING SYNESTHESIA-- THE SEEMINGLY RANDOM REWIRING OF THE SENSES.
WHEN YOUR BRAIN DETECTS THE PHYSIOLOGICAL REACTION OF A LIAR, YOU SMELL STRAWBERRIES.
NOW ASK A QUESTION AND ROGUE WILL REPLY WITH THE TRUTH.
ARE YOU AN AVENGER?
YES.
THE TRUTH SMELLS LIKE... THE SEA. NO, SEAWEED.
I THOUGHT I WAS GOING CRAZY.
HOW IS THIS SUPPOSED TO MAKE ME A BETTER AVENGER?
I'M MAKING YOU A BETTER SOLDIER BY MAKING YOU A LIVING LIE DETECTOR.
YOU COULD POTENTIALLY REWRITE WHAT WE UNDERSTAND ABOUT NEUROLOGY. THE BODY HAS PHYSIOLOGICAL REACTIONS TO LYING, AND YOU'RE ATTUNED TO THOSE REACTIONS.
I'M COMPILING A LIST OF WAYS YOUR GIFTS CAN BE USED TACTICALLY.
YOUR SCIENCE CLUB WILL HAVE TO WAIT--WE'RE ALMOST TO THE KILL-DOZER EMERGENCY IN CONNECTICUT.
DEADPOOL, WHY ARE YOU DRESSED LIKE YOU'RE IN CADDYSHACK?

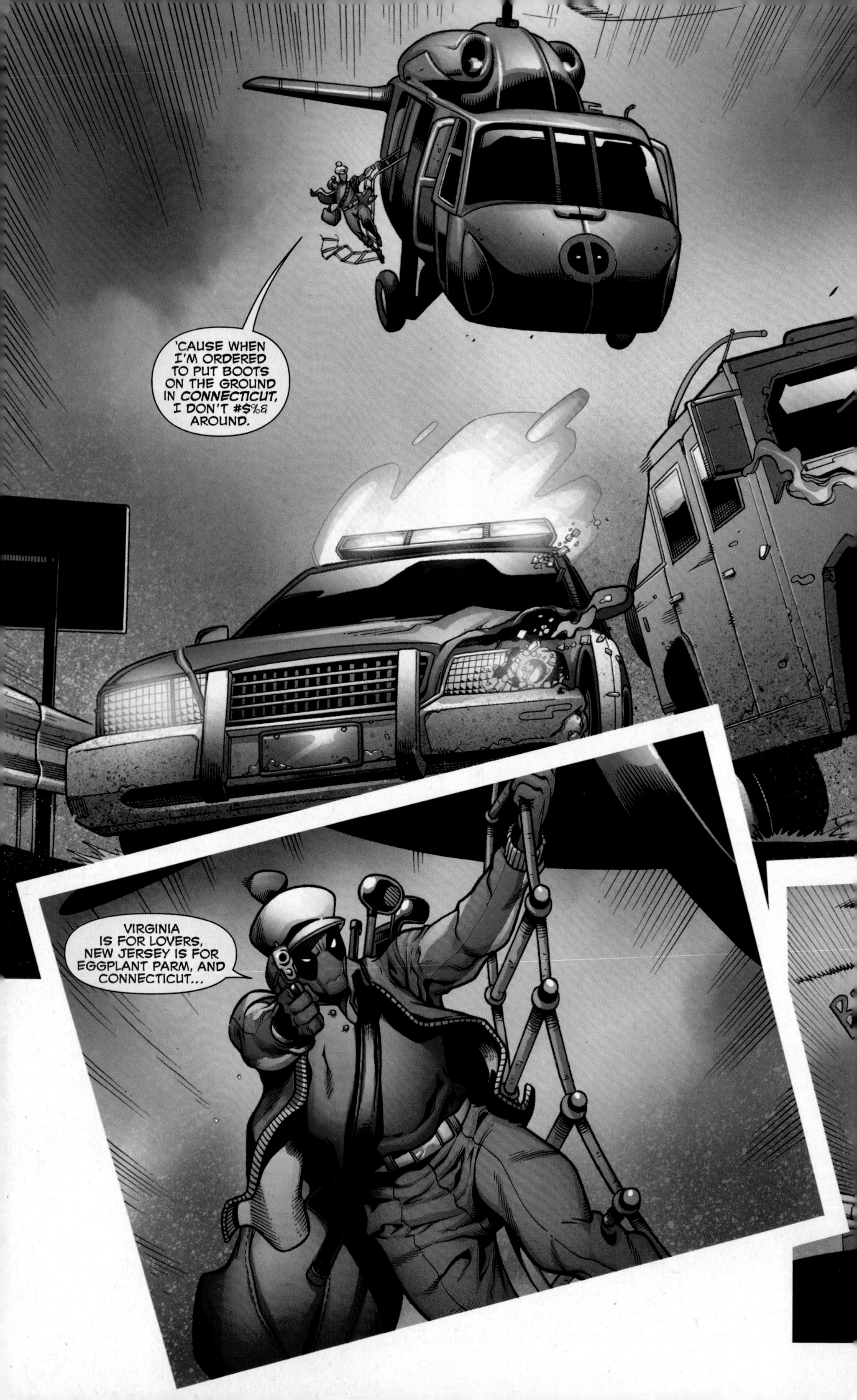
'CAUSE WHEN I'M ORDERED TO PUT BOOTS ON THE GROUND IN CONNECTICUT, I DON'T #$%& AROUND.
VIRGINIA IS FOR LOVERS, NEW JERSEY IS FOR EGGPLANT PARM, AND CONNECTICUT...

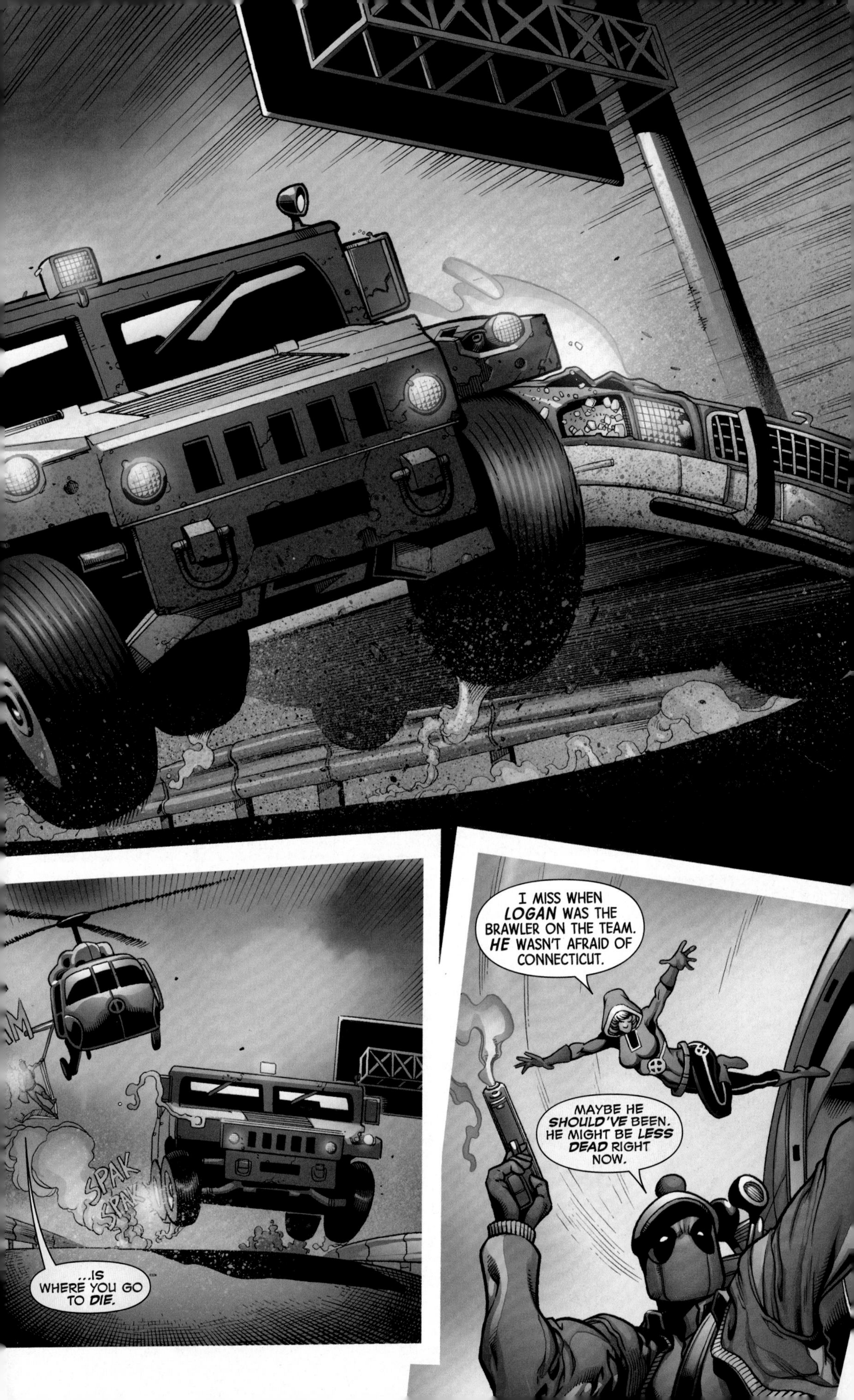
SPAK
SPAK
...IS WHERE YOU GO TO DIE.
I MISS WHEN LOGAN WAS THE BRAWLER ON THE TEAM. HE WASN'T AFRAID OF CONNECTICUT.
MAYBE HE SHOULD'VE BEEN. HE MIGHT BE LESS DEAD RIGHT NOW.

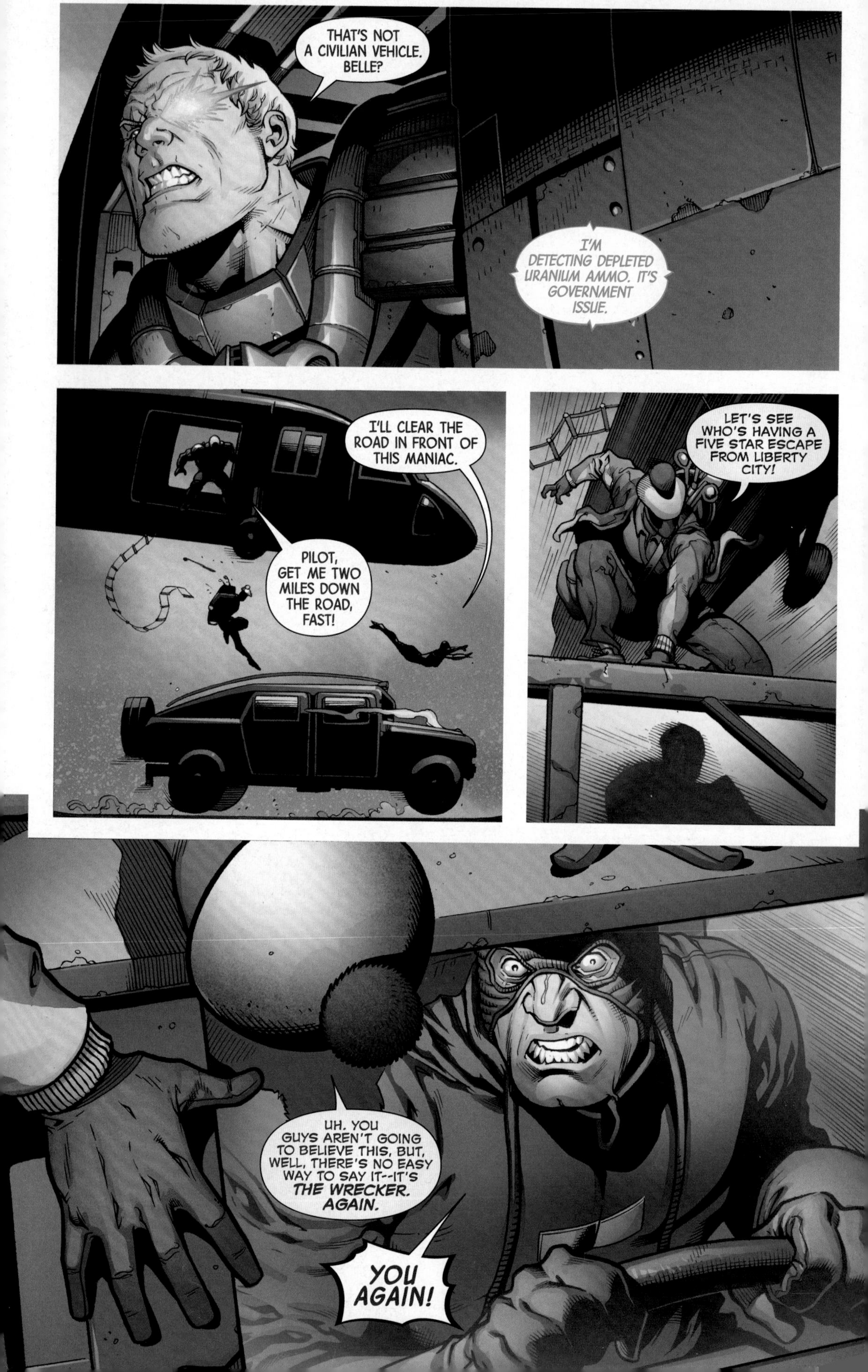
THAT'S NOT A CIVILIAN VEHICLE. BELLE?
I'M DETECTING DEPLETED URANIUM AMMO. IT'S GOVERNMENT ISSUE.
I'LL CLEAR THE ROAD IN FRONT OF THIS MANIAC.
PILOT, GET ME TWO MILES DOWN THE ROAD, FAST!
LET'S SEE WHO'S HAVING A FIVE STAR ESCAPE FROM LIBERTY CITY!
UH. YOU GUYS AREN'T GOING TO BELIEVE THIS, BUT, WELL, THERE'S NO EASY WAY TO SAY IT--IT'S THE WRECKER. AGAIN.
YOU AGAIN!

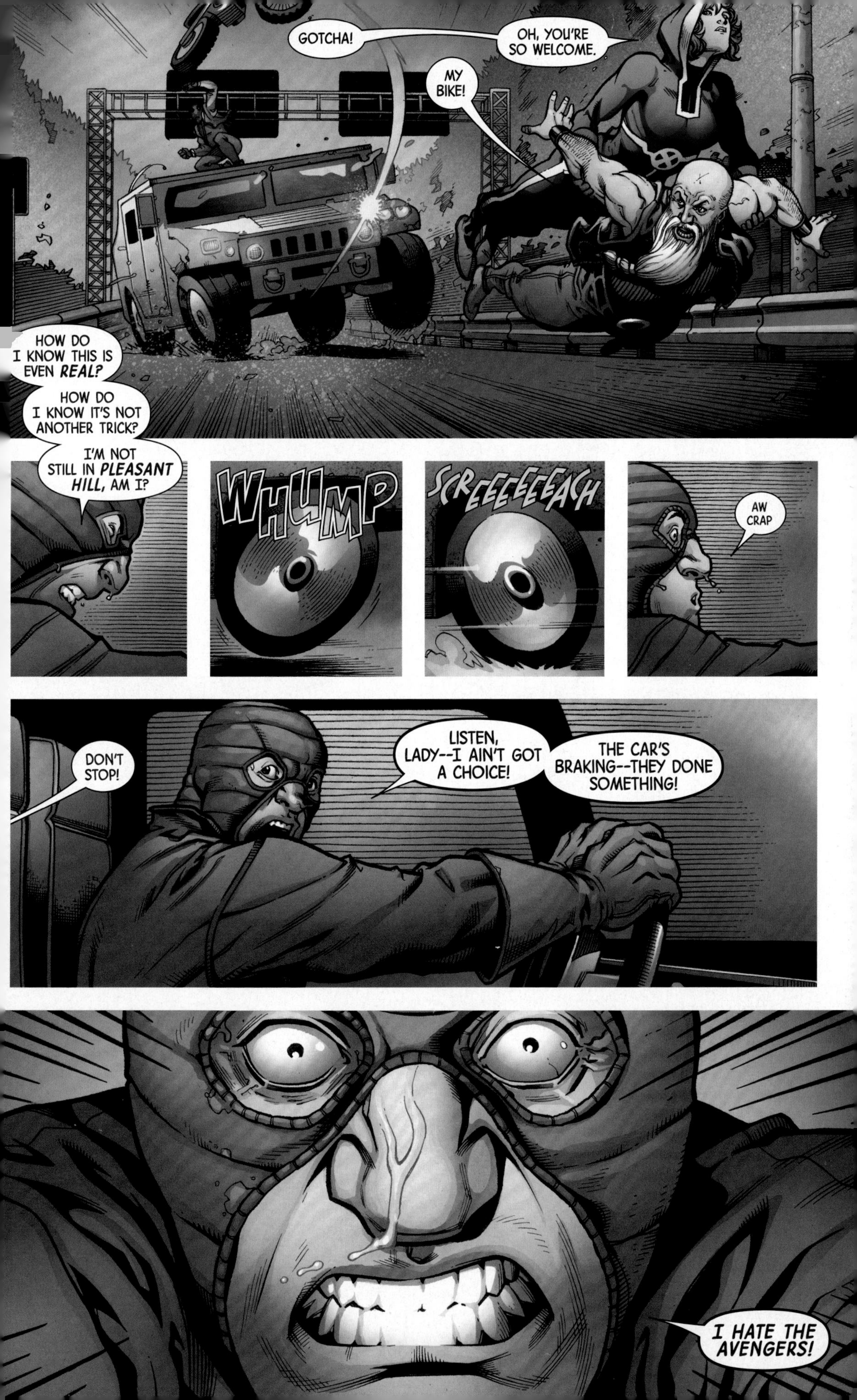
GOTCHA!
OH, YOU'RE SO WELCOME.
MY BIKE!
HOW DO I KNOW THIS IS EVEN REAL?
HOW DO I KNOW IT'S NOT ANOTHER TRICK?
I'M NOT STILL IN PLEASANT HILL, AM I?
WHUMP
SCREEEEEEACH
AW CRAP
DON'T STOP!
LISTEN, LADY--I AIN'T GOT A CHOICE!
THE CAR'S BRAKING--THEY DONE SOMETHING!
I HATE THE AVENGERS!

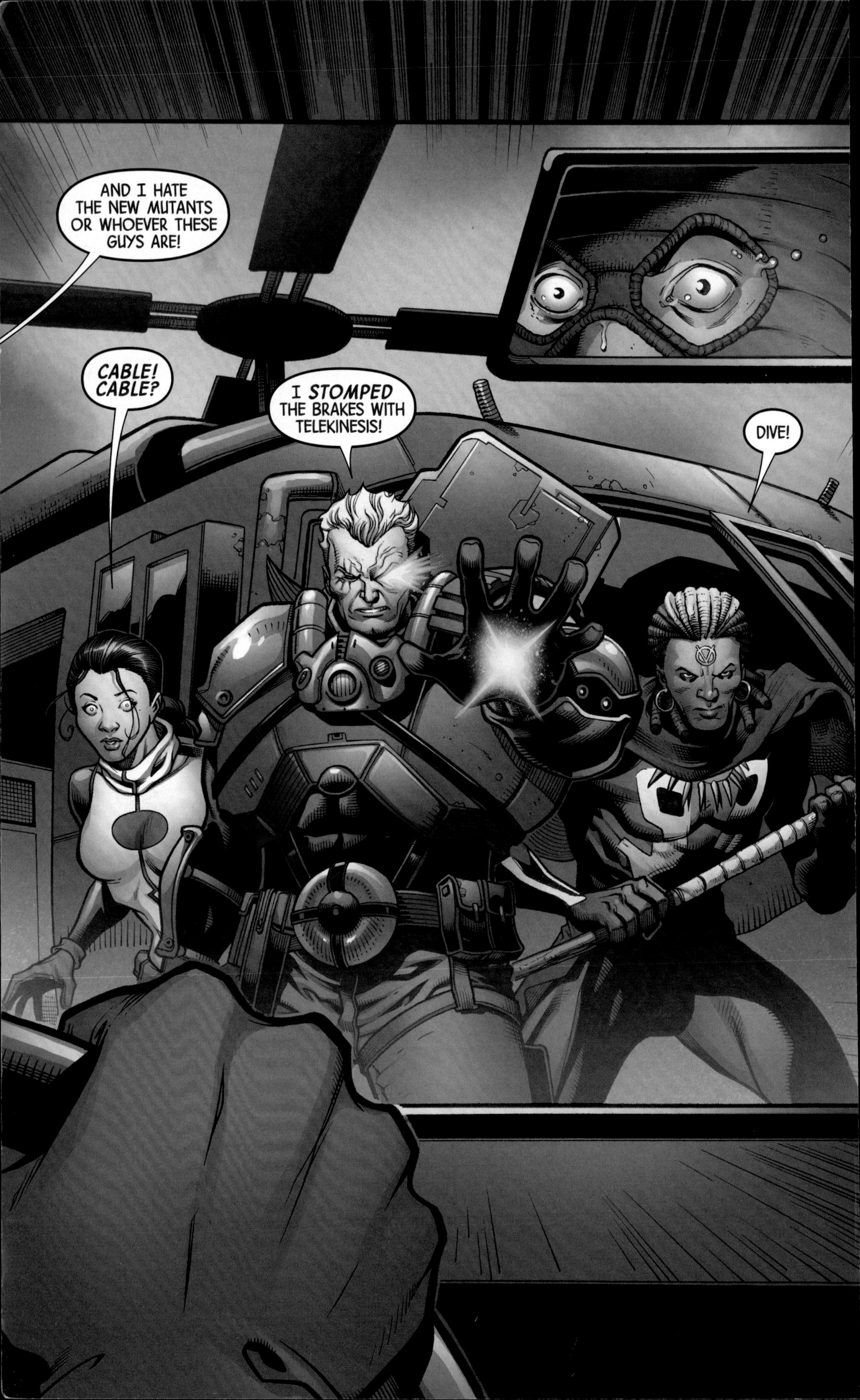
AND I HATE THE NEW MUTANTS OR WHOEVER THESE GUYS ARE!
CABLE! CABLE?
I STOMPED THE BRAKES WITH TELEKINESIS!
DIVE!

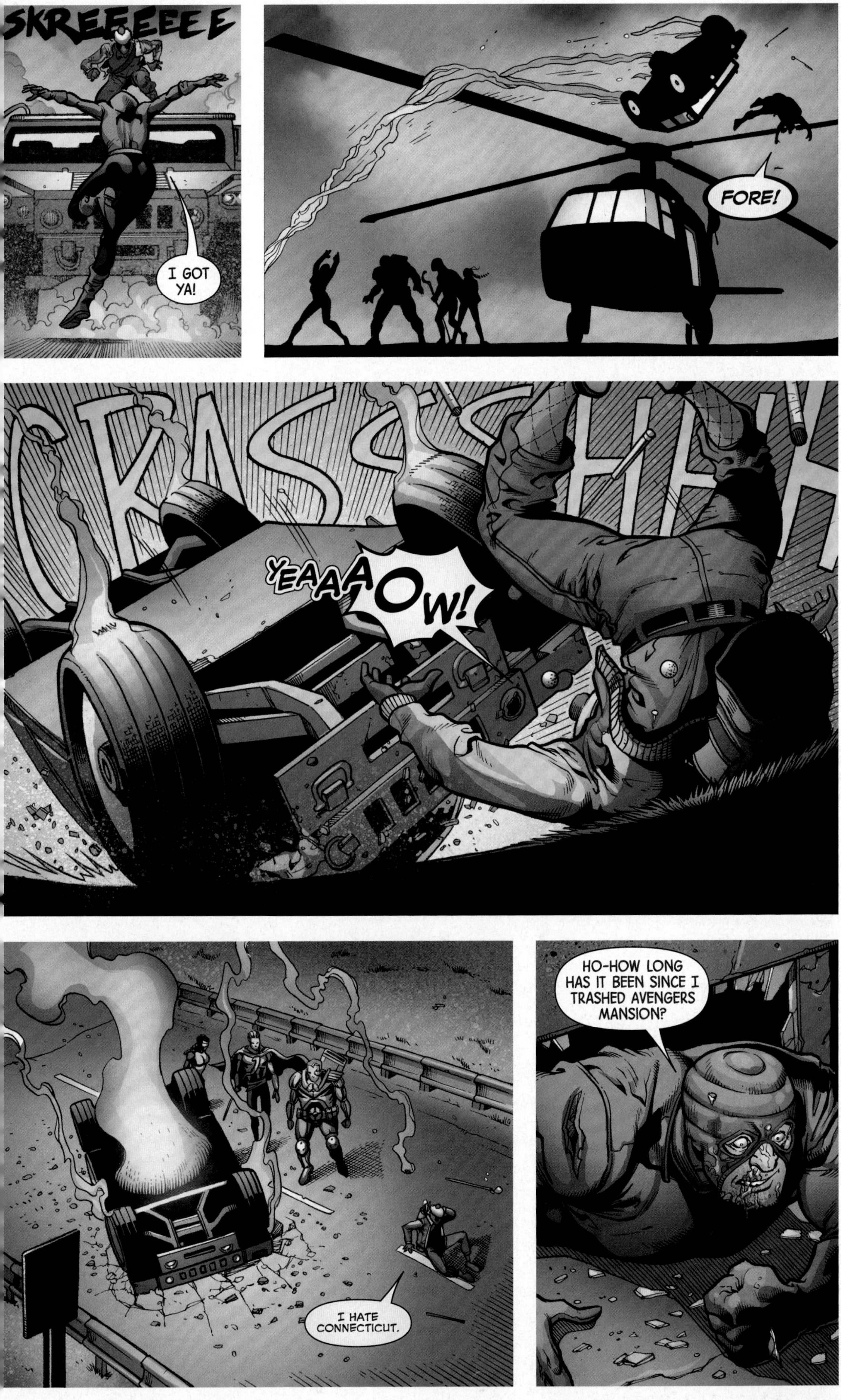
SKREEEEEE
I GOT YA!
FORE!
CRASSSHHH
YEAAAAOW!
I HATE CONNECTICUT.
HO-HOW LONG HAS IT BEEN SINCE I TRASHED AVENGERS MANSION?

I DUNNO-- A COUPLE OF WEEKS?

NO!

JIM'S BEEN INSIDE ALONE!

WEREN'T YOU SUPPOSED TO BE LOOKING THROUGH THE UNDERWORLD FOR THE RED SKULL FOR ME?

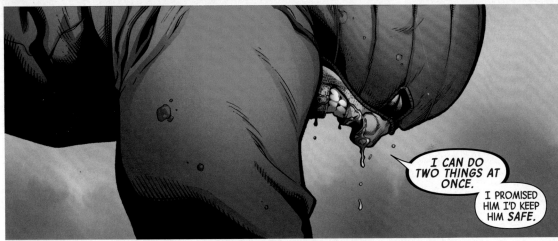

I CAN DO TWO THINGS AT ONCE.

I PROMISED HIM I'D KEEP HIM SAFE.

KEEP WHO SAFE?

I UNDERSTAND NOW.

YOU WANTED TO BE SENT BACK TO PRISON BECAUSE YOU WERE HELPING SOMEONE SURVIVE INSIDE.

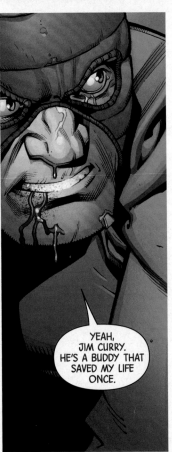

YEAH, JIM CURRY. HE'S A BUDDY THAT SAVED MY LIFE ONCE.

AH. YOU TRASHED AVENGERS MANSION FOR A QUICK RETURN TICKET. ONLY, YOU WEREN'T RETURNED TO JAIL, WERE YOU? THEY SENT YOU SOMEPLACE ELSE.

I'M SORRY TO TELL YOU THIS...

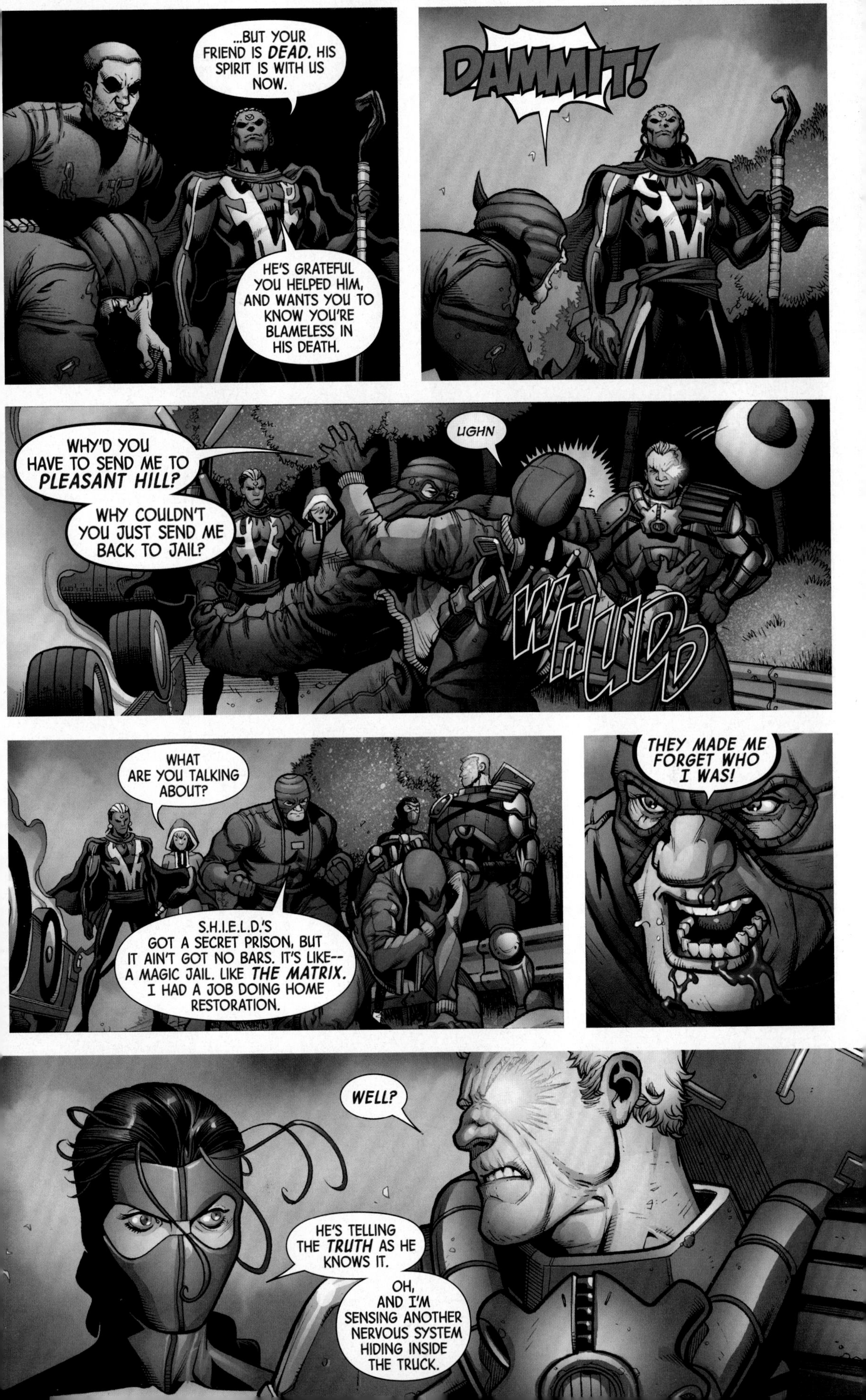
...BUT YOUR FRIEND IS DEAD. HIS SPIRIT IS WITH US NOW.
HE'S GRATEFUL YOU HELPED HIM, AND WANTS YOU TO KNOW YOU'RE BLAMELESS IN HIS DEATH.
DAMMIT!
WHY'D YOU HAVE TO SEND ME TO PLEASANT HILL?
WHY COULDN'T YOU JUST SEND ME BACK TO JAIL?
UGHN
WHUDD
WHAT ARE YOU TALKING ABOUT?
S.H.I.E.L.D.'S GOT A SECRET PRISON, BUT IT AIN'T GOT NO BARS. IT'S LIKE-- A MAGIC JAIL. LIKE THE MATRIX. I HAD A JOB DOING HOME RESTORATION.
THEY MADE ME FORGET WHO I WAS!
WELL?
HE'S TELLING THE TRUTH AS HE KNOWS IT.
OH, AND I'M SENSING ANOTHER NERVOUS SYSTEM HIDING INSIDE THE TRUCK.

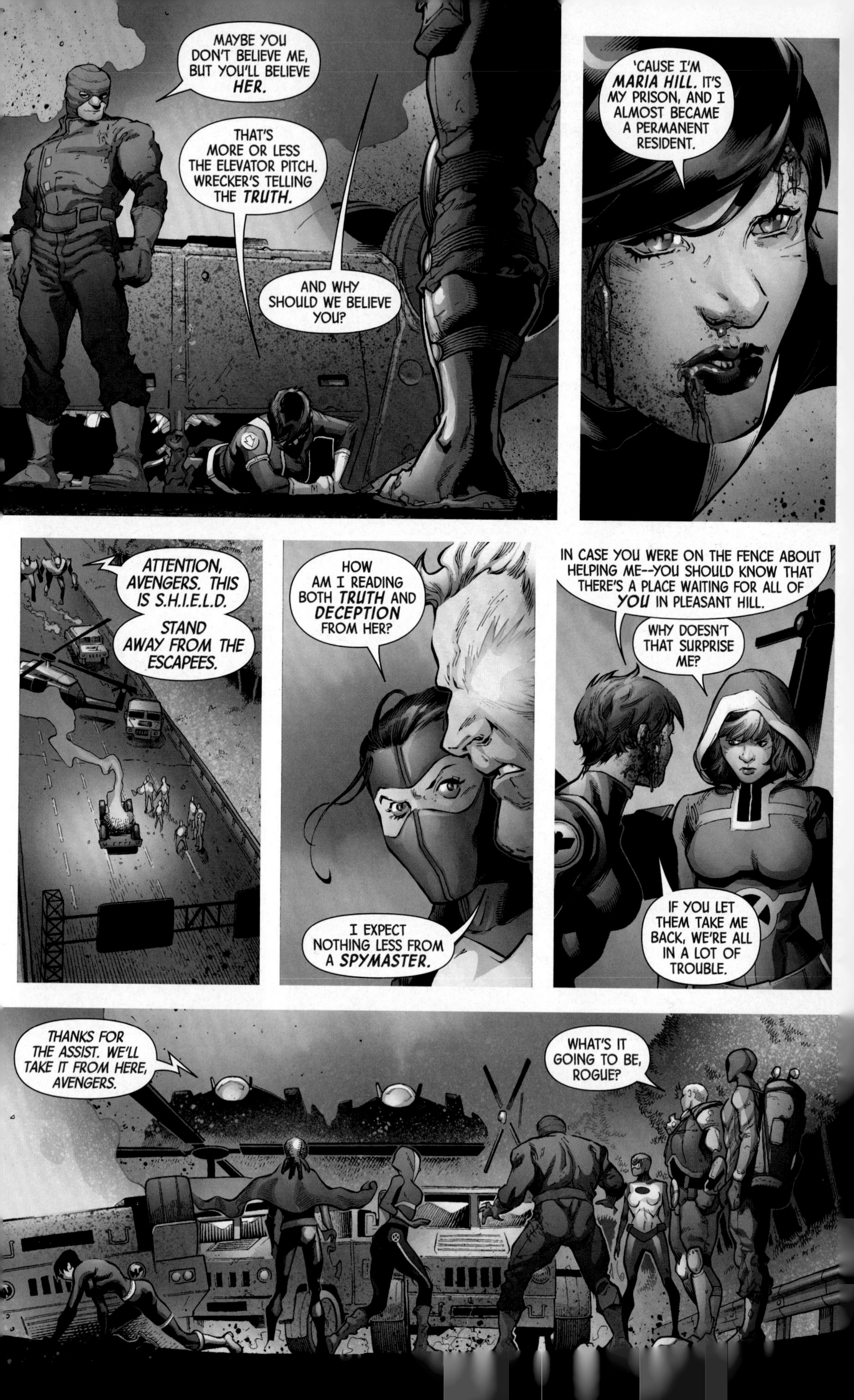
MAYBE YOU DON'T BELIEVE ME, BUT YOU'LL BELIEVE HER.
THAT'S MORE OR LESS THE ELEVATOR PITCH. WRECKER'S TELLING THE TRUTH.
AND WHY SHOULD WE BELIEVE YOU?
'CAUSE I'M MARIA HILL. IT'S MY PRISON, AND I ALMOST BECAME A PERMANENT RESIDENT.
ATTENTION, AVENGERS. THIS IS S.H.I.E.L.D.
STAND AWAY FROM THE ESCAPEES.
HOW AM I READING BOTH TRUTH AND DECEPTION FROM HER?
I EXPECT NOTHING LESS FROM A SPYMASTER.
IN CASE YOU WERE ON THE FENCE ABOUT HELPING ME--YOU SHOULD KNOW THAT THERE'S A PLACE WAITING FOR ALL OF YOU IN PLEASANT HILL.
WHY DOESN'T THAT SURPRISE ME?
IF YOU LET THEM TAKE ME BACK, WE'RE ALL IN A LOT OF TROUBLE.
THANKS FOR THE ASSIST. WE'LL TAKE IT FROM HERE, AVENGERS.
WHAT'S IT GOING TO BE, ROGUE?

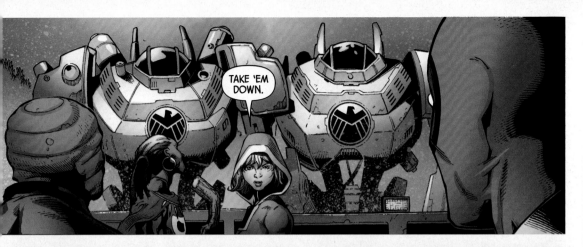

TAKE 'EM DOWN.

I KEPT THIS WARM FOR YOU FROM LAST TIME.

BARBARA.

ARE WE SERIOUSLY ABOUT TO DO WHAT I THINK WE'RE ABOUT TO DO?

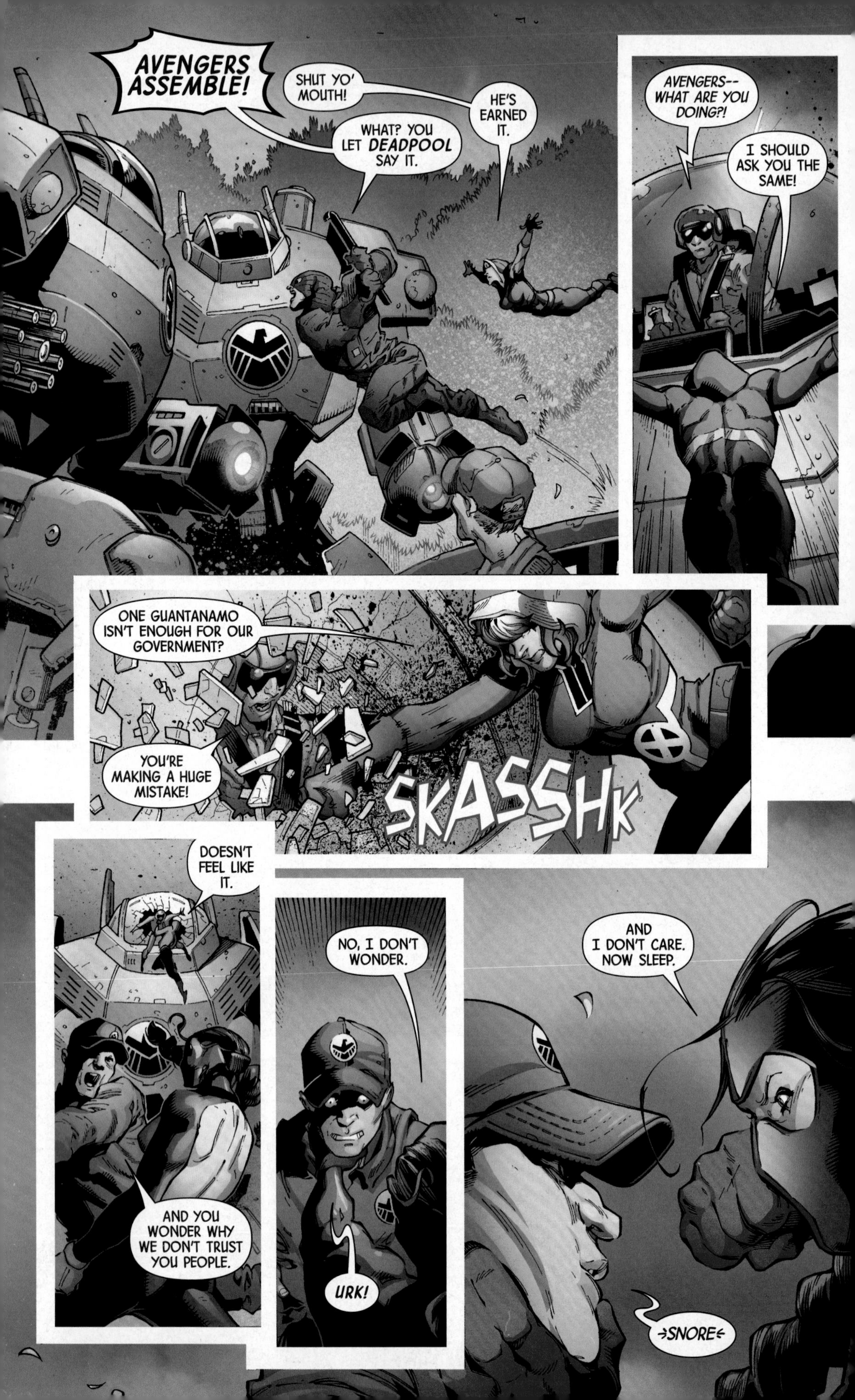
AVENGERS ASSEMBLE!
SHUT YO' MOUTH!
WHAT? YOU LET DEADPOOL SAY IT.
HE'S EARNED IT.
AVENGERS-- WHAT ARE YOU DOING?!
I SHOULD ASK YOU THE SAME!
ONE GUANTANAMO ISN'T ENOUGH FOR OUR GOVERNMENT?
YOU'RE MAKING A HUGE MISTAKE!
SKASSHK
DOESN'T FEEL LIKE IT.
AND YOU WONDER WHY WE DON'T TRUST YOU PEOPLE.
NO, I DON'T WONDER.
URK!
AND I DON'T CARE. NOW SLEEP.
SNORE

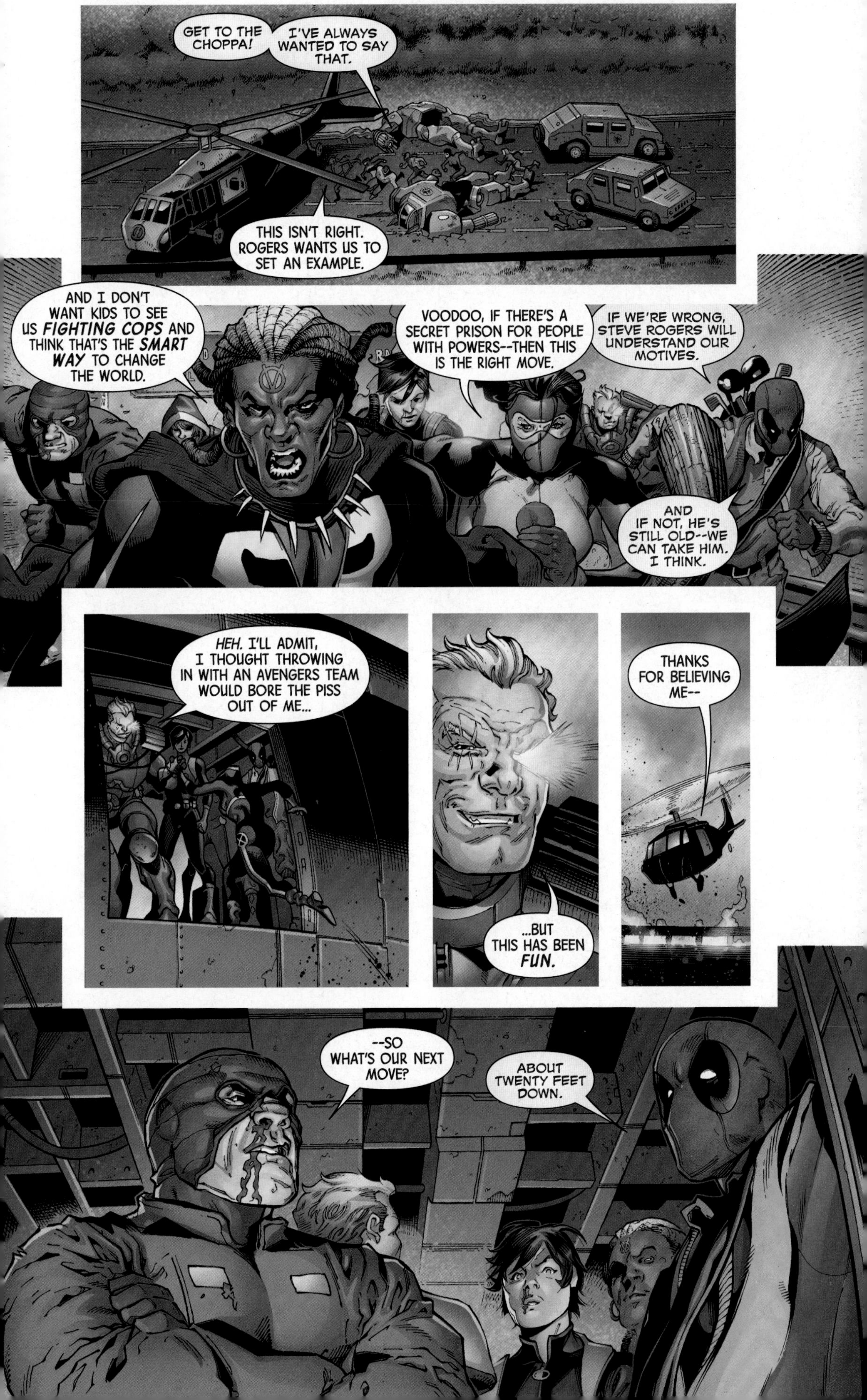
GET TO THE CHOPPA!
I'VE ALWAYS WANTED TO SAY THAT.
THIS ISN'T RIGHT. ROGERS WANTS US TO SET AN EXAMPLE.
AND I DON'T WANT KIDS TO SEE US FIGHTING COPS AND THINK THAT'S THE SMART WAY TO CHANGE THE WORLD.
VOODOO, IF THERE'S A SECRET PRISON FOR PEOPLE WITH POWERS--THEN THIS IS THE RIGHT MOVE.
IF WE'RE WRONG, STEVE ROGERS WILL UNDERSTAND OUR MOTIVES.
AND IF NOT, HE'S STILL OLD--WE CAN TAKE HIM. I THINK.
HEH. I'LL ADMIT, I THOUGHT THROWING IN WITH AN AVENGERS TEAM WOULD BORE THE PISS OUT OF ME...
...BUT THIS HAS BEEN FUN.
THANKS FOR BELIEVING ME--
--SO WHAT'S OUR NEXT MOVE?
ABOUT TWENTY FEET DOWN.

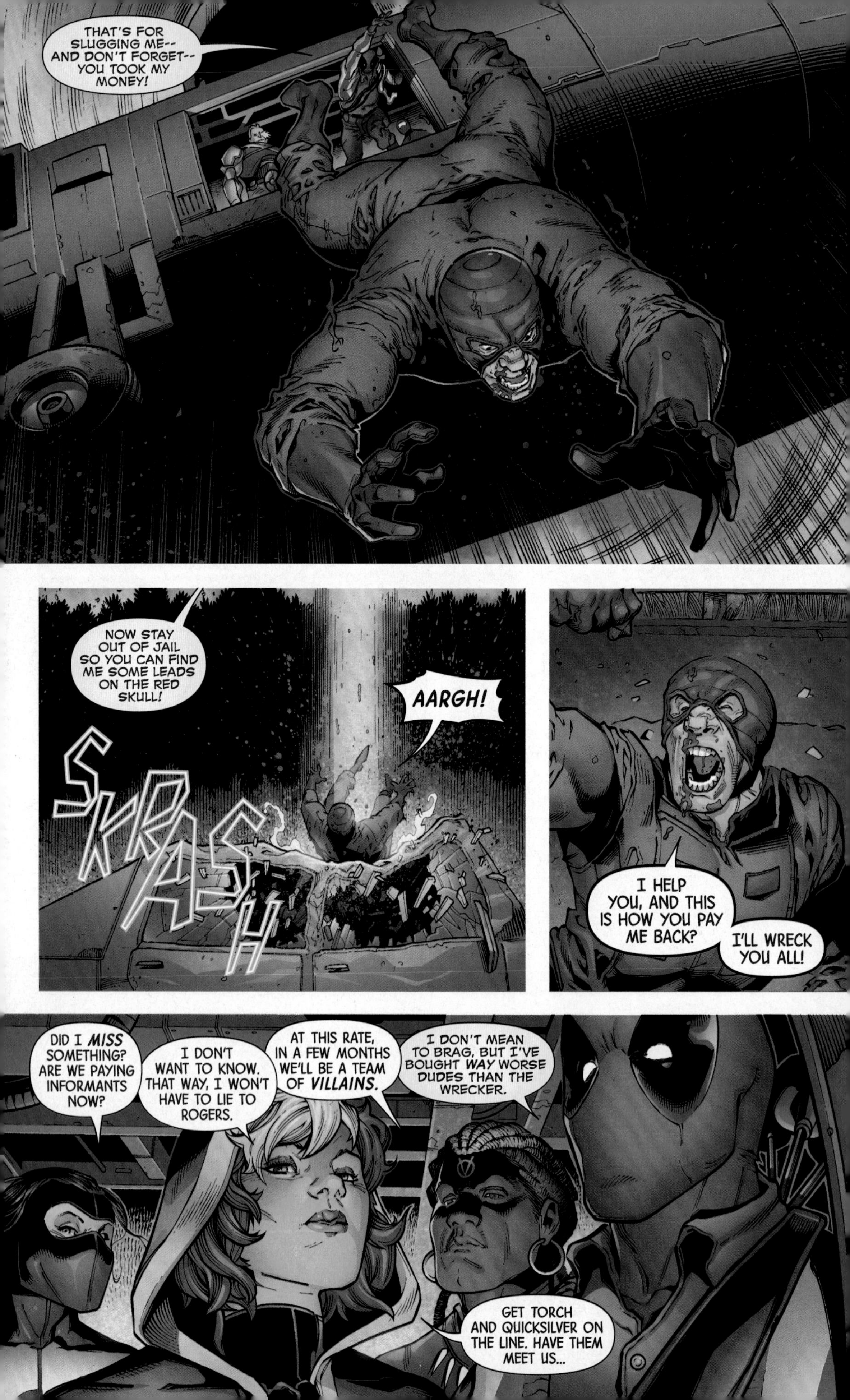
THAT'S FOR SLUGGING ME-- AND DON'T FORGET-- YOU TOOK MY MONEY!
NOW STAY OUT OF JAIL SO YOU CAN FIND ME SOME LEADS ON THE RED SKULL!
AARGH!
SKRASH
I HELP YOU, AND THIS IS HOW YOU PAY ME BACK?
I'LL WRECK YOU ALL!
DID I MISS SOMETHING? ARE WE PAYING INFORMANTS NOW?
I DON'T WANT TO KNOW. THAT WAY, I WON'T HAVE TO LIE TO ROGERS.
AT THIS RATE, IN A FEW MONTHS WE'LL BE A TEAM OF VILLAINS.
I DON'T MEAN TO BRAG, BUT I'VE BOUGHT WAY WORSE DUDES THAN THE WRECKER.
GET TORCH AND QUICKSILVER ON THE LINE. HAVE THEM MEET US...

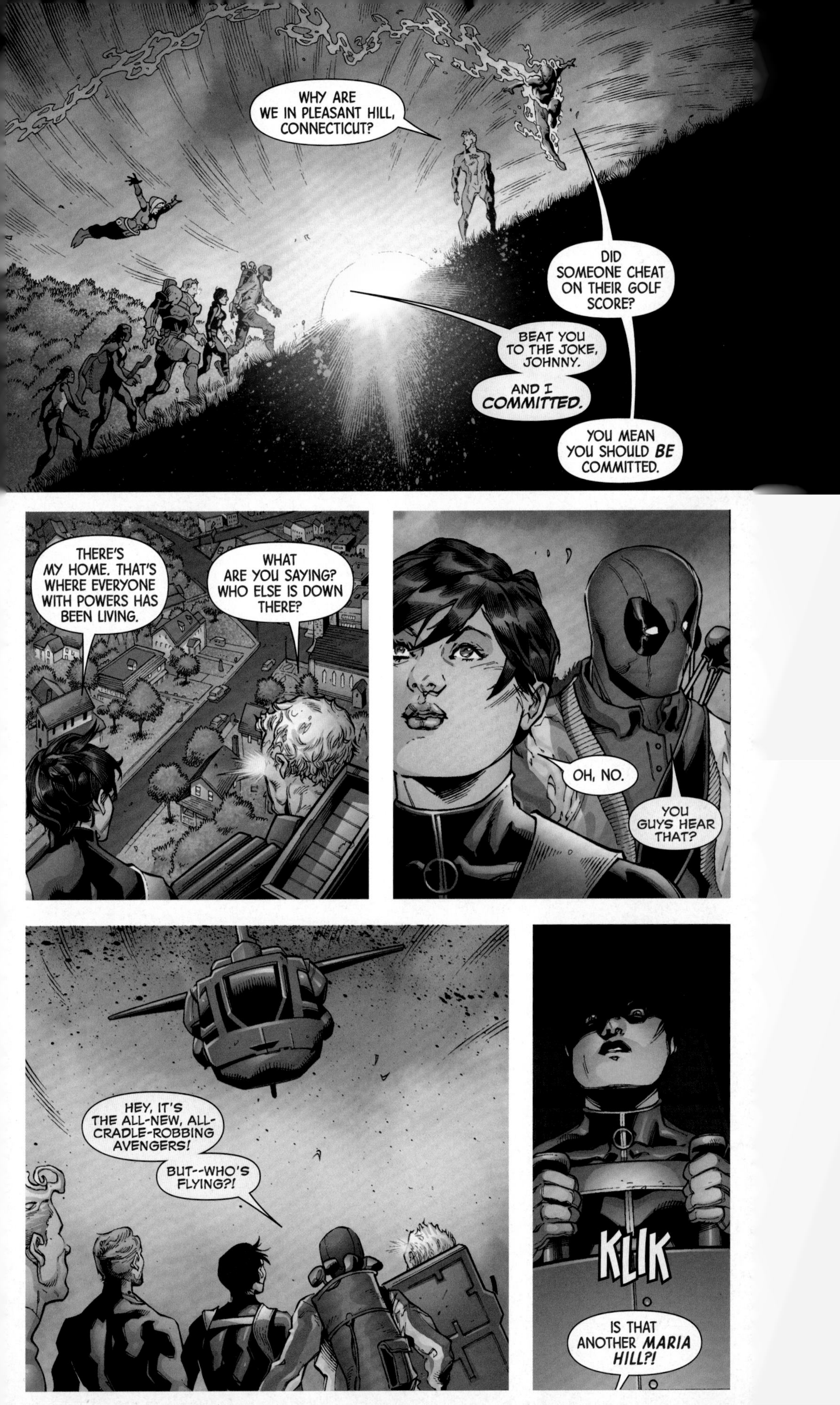
WHY ARE WE IN PLEASANT HILL, CONNECTICUT?
DID SOMEONE CHEAT ON THEIR GOLF SCORE?
BEAT YOU TO THE JOKE, JOHNNY.
AND I COMMITTED.
YOU MEAN YOU SHOULD BE COMMITTED.
THERE'S MY HOME. THAT'S WHERE EVERYONE WITH POWERS HAS BEEN LIVING.
WHAT ARE YOU SAYING? WHO ELSE IS DOWN THERE?
OH, NO.
YOU GUYS HEAR THAT?
HEY, IT'S THE ALL-NEW, ALL-CRADLE-ROBBING AVENGERS!
BUT--WHO'S FLYING?!
KLIK
IS THAT ANOTHER MARIA HILL?!

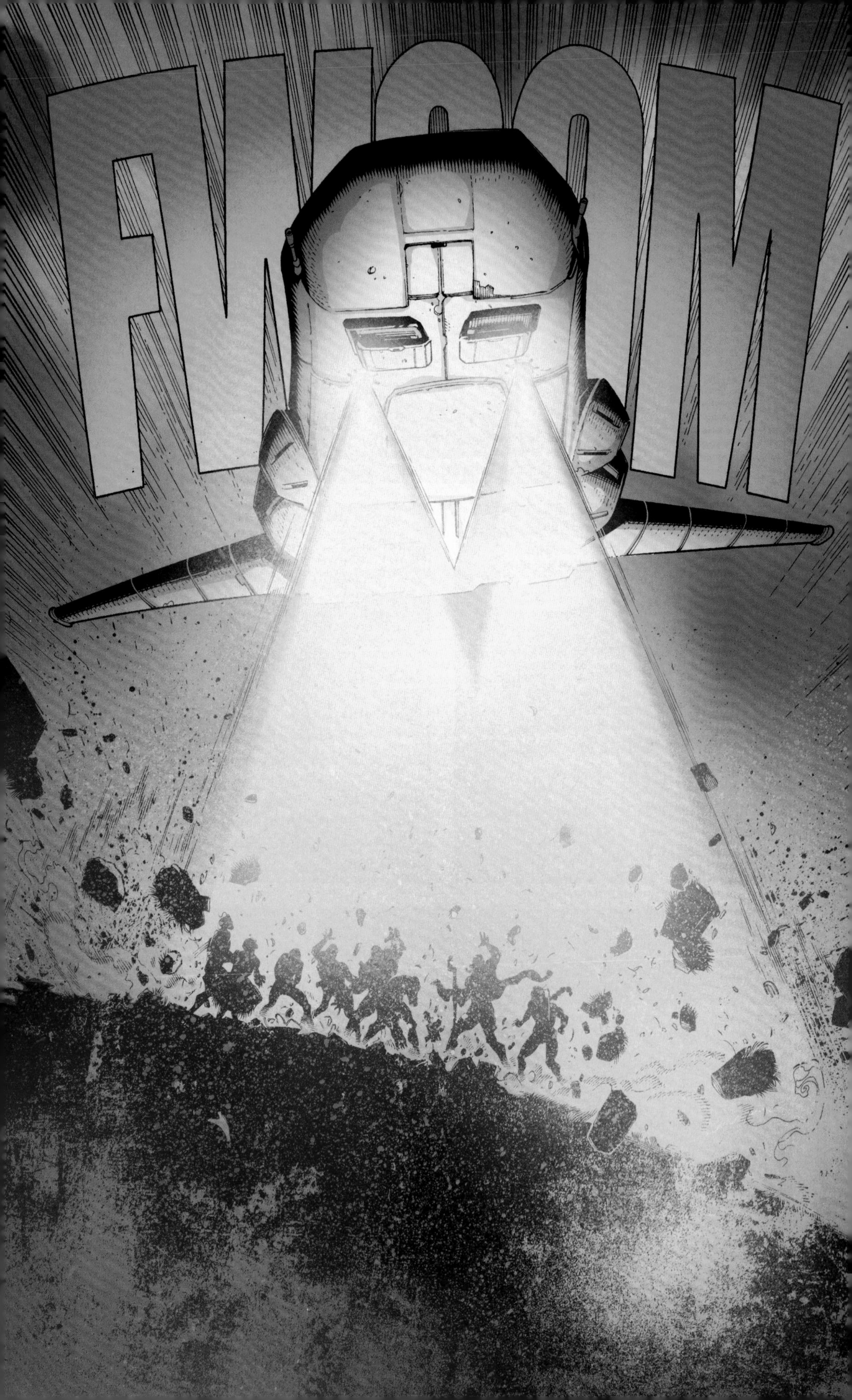
FWOOM!

8

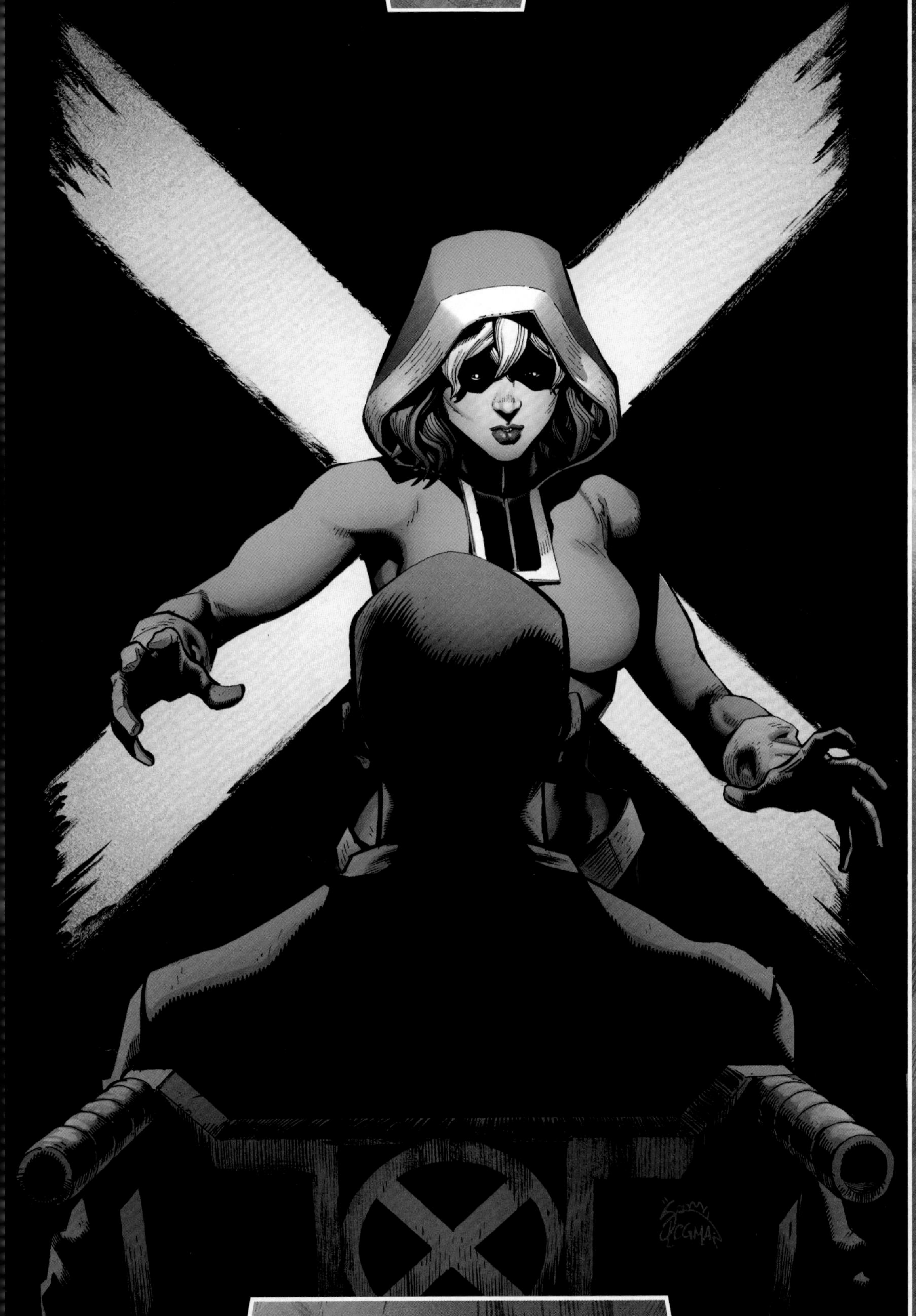

"STUDENT DEBT"

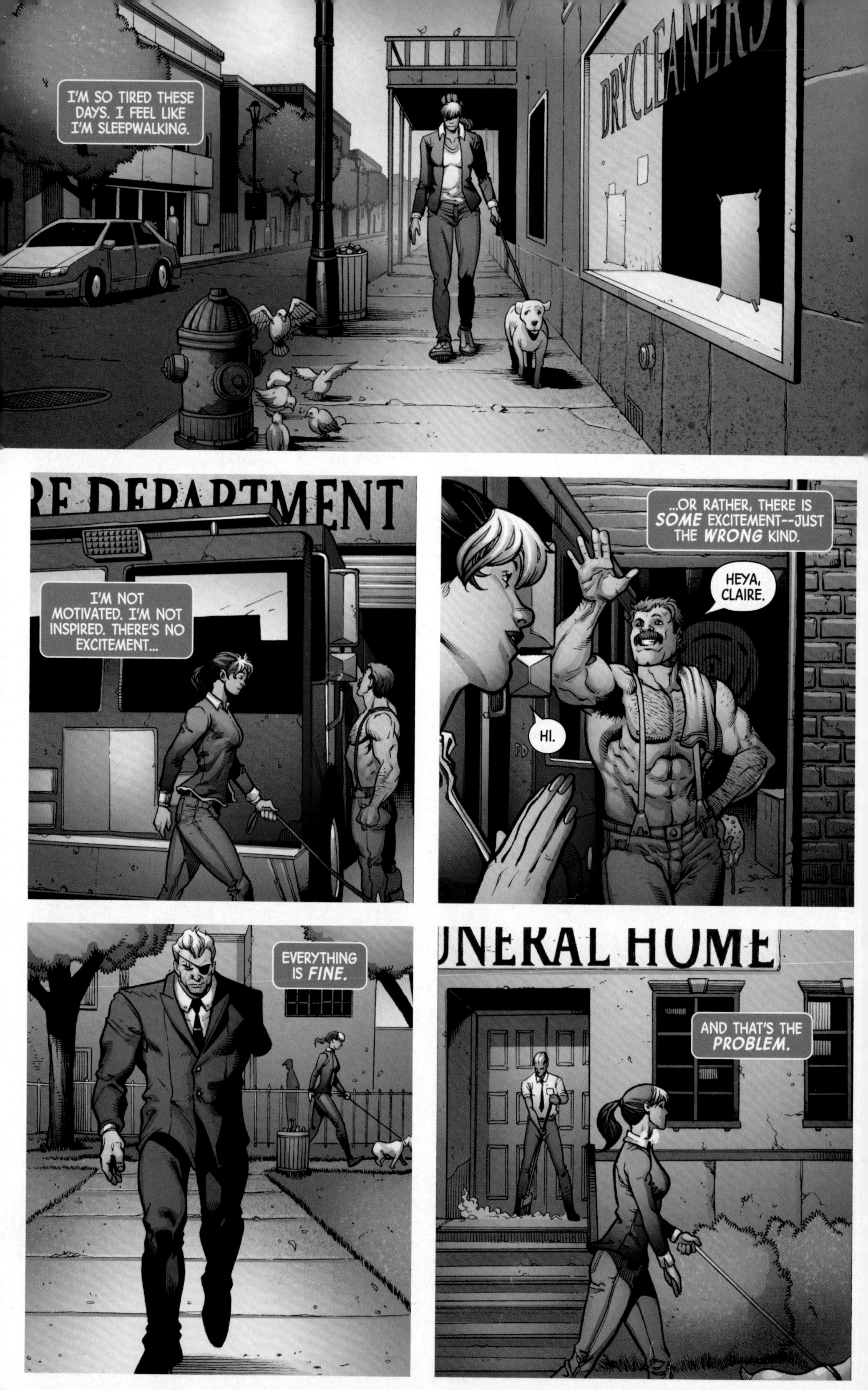

I'M SO TIRED THESE DAYS. I FEEL LIKE I'M SLEEPWALKING.
DRYCLEANERS
DEPARTMENT
I'M NOT MOTIVATED. I'M NOT INSPIRED. THERE'S NO EXCITEMENT...
...OR RATHER, THERE IS *SOME* EXCITEMENT--JUST THE *WRONG* KIND.
HEYA, CLAIRE.
HI.
EVERYTHING IS *FINE.*
AND THAT'S THE *PROBLEM.*

PLEASANT HILL IS ALMOST *INSIPIDLY* PLEASANT.

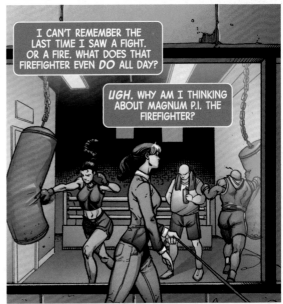

I CAN'T REMEMBER THE LAST TIME I SAW A FIGHT. OR A FIRE. WHAT DOES THAT FIREFIGHTER EVEN *DO* ALL DAY?

UGH. WHY AM I THINKING ABOUT MAGNUM P.I. THE FIREFIGHTER?

THERE IS ONE *UNPLEASANT* THING IN *MY* LIFE NOWADAYS.

IF THAT WEIRDO WHO'S BEEN HARASSING ME CALLS AGAIN, I'M *NOT* ANSWERING.

DAMMIT, I'M NOT ANSWERING THE PHONE TODAY!

DEET DEET DEET

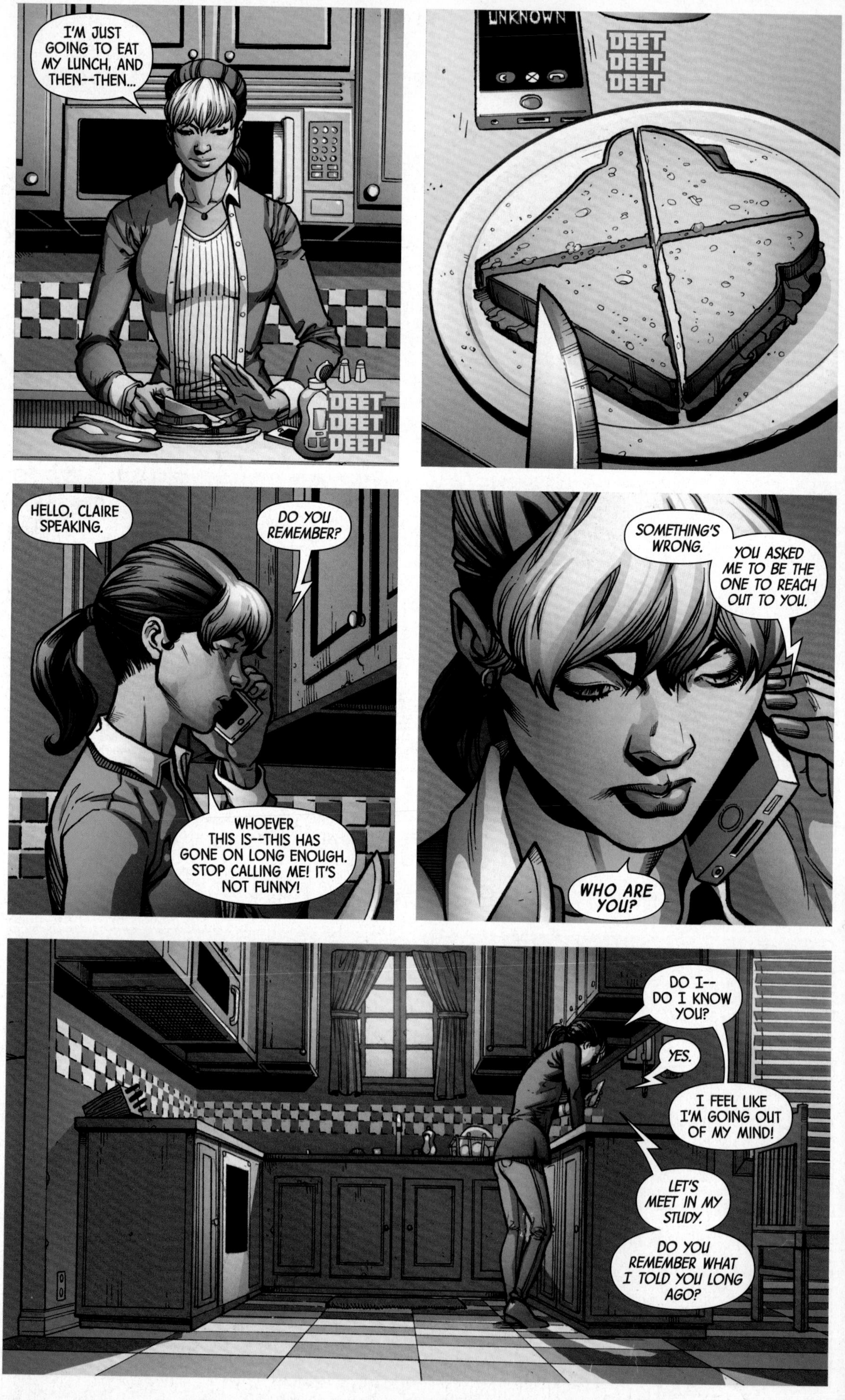
I'M JUST GOING TO EAT MY LUNCH, AND THEN--THEN...
DEET DEET DEET
UNKNOWN
DEET DEET DEET
HELLO, CLAIRE SPEAKING.
DO YOU REMEMBER?
WHOEVER THIS IS--THIS HAS GONE ON LONG ENOUGH. STOP CALLING ME! IT'S NOT FUNNY!
SOMETHING'S WRONG.
YOU ASKED ME TO BE THE ONE TO REACH OUT TO YOU.
WHO ARE YOU?
DO I-- DO I KNOW YOU?
YES.
I FEEL LIKE I'M GOING OUT OF MY MIND!
LET'S MEET IN MY STUDY.
DO YOU REMEMBER WHAT I TOLD YOU LONG AGO?

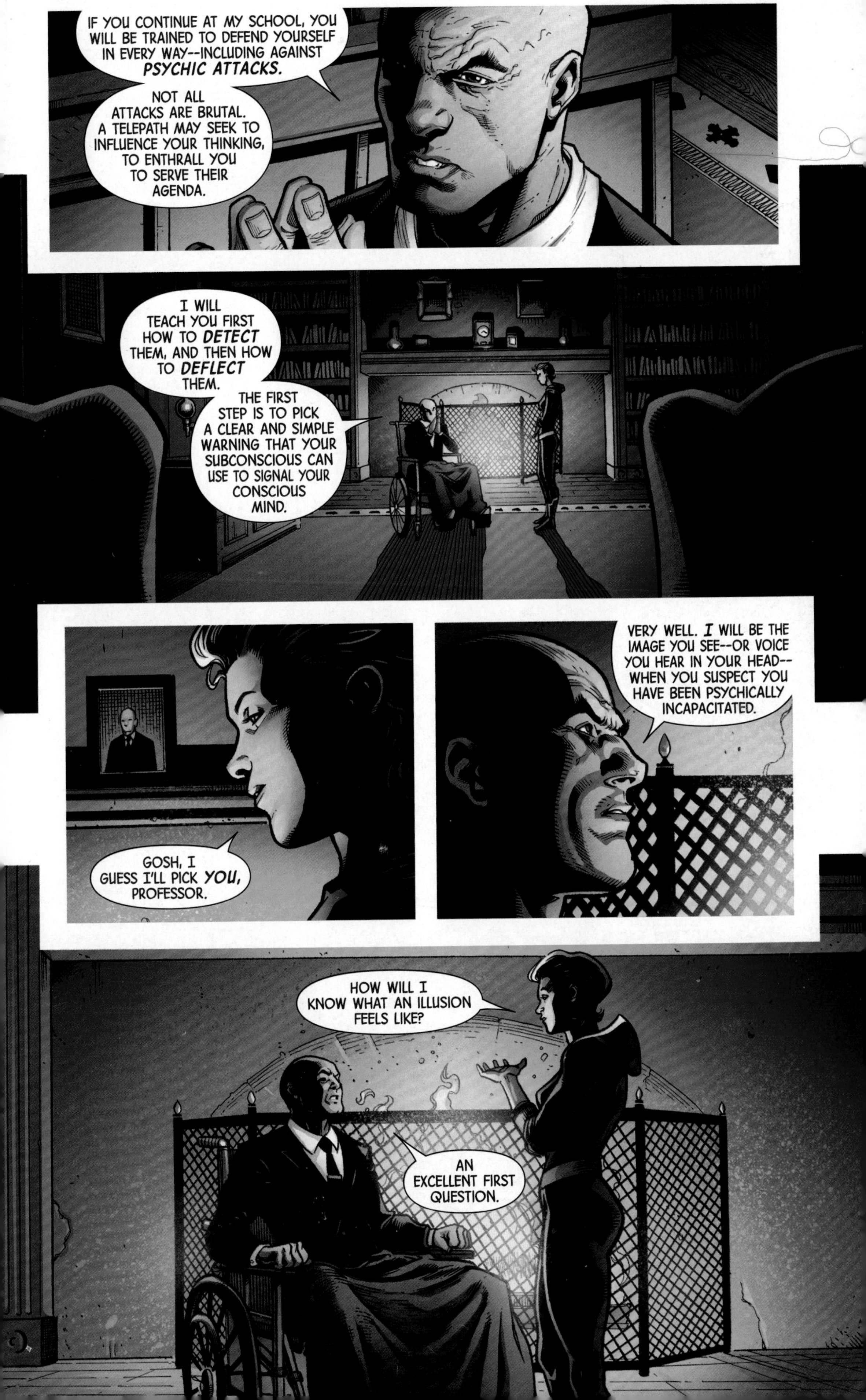
IF YOU CONTINUE AT MY SCHOOL, YOU WILL BE TRAINED TO DEFEND YOURSELF IN EVERY WAY--INCLUDING AGAINST PSYCHIC ATTACKS.
NOT ALL ATTACKS ARE BRUTAL. A TELEPATH MAY SEEK TO INFLUENCE YOUR THINKING, TO ENTHRALL YOU TO SERVE THEIR AGENDA.
I WILL TEACH YOU FIRST HOW TO DETECT THEM, AND THEN HOW TO DEFLECT THEM.
THE FIRST STEP IS TO PICK A CLEAR AND SIMPLE WARNING THAT YOUR SUBCONSCIOUS CAN USE TO SIGNAL YOUR CONSCIOUS MIND.
GOSH, I GUESS I'LL PICK YOU, PROFESSOR.
VERY WELL. I WILL BE THE IMAGE YOU SEE--OR VOICE YOU HEAR IN YOUR HEAD--WHEN YOU SUSPECT YOU HAVE BEEN PSYCHICALLY INCAPACITATED.
HOW WILL I KNOW WHAT AN ILLUSION FEELS LIKE?
AN EXCELLENT FIRST QUESTION.

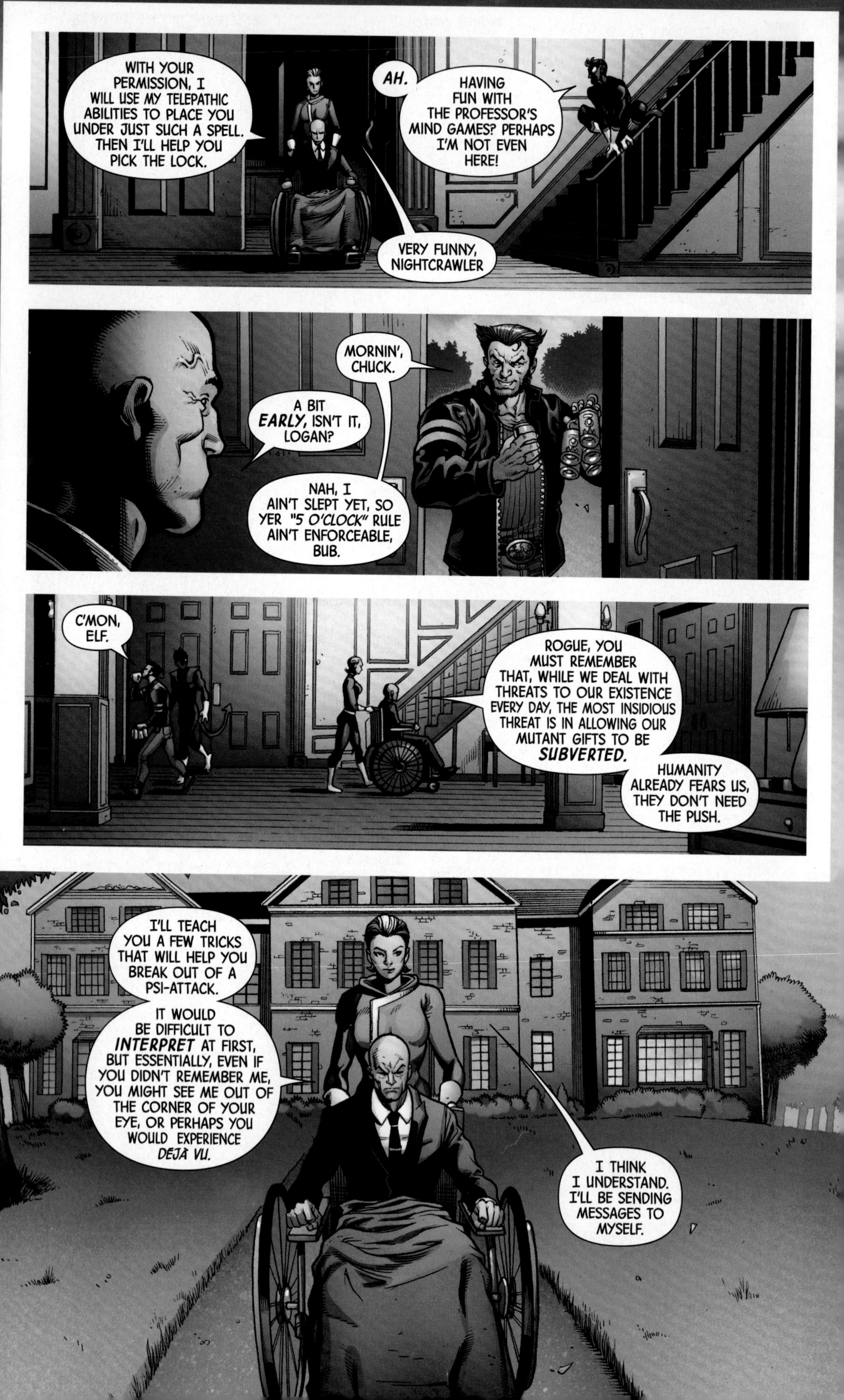
WITH YOUR PERMISSION, I WILL USE MY TELEPATHIC ABILITIES TO PLACE YOU UNDER JUST SUCH A SPELL. THEN I'LL HELP YOU PICK THE LOCK.
AH.
HAVING FUN WITH THE PROFESSOR'S MIND GAMES? PERHAPS I'M NOT EVEN HERE!
VERY FUNNY, NIGHTCRAWLER
MORNIN', CHUCK.
A BIT EARLY, ISN'T IT, LOGAN?
NAH, I AIN'T SLEPT YET, SO YER "5 O'CLOCK" RULE AIN'T ENFORCEABLE, BUB.
C'MON, ELF.
ROGUE, YOU MUST REMEMBER THAT, WHILE WE DEAL WITH THREATS TO OUR EXISTENCE EVERY DAY, THE MOST INSIDIOUS THREAT IS IN ALLOWING OUR MUTANT GIFTS TO BE SUBVERTED.
HUMANITY ALREADY FEARS US, THEY DON'T NEED THE PUSH.
I'LL TEACH YOU A FEW TRICKS THAT WILL HELP YOU BREAK OUT OF A PSI-ATTACK.
IT WOULD BE DIFFICULT TO INTERPRET AT FIRST, BUT ESSENTIALLY, EVEN IF YOU DIDN'T REMEMBER ME, YOU MIGHT SEE ME OUT OF THE CORNER OF YOUR EYE, OR PERHAPS YOU WOULD EXPERIENCE DEJÀ VU.
I THINK I UNDERSTAND. I'LL BE SENDING MESSAGES TO MYSELF.

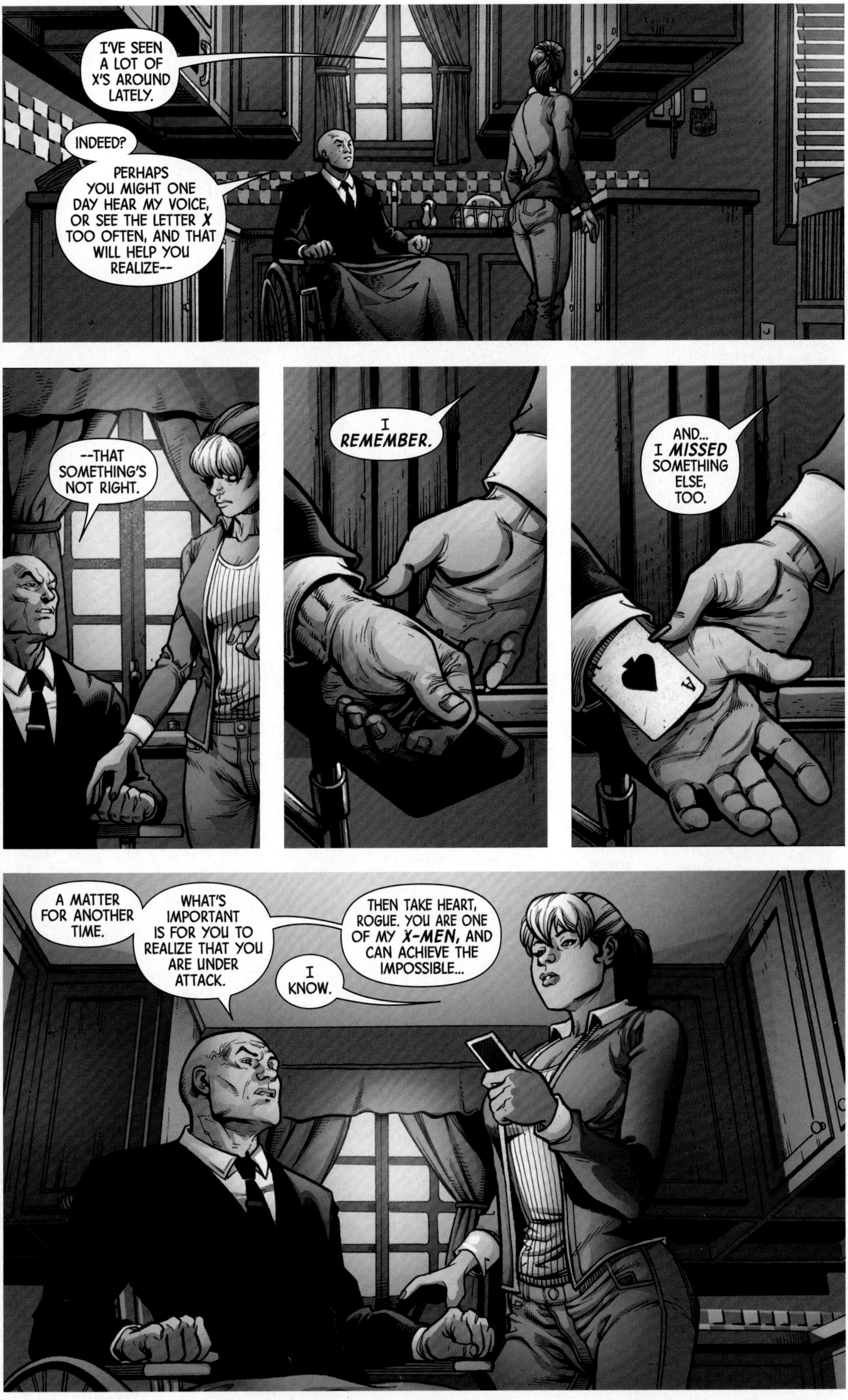
I'VE SEEN A LOT OF X'S AROUND LATELY.
INDEED?
PERHAPS YOU MIGHT ONE DAY HEAR MY VOICE, OR SEE THE LETTER X TOO OFTEN, AND THAT WILL HELP YOU REALIZE--
--THAT SOMETHING'S NOT RIGHT.
I REMEMBER.
AND... I MISSED SOMETHING ELSE, TOO.
A MATTER FOR ANOTHER TIME.
WHAT'S IMPORTANT IS FOR YOU TO REALIZE THAT YOU ARE UNDER ATTACK.
I KNOW.
THEN TAKE HEART, ROGUE. YOU ARE ONE OF MY X-MEN, AND CAN ACHIEVE THE IMPOSSIBLE...

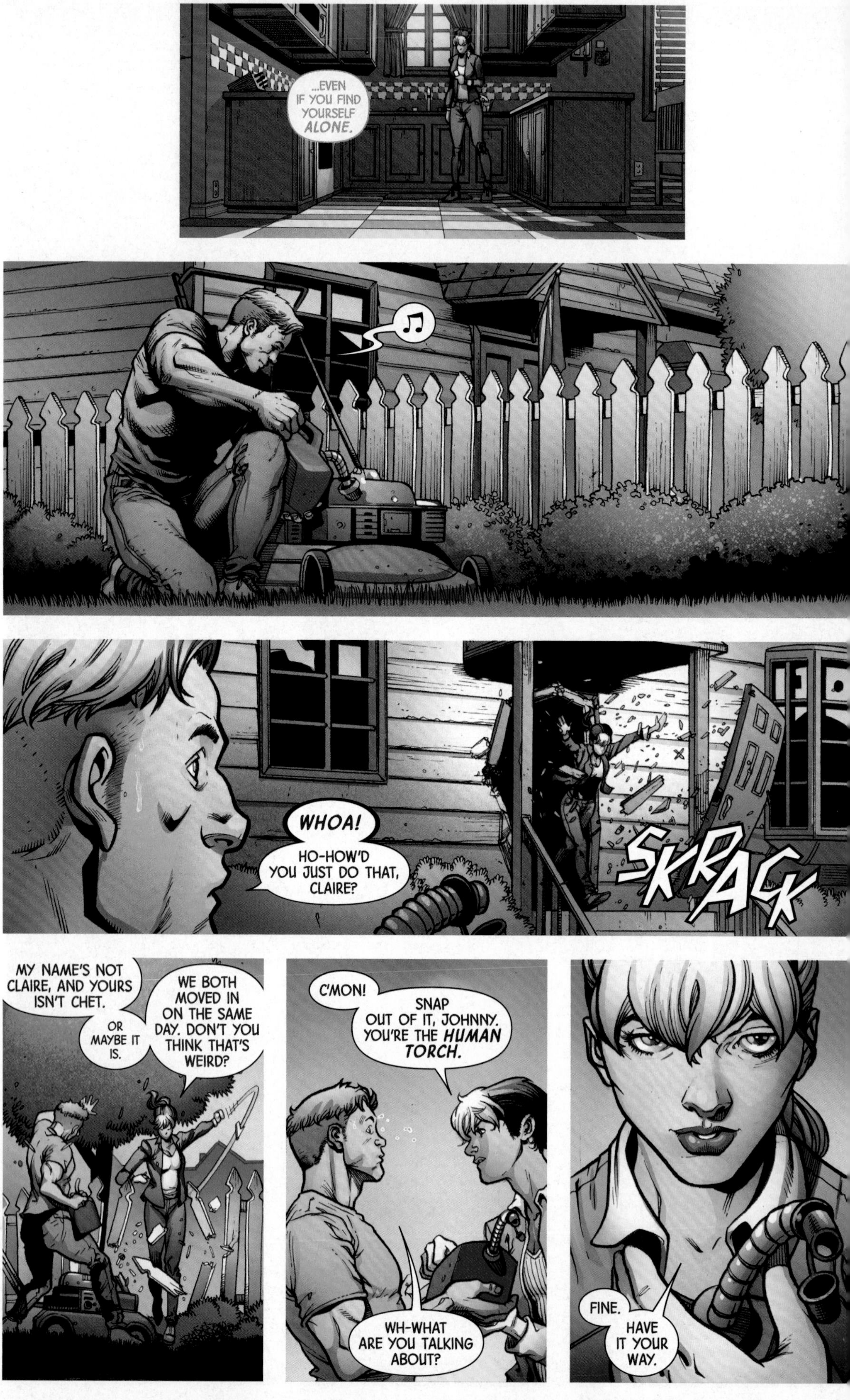
...EVEN IF YOU FIND YOURSELF ALONE.
♫
WHOA!
HO-HOW'D YOU JUST DO THAT, CLAIRE?
SKRACK
MY NAME'S NOT CLAIRE, AND YOURS ISN'T CHET.
OR MAYBE IT IS.
WE BOTH MOVED IN ON THE SAME DAY. DON'T YOU THINK THAT'S WEIRD?
C'MON!
SNAP OUT OF IT, JOHNNY. YOU'RE THE HUMAN TORCH.
WH-WHAT ARE YOU TALKING ABOUT?
FINE.
HAVE IT YOUR WAY.

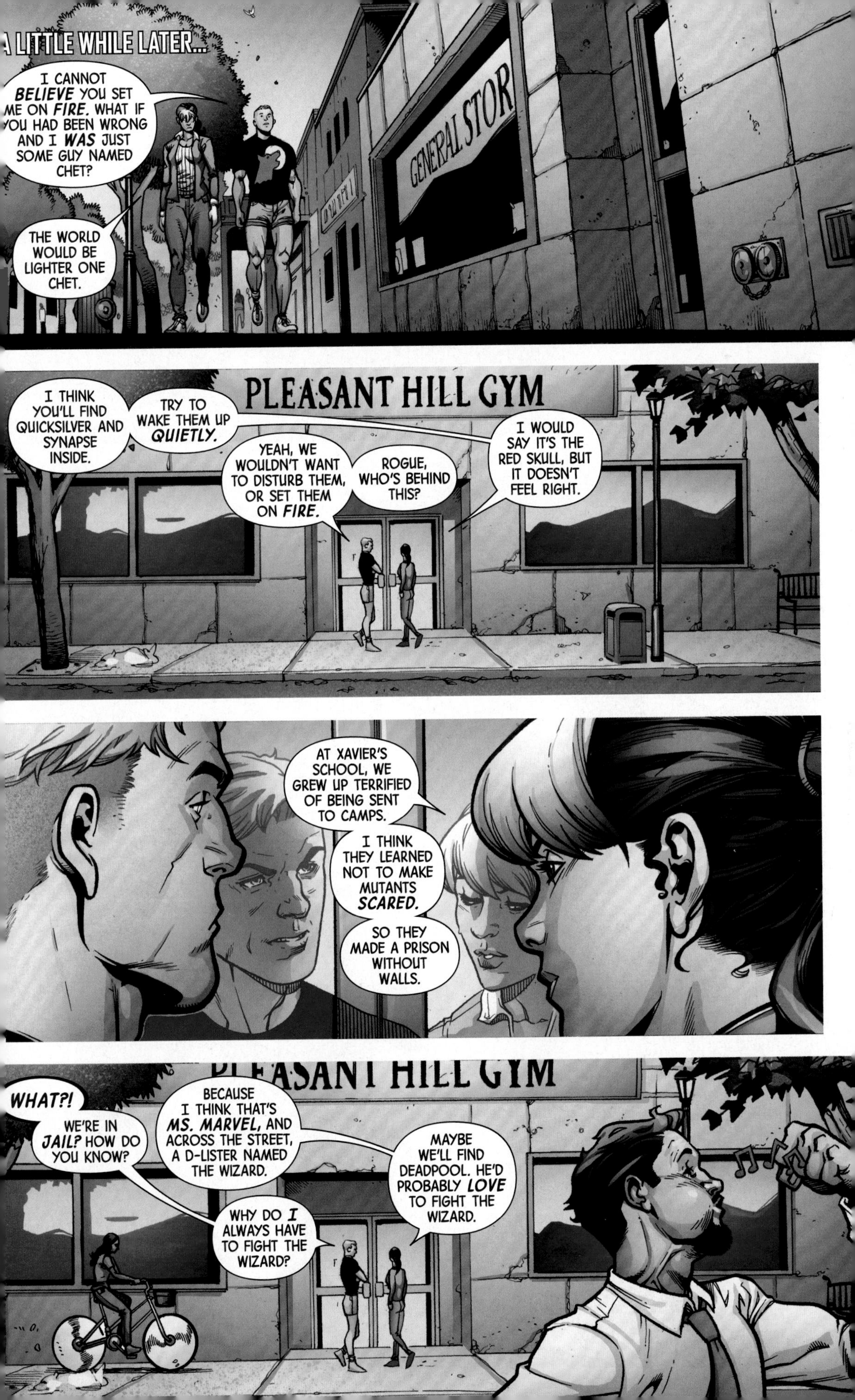
A LITTLE WHILE LATER...
I CANNOT BELIEVE YOU SET ME ON FIRE. WHAT IF YOU HAD BEEN WRONG AND I WAS JUST SOME GUY NAMED CHET?
THE WORLD WOULD BE LIGHTER ONE CHET.
GENERAL STOR
PLEASANT HILL GYM
I THINK YOU'LL FIND QUICKSILVER AND SYNAPSE INSIDE.
TRY TO WAKE THEM UP QUIETLY.
YEAH, WE WOULDN'T WANT TO DISTURB THEM, OR SET THEM ON FIRE.
ROGUE, WHO'S BEHIND THIS?
I WOULD SAY IT'S THE RED SKULL, BUT IT DOESN'T FEEL RIGHT.
AT XAVIER'S SCHOOL, WE GREW UP TERRIFIED OF BEING SENT TO CAMPS.
I THINK THEY LEARNED NOT TO MAKE MUTANTS SCARED.
SO THEY MADE A PRISON WITHOUT WALLS.
PLEASANT HILL GYM
WHAT?!
WE'RE IN JAIL? HOW DO YOU KNOW?
BECAUSE I THINK THAT'S MS. MARVEL, AND ACROSS THE STREET, A D-LISTER NAMED THE WIZARD.
WHY DO I ALWAYS HAVE TO FIGHT THE WIZARD?
MAYBE WE'LL FIND DEADPOOL. HE'D PROBABLY LOVE TO FIGHT THE WIZARD.

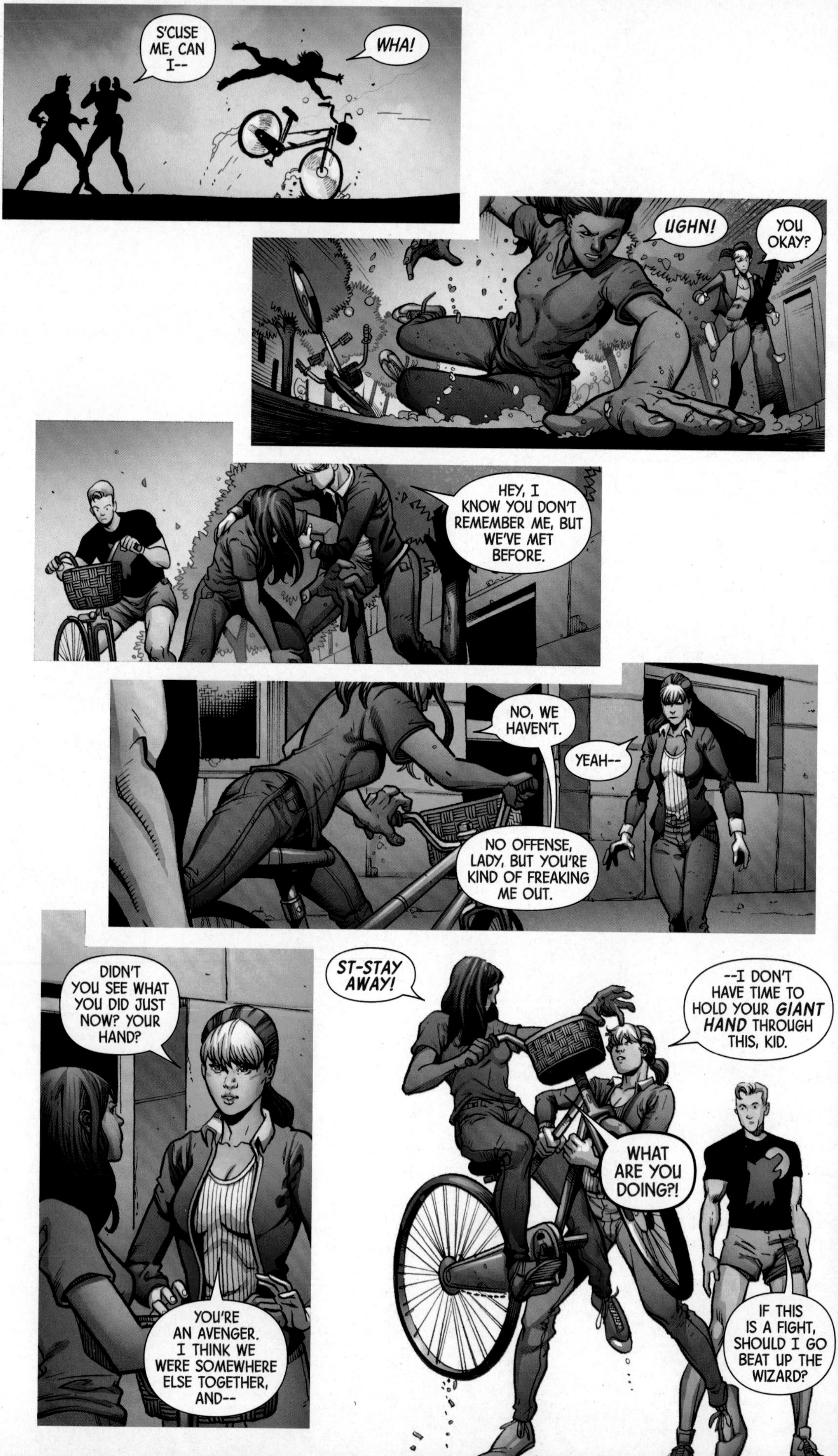

S'CUSE ME, CAN I--
WHA!
UGHN!
YOU OKAY?
HEY, I KNOW YOU DON'T REMEMBER ME, BUT WE'VE MET BEFORE.
NO, WE HAVEN'T.
YEAH--
NO OFFENSE, LADY, BUT YOU'RE KIND OF FREAKING ME OUT.
DIDN'T YOU SEE WHAT YOU DID JUST NOW? YOUR HAND?
YOU'RE AN AVENGER. I THINK WE WERE SOMEWHERE ELSE TOGETHER, AND--
ST-STAY AWAY!
--I DON'T HAVE TIME TO HOLD YOUR GIANT HAND THROUGH THIS, KID.
WHAT ARE YOU DOING?!
IF THIS IS A FIGHT, SHOULD I GO BEAT UP THE WIZARD?

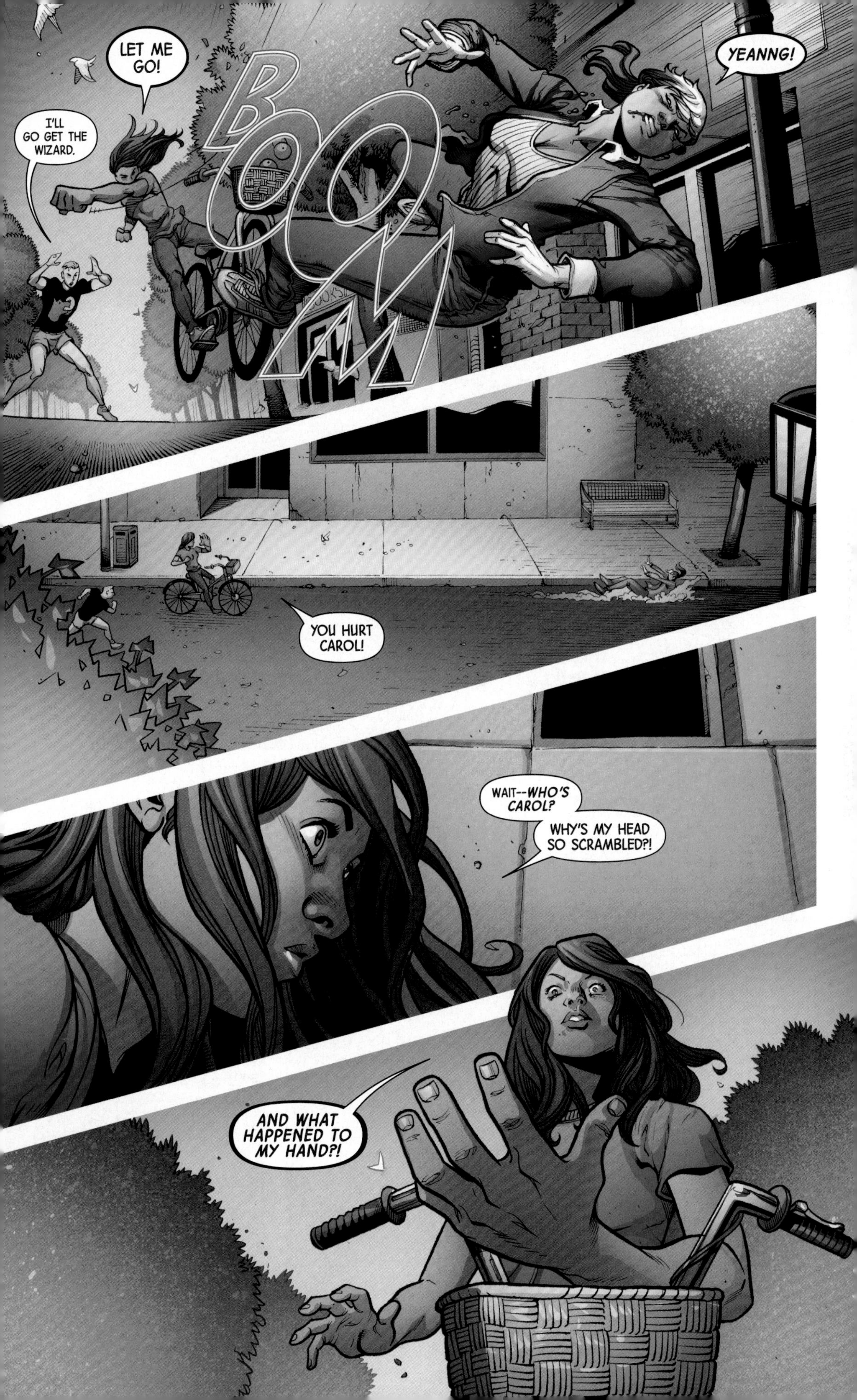
LET ME GO!
I'LL GO GET THE WIZARD.
BOOM
YEANNG!
YOU HURT CAROL!
WAIT--WHO'S CAROL?
WHY'S MY HEAD SO SCRAMBLED?!
AND WHAT HAPPENED TO MY HAND?!

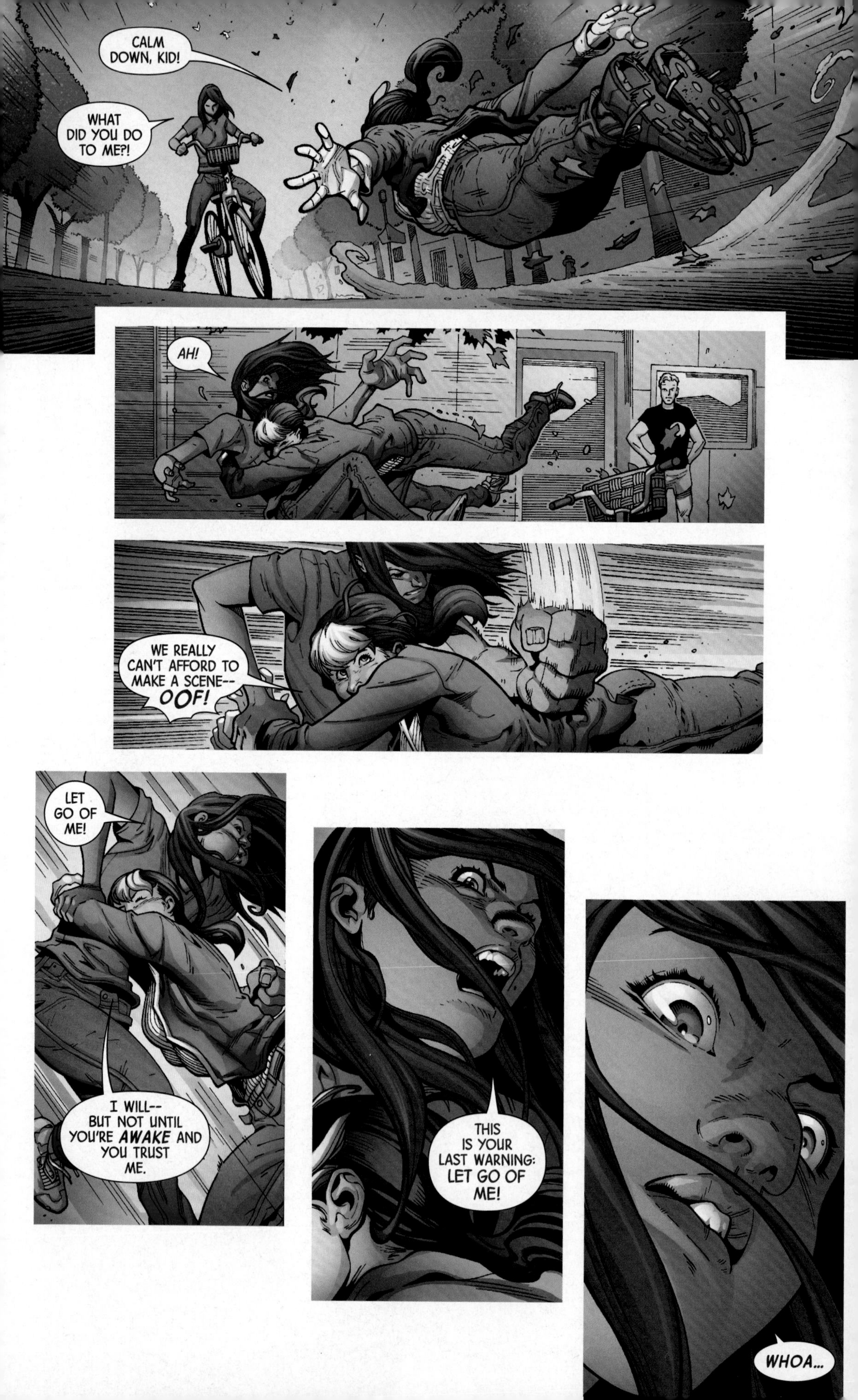
CALM DOWN, KID!
WHAT DID YOU DO TO ME?!
AH!
WE REALLY CAN'T AFFORD TO MAKE A SCENE-- OOF!
LET GO OF ME!
I WILL-- BUT NOT UNTIL YOU'RE AWAKE AND YOU TRUST ME.
THIS IS YOUR LAST WARNING: LET GO OF ME!
WHOA...

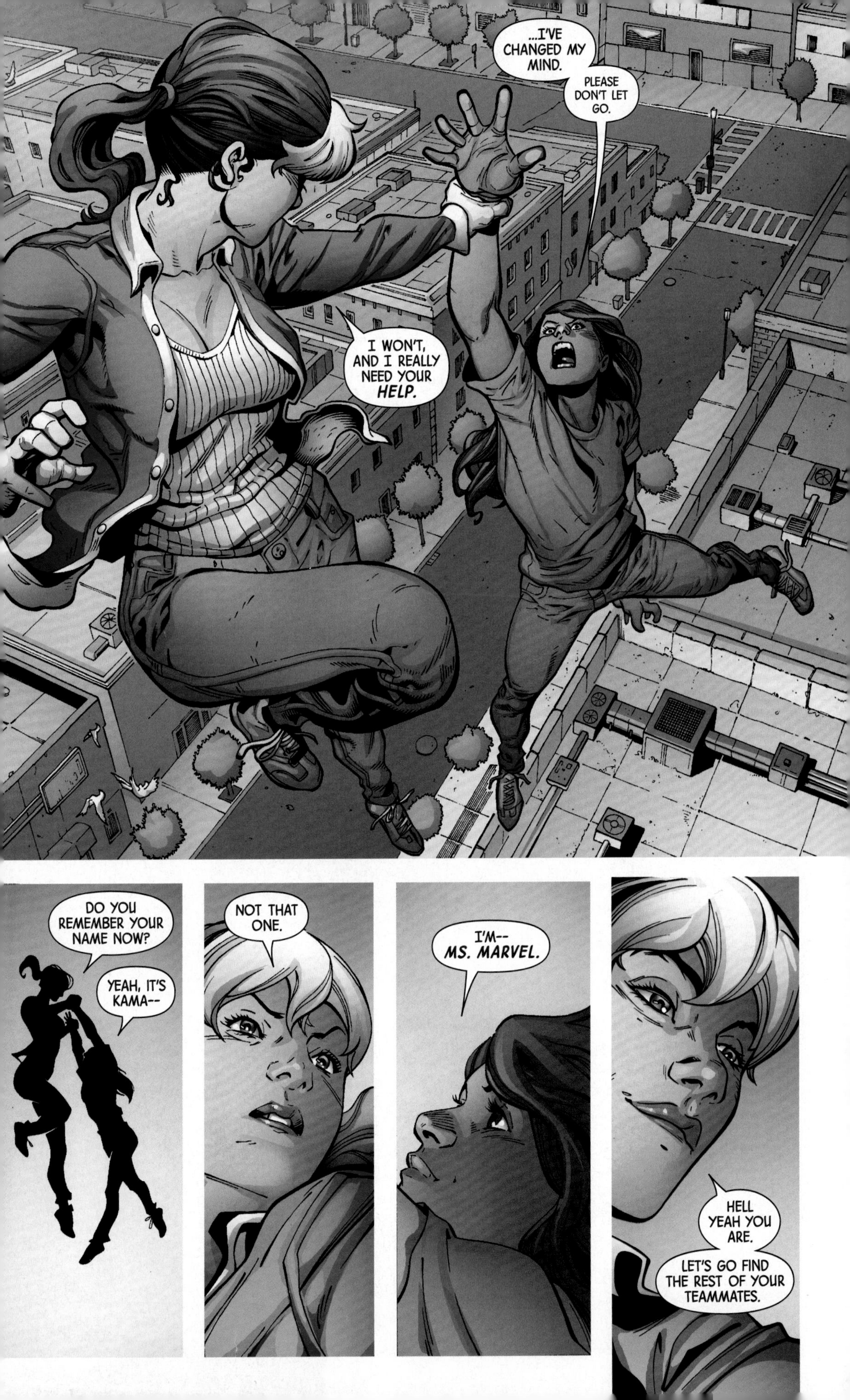
...I'VE CHANGED MY MIND.
PLEASE DON'T LET GO.
I WON'T, AND I REALLY NEED YOUR HELP.
DO YOU REMEMBER YOUR NAME NOW?
YEAH, IT'S KAMA--
NOT THAT ONE.
I'M-- MS. MARVEL.
HELL YEAH YOU ARE.
LET'S GO FIND THE REST OF YOUR TEAMMATES.

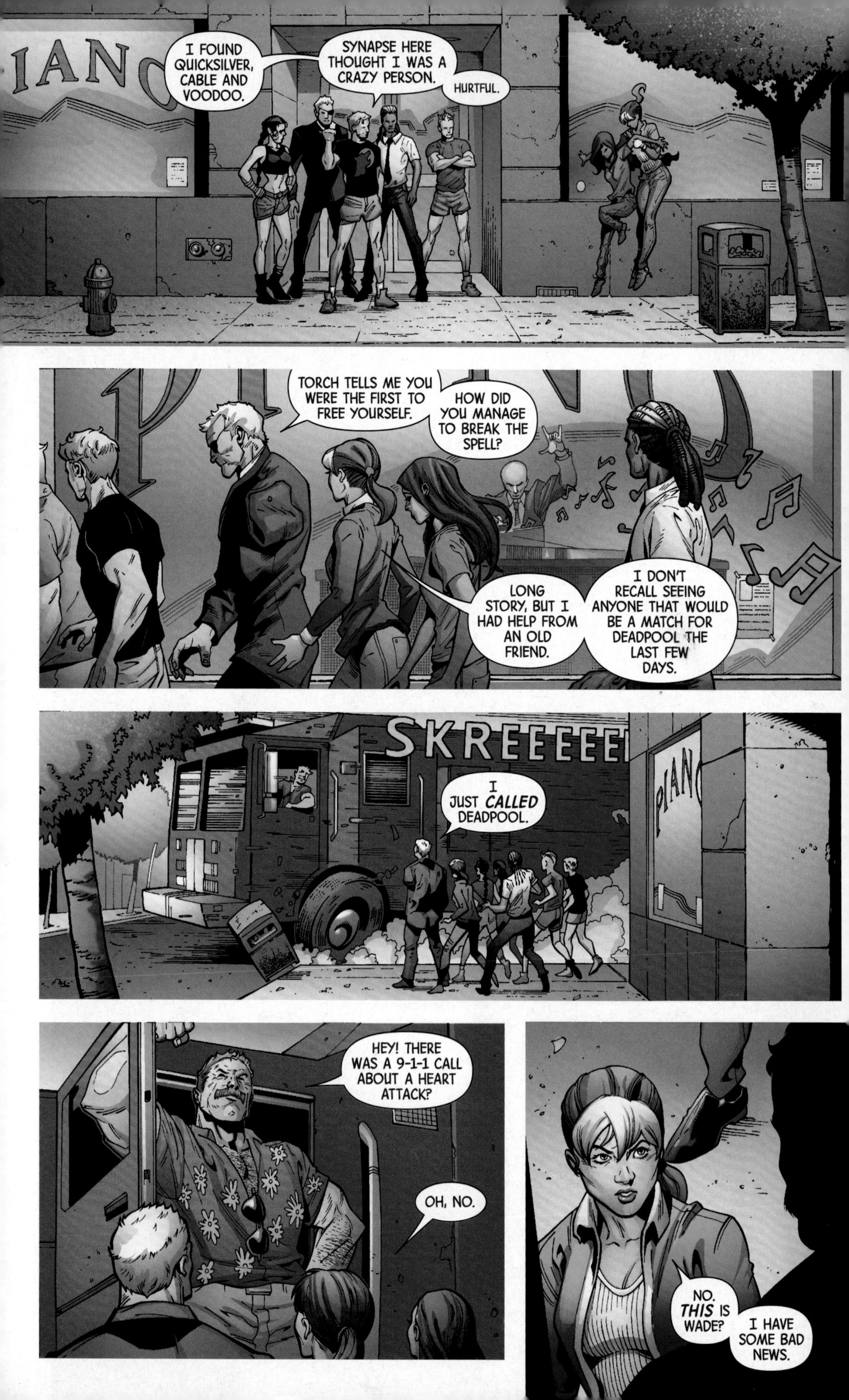
IAN
I FOUND QUICKSILVER, CABLE AND VOODOO.
SYNAPSE HERE THOUGHT I WAS A CRAZY PERSON.
HURTFUL.
TORCH TELLS ME YOU WERE THE FIRST TO FREE YOURSELF.
HOW DID YOU MANAGE TO BREAK THE SPELL?
LONG STORY, BUT I HAD HELP FROM AN OLD FRIEND.
I DON'T RECALL SEEING ANYONE THAT WOULD BE A MATCH FOR DEADPOOL THE LAST FEW DAYS.
SKREEEEEE
I JUST CALLED DEADPOOL.
PIAN
HEY! THERE WAS A 9-1-1 CALL ABOUT A HEART ATTACK?
OH, NO.
NO. THIS IS WADE?
I HAVE SOME BAD NEWS.

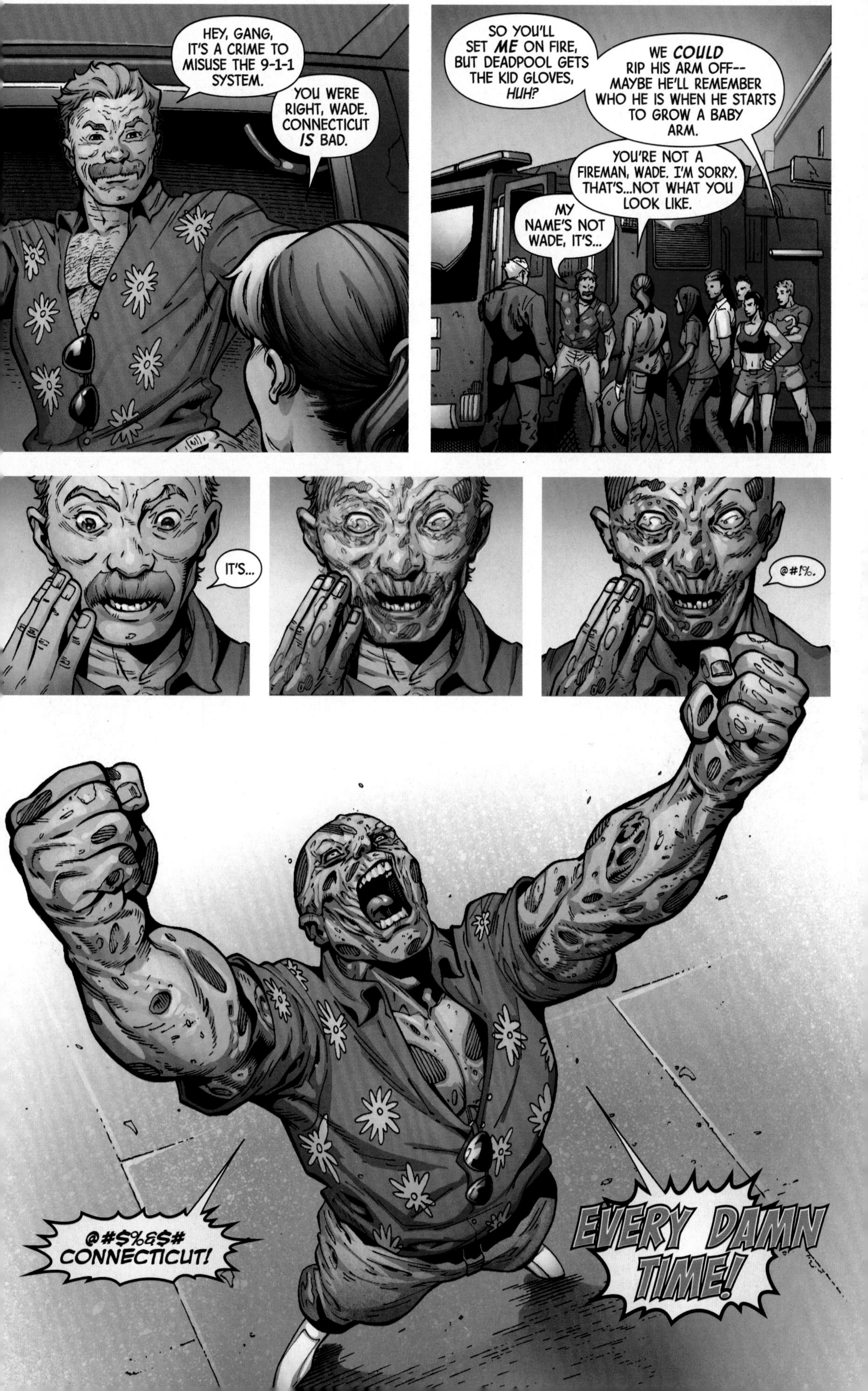

HEY, GANG, IT'S A CRIME TO MISUSE THE 9-1-1 SYSTEM.
YOU WERE RIGHT, WADE. CONNECTICUT IS BAD.
SO YOU'LL SET ME ON FIRE, BUT DEADPOOL GETS THE KID GLOVES, HUH?
WE COULD RIP HIS ARM OFF-- MAYBE HE'LL REMEMBER WHO HE IS WHEN HE STARTS TO GROW A BABY ARM.
YOU'RE NOT A FIREMAN, WADE. I'M SORRY. THAT'S...NOT WHAT YOU LOOK LIKE.
MY NAME'S NOT WADE, IT'S...
IT'S...
@#!%.
@#$%&$# CONNECTICUT!
EVERY DAMN TIME!

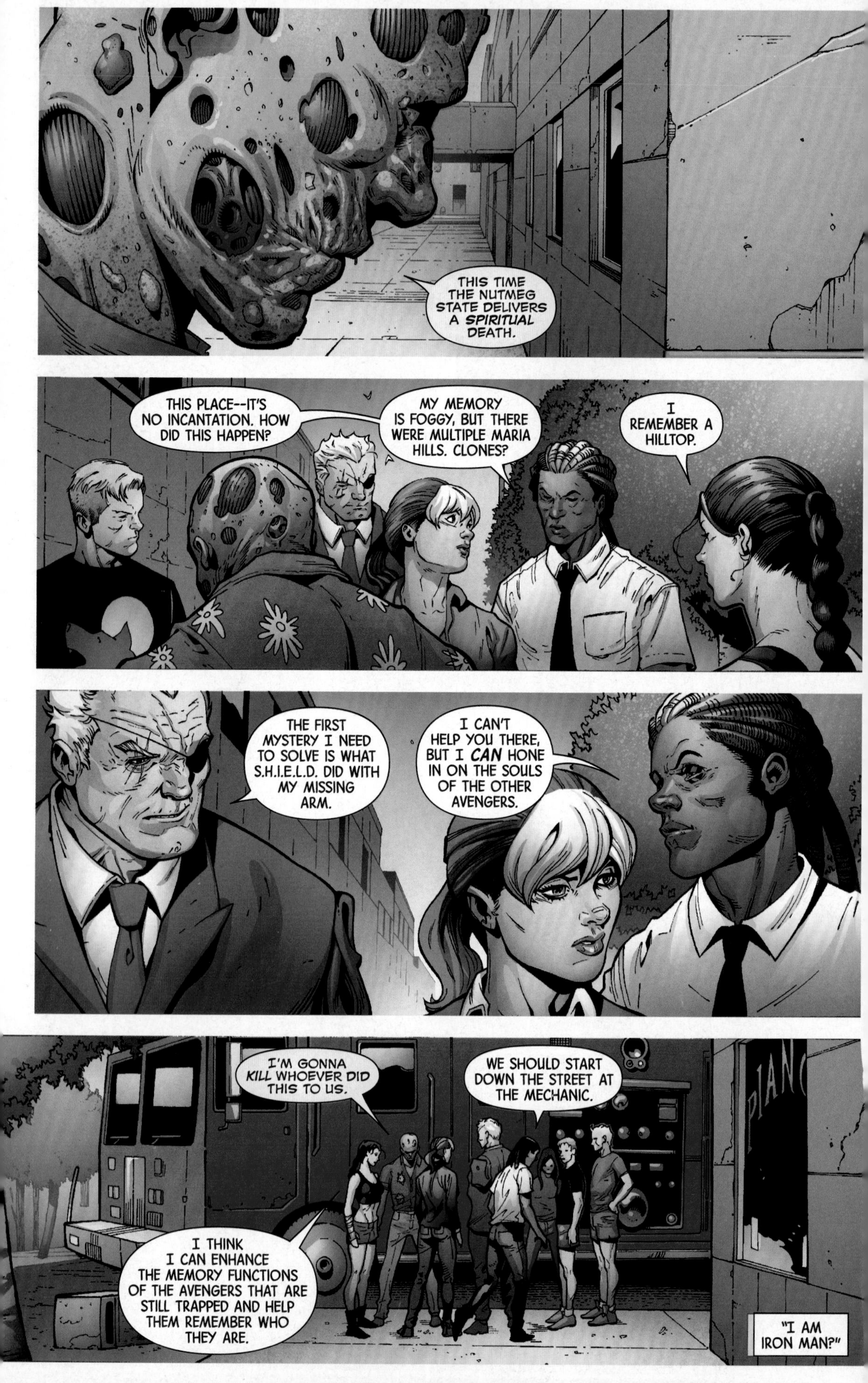

THIS TIME THE NUTMEG STATE DELIVERS A SPIRITUAL DEATH.
THIS PLACE--IT'S NO INCANTATION. HOW DID THIS HAPPEN?
MY MEMORY IS FOGGY, BUT THERE WERE MULTIPLE MARIA HILLS. CLONES?
I REMEMBER A HILLTOP.
THE FIRST MYSTERY I NEED TO SOLVE IS WHAT S.H.I.E.L.D. DID WITH MY MISSING ARM.
I CAN'T HELP YOU THERE, BUT I CAN HONE IN ON THE SOULS OF THE OTHER AVENGERS.
I'M GONNA KILL WHOEVER DID THIS TO US.
WE SHOULD START DOWN THE STREET AT THE MECHANIC.
I THINK I CAN ENHANCE THE MEMORY FUNCTIONS OF THE AVENGERS THAT ARE STILL TRAPPED AND HELP THEM REMEMBER WHO THEY ARE.
"I AM IRON MAN?"

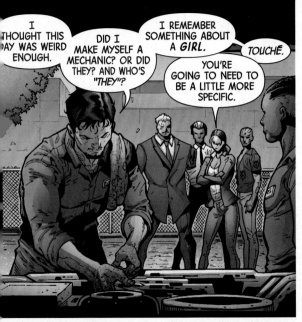

I THOUGHT THIS DAY WAS WEIRD ENOUGH.

DID I MAKE MYSELF A MECHANIC? OR DID THEY? AND WHO'S "THEY"?

I REMEMBER SOMETHING ABOUT A GIRL.

TOUCHE.

YOU'RE GOING TO NEED TO BE A LITTLE MORE SPECIFIC.

I REMEMBER A GIRL, TOO.

UNTIL WE KNOW WHAT WE'RE UP AGAINST, LET'S PLAY IT SLOW. NO REASON TO LET ANYONE KNOW THAT WE'RE AWAKE.

I SENT QUICKSILVER OUT ON RECON. WE'RE SURROUNDED BY SOME KIND OF FORCE-FIELD.

GARAGE

DAMMIT. WHERE'S MY ARMOR?

WHERE'S MY ARM?

I THINK MARIA HILL LURED US RIGHT INTO THIS TRAP.

WHERE ARE SAM WILSON AND STEVE ROGERS? HAVE THEY BEEN HIT WITH THE WHAMMY STICK, TOO?

AT LEAST IF STEVE WERE BRAINWASHED IT WOULD EXPLAIN WHY HE MADE YOU AN AVENGER.

THAT WAS NEVER ABOUT ME, IT WAS ABOUT ALL OF YOU.

I'M SORRY?

ROGERS TOLD ME I WAS AROUND TO REMIND ALL OF YOU ALL THAT NOT EVERYONE IS A GOD.

BUT WHILE WE'RE ON THE SUBJECT OF QUESTIONABLE ROSTERS, MAYBE FORMING THE *"TINY TONY URBAN ACHIEVERS"*--YES, AND *PROUD WE ARE OF ALL OF THEM*--WASN'T YOUR FINEST HOUR, MAN.

I'M *FINISHED* APOLOGIZING FOR BEING AN AVENGER. THE DECISION WAS MADE *FOR* ME BY STEVE ROGERS. YOU GOT A PROBLEM WITH IT, HEAD ON OVER TO THE PLEASANT HILL NURSING HOME AND TAKE IT UP WITH *HIM.*

WELL-- HE SHUT *ME* UP.

LET'S FIND WHERE MY ARMOR IS STOWED. NOVA'S HELMET. JOHNNY'S ASBESTOS PAJAMAS.

I COULD TELEPORT US AWAY SO WE CAN REGROUP.

THAT'LL BE OUR BACKUP PLAN. LET'S NOT GIVE UP THE ELEMENT OF SURPRISE.

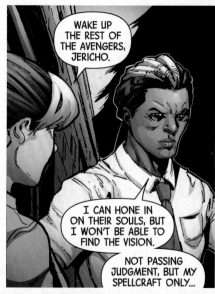

WAKE UP THE REST OF THE AVENGERS, JERICHO.

I CAN HONE IN ON THEIR SOULS, BUT I WON'T BE ABLE TO FIND THE VISION.

NOT PASSING JUDGMENT, BUT MY SPELLCRAFT ONLY...

I THINK I KNOW WHERE TO FIND HIM. MEET ME AT THE MUSIC STORE WHEN YOU'RE DONE.

MS. MARVEL, WOULD YOU JOIN ME?

"LET'S SAY FOR THE SAKE OF ARGUMENT THAT I BELIEVE YOU..."

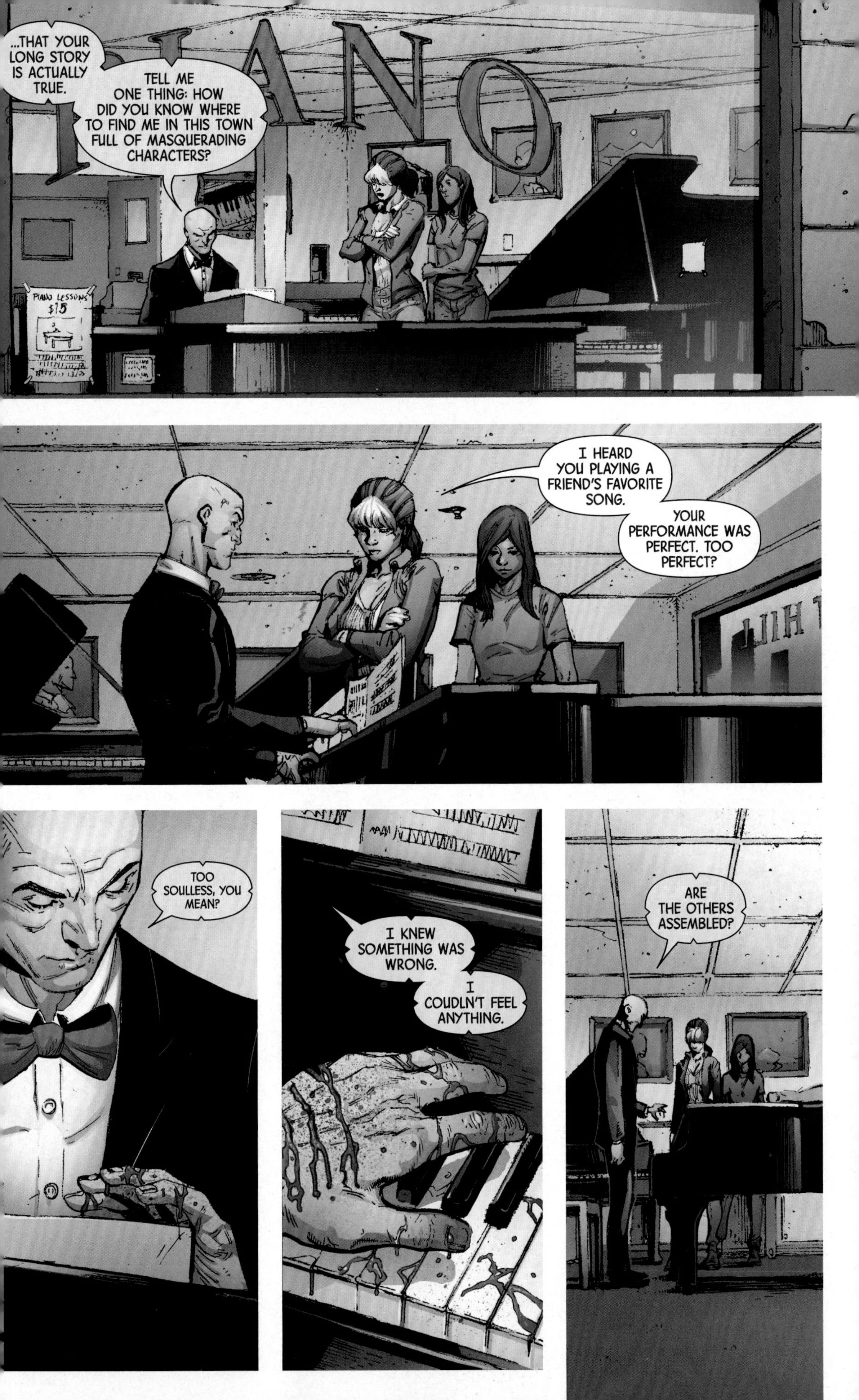

PIANO
...THAT YOUR LONG STORY IS ACTUALLY TRUE.
TELL ME ONE THING: HOW DID YOU KNOW WHERE TO FIND ME IN THIS TOWN FULL OF MASQUERADING CHARACTERS?
PIANO LESSONS $15
I HEARD YOU PLAYING A FRIEND'S FAVORITE SONG.
YOUR PERFORMANCE WAS PERFECT. TOO PERFECT?
TOO SOULLESS, YOU MEAN?
I KNEW SOMETHING WAS WRONG.
I COUDLN'T FEEL ANYTHING.
ARE THE OTHERS ASSEMBLED?

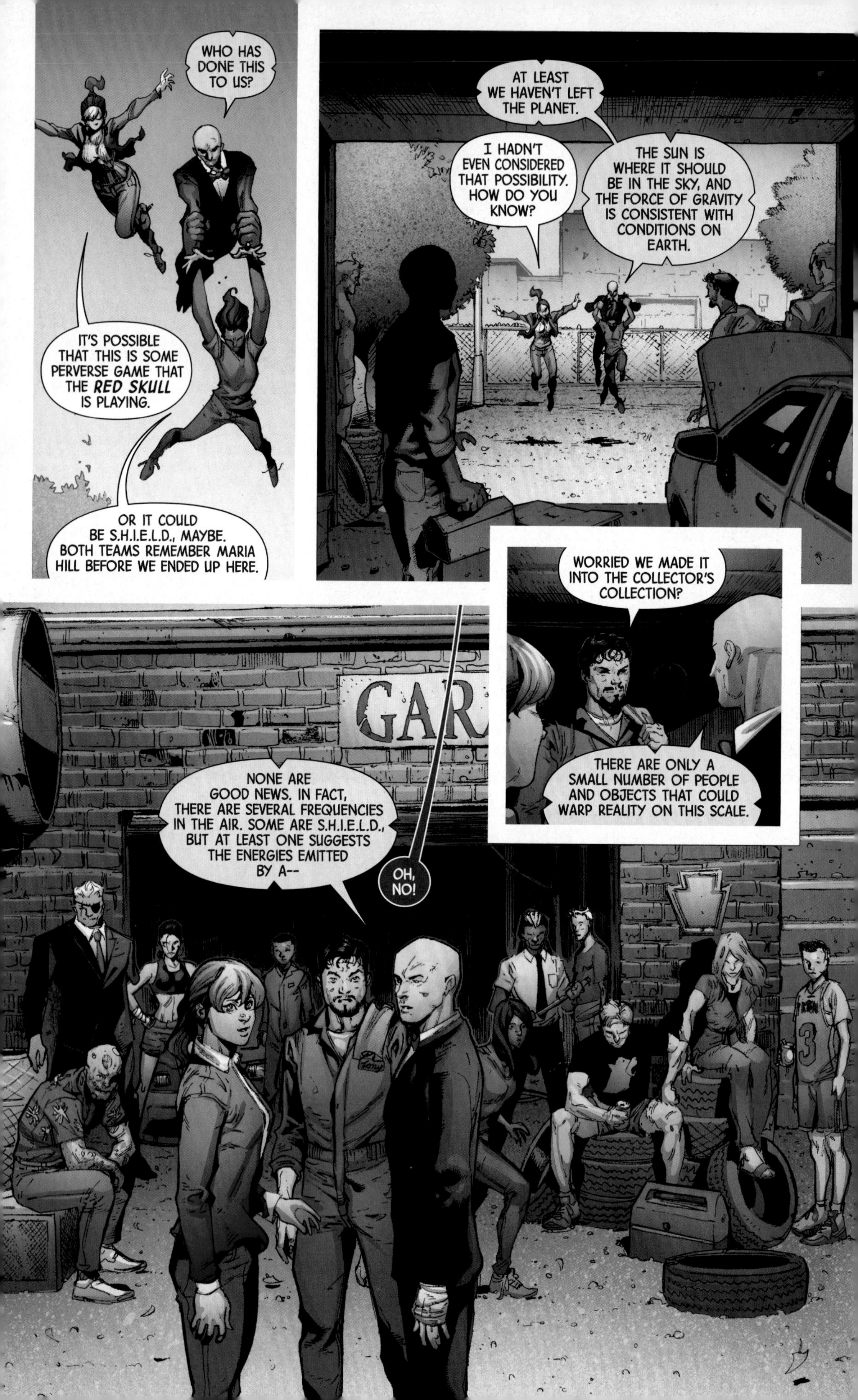
WHO HAS DONE THIS TO US?
IT'S POSSIBLE THAT THIS IS SOME PERVERSE GAME THAT THE ***RED SKULL*** IS PLAYING.
OR IT COULD BE S.H.I.E.L.D., MAYBE. BOTH TEAMS REMEMBER MARIA HILL BEFORE WE ENDED UP HERE.
AT LEAST WE HAVEN'T LEFT THE PLANET.
I HADN'T EVEN CONSIDERED THAT POSSIBILITY. HOW DO YOU KNOW?
THE SUN IS WHERE IT SHOULD BE IN THE SKY, AND THE FORCE OF GRAVITY IS CONSISTENT WITH CONDITIONS ON EARTH.
WORRIED WE MADE IT INTO THE COLLECTOR'S COLLECTION?
THERE ARE ONLY A SMALL NUMBER OF PEOPLE AND OBJECTS THAT COULD WARP REALITY ON THIS SCALE.
NONE ARE GOOD NEWS. IN FACT, THERE ARE SEVERAL FREQUENCIES IN THE AIR. SOME ARE S.H.I.E.L.D., BUT AT LEAST ONE SUGGESTS THE ENERGIES EMITTED BY A--
OH, NO!
GAR

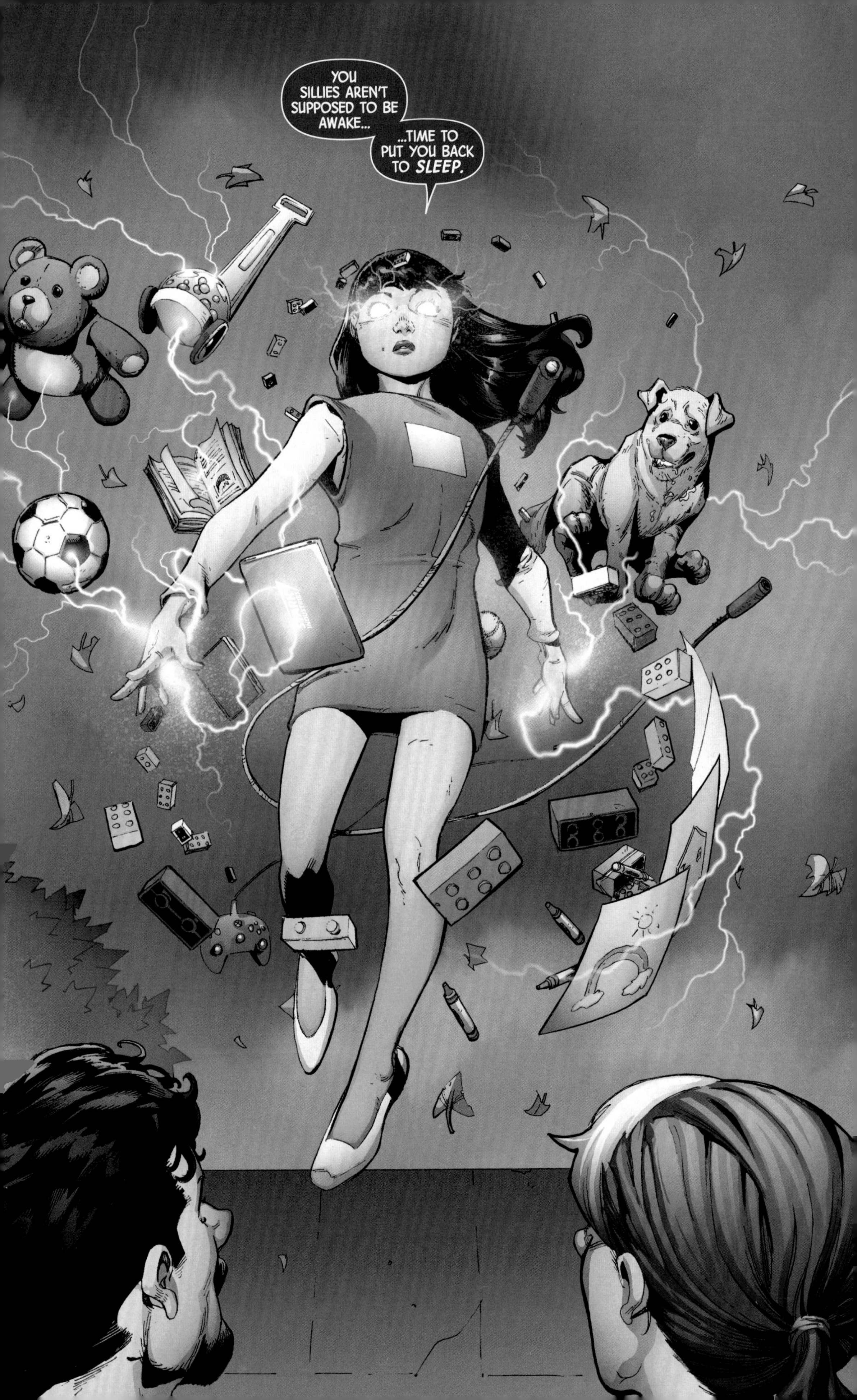
YOU SILLIES AREN'T SUPPOSED TO BE AWAKE...
...TIME TO PUT YOU BACK TO SLEEP.

9

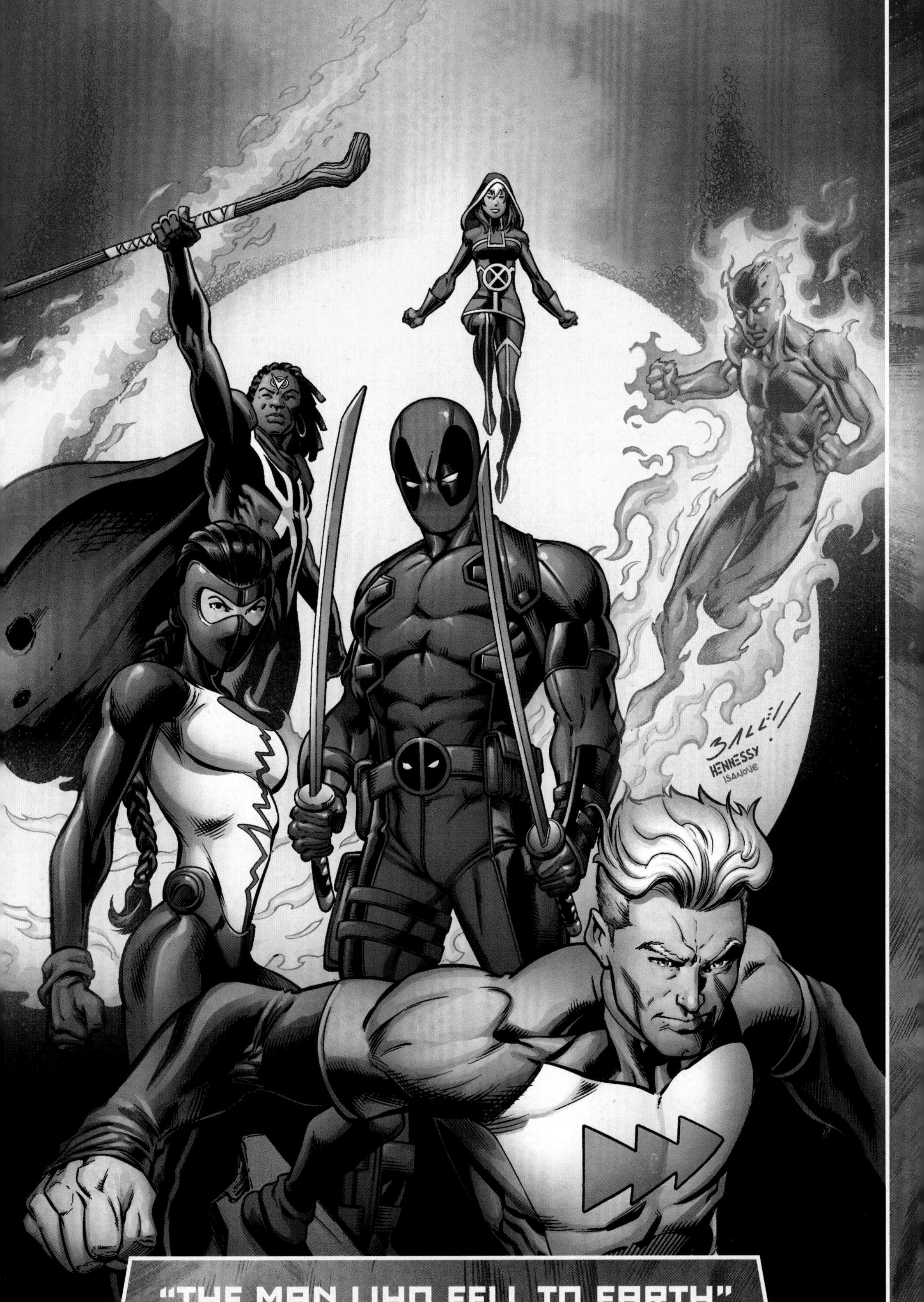

"THE MAN WHO FELL TO EARTH"

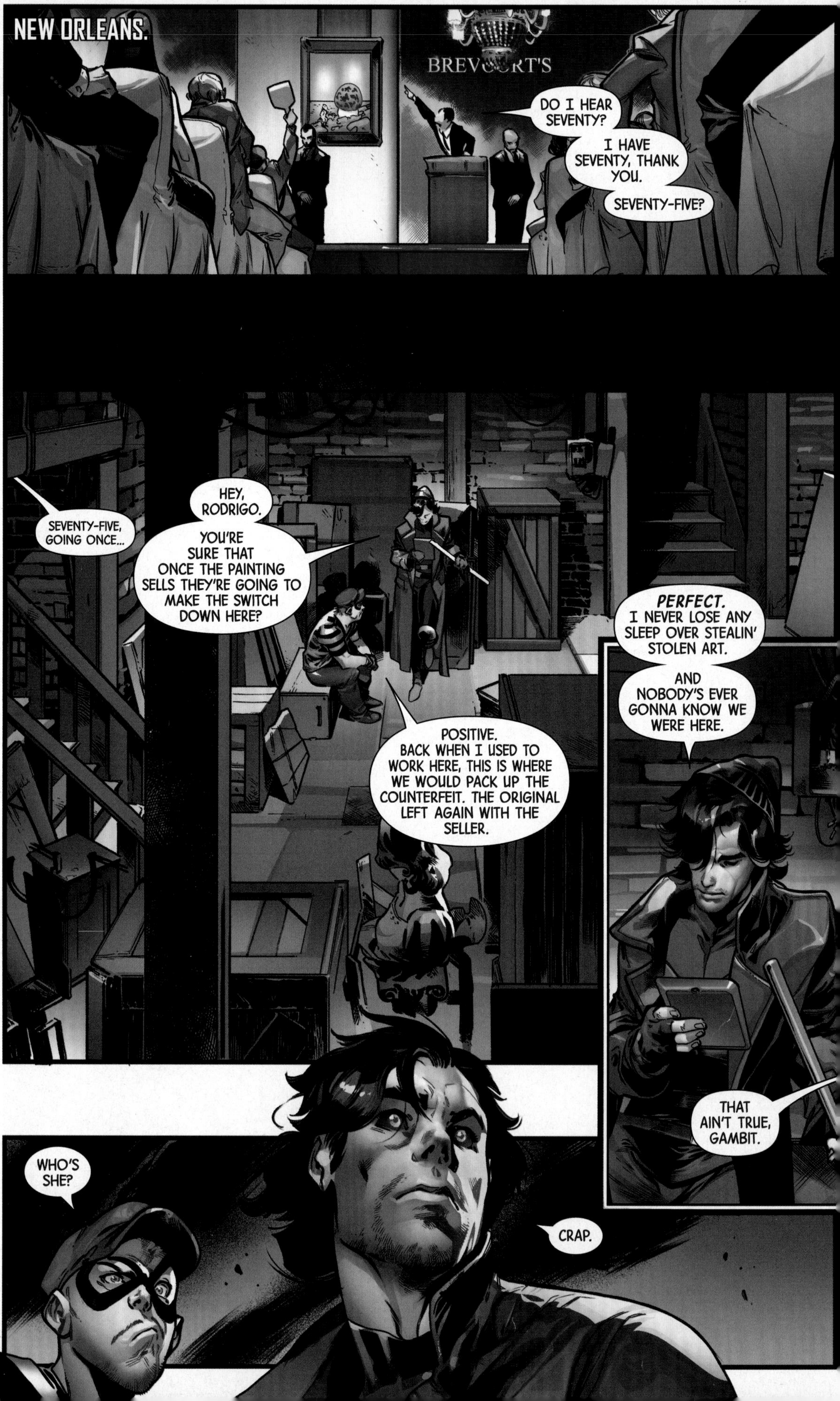

NEW ORLEANS.
BREVOORT'S
DO I HEAR SEVENTY?
I HAVE SEVENTY, THANK YOU.
SEVENTY-FIVE?
SEVENTY-FIVE, GOING ONCE...
HEY, RODRIGO.
YOU'RE SURE THAT ONCE THE PAINTING SELLS THEY'RE GOING TO MAKE THE SWITCH DOWN HERE?
POSITIVE. BACK WHEN I USED TO WORK HERE, THIS IS WHERE WE WOULD PACK UP THE COUNTERFEIT. THE ORIGINAL LEFT AGAIN WITH THE SELLER.
PERFECT. I NEVER LOSE ANY SLEEP OVER STEALIN' STOLEN ART.
AND NOBODY'S EVER GONNA KNOW WE WERE HERE.
THAT AIN'T TRUE, GAMBIT.
WHO'S SHE?
CRAP.

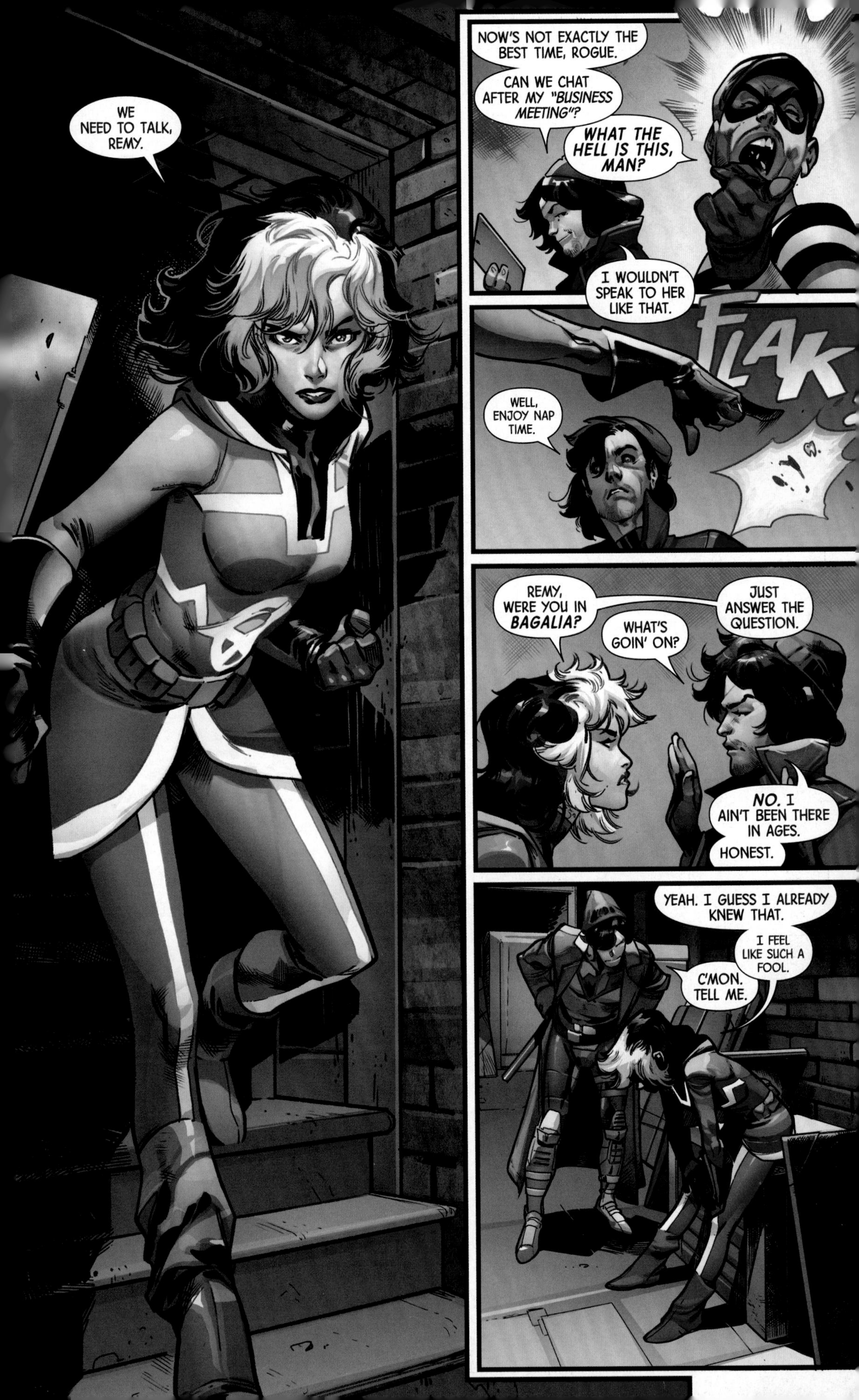
WE NEED TO TALK, REMY.
NOW'S NOT EXACTLY THE BEST TIME, ROGUE.
CAN WE CHAT AFTER MY "BUSINESS MEETING"?
WHAT THE HELL IS THIS, MAN?
I WOULDN'T SPEAK TO HER LIKE THAT.
FLAK
WELL, ENJOY NAP TIME.
REMY, WERE YOU IN BAGALIA?
WHAT'S GOIN' ON?
JUST ANSWER THE QUESTION.
NO. I AIN'T BEEN THERE IN AGES.
HONEST.
YEAH. I GUESS I ALREADY KNEW THAT.
I FEEL LIKE SUCH A FOOL.
C'MON. TELL ME.

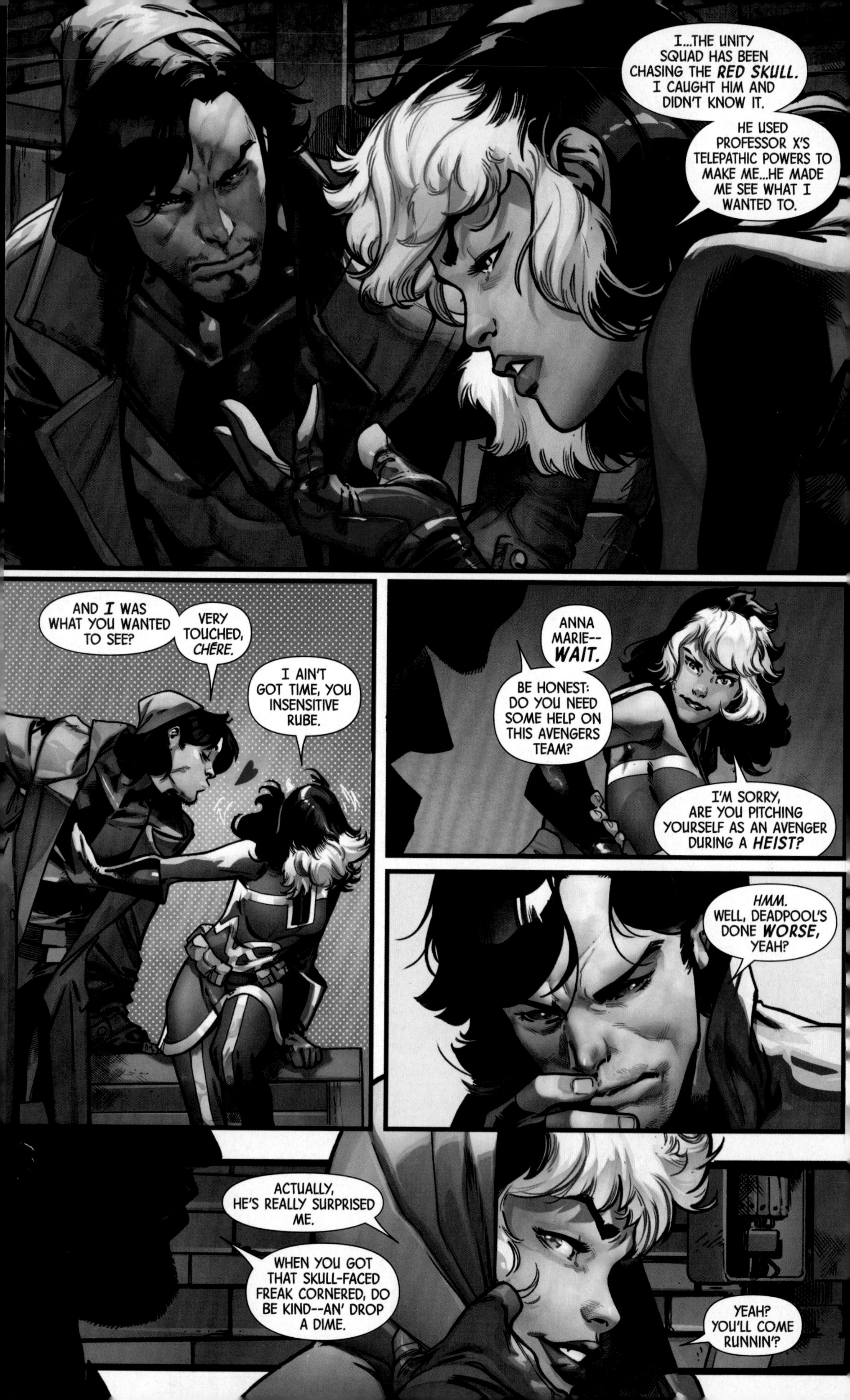
I...THE UNITY SQUAD HAS BEEN CHASING THE RED SKULL. I CAUGHT HIM AND DIDN'T KNOW IT.
HE USED PROFESSOR X'S TELEPATHIC POWERS TO MAKE ME...HE MADE ME SEE WHAT I WANTED TO.
AND I WAS WHAT YOU WANTED TO SEE?
VERY TOUCHED, CHÉRE.
I AIN'T GOT TIME, YOU INSENSITIVE RUBE.
ANNA MARIE-- WAIT.
BE HONEST: DO YOU NEED SOME HELP ON THIS AVENGERS TEAM?
I'M SORRY, ARE YOU PITCHING YOURSELF AS AN AVENGER DURING A HEIST?
HMM. WELL, DEADPOOL'S DONE WORSE, YEAH?
ACTUALLY, HE'S REALLY SURPRISED ME.
WHEN YOU GOT THAT SKULL-FACED FREAK CORNERED, DO BE KIND--AN' DROP A DIME.
YEAH? YOU'LL COME RUNNIN'?

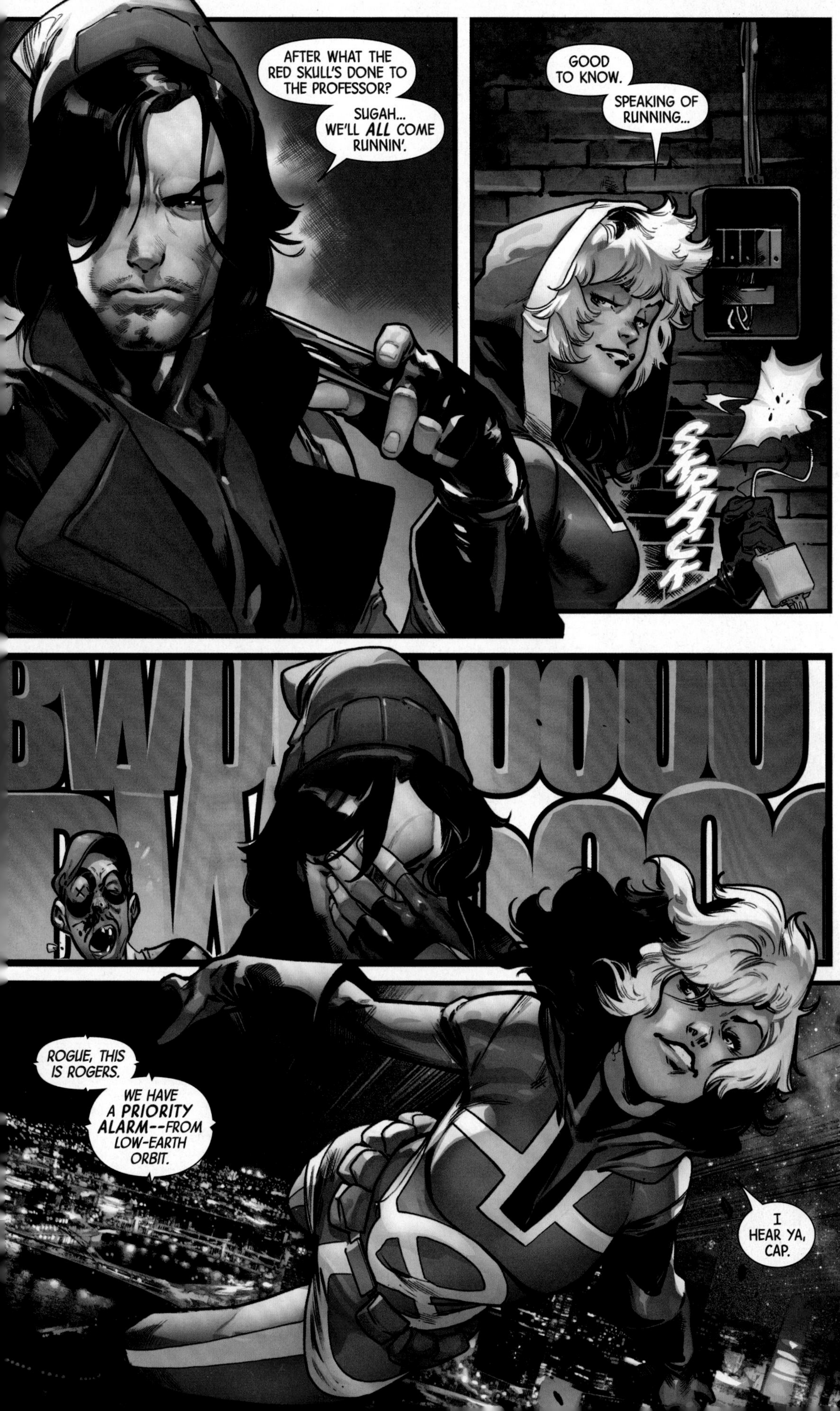
AFTER WHAT THE RED SKULL'S DONE TO THE PROFESSOR?
SUGAH... WE'LL ALL COME RUNNIN'.
GOOD TO KNOW.
SPEAKING OF RUNNING...
SKRACK
ROGUE, THIS IS ROGERS.
WE HAVE A PRIORITY ALARM--FROM LOW-EARTH ORBIT.
I HEAR YA, CAP.

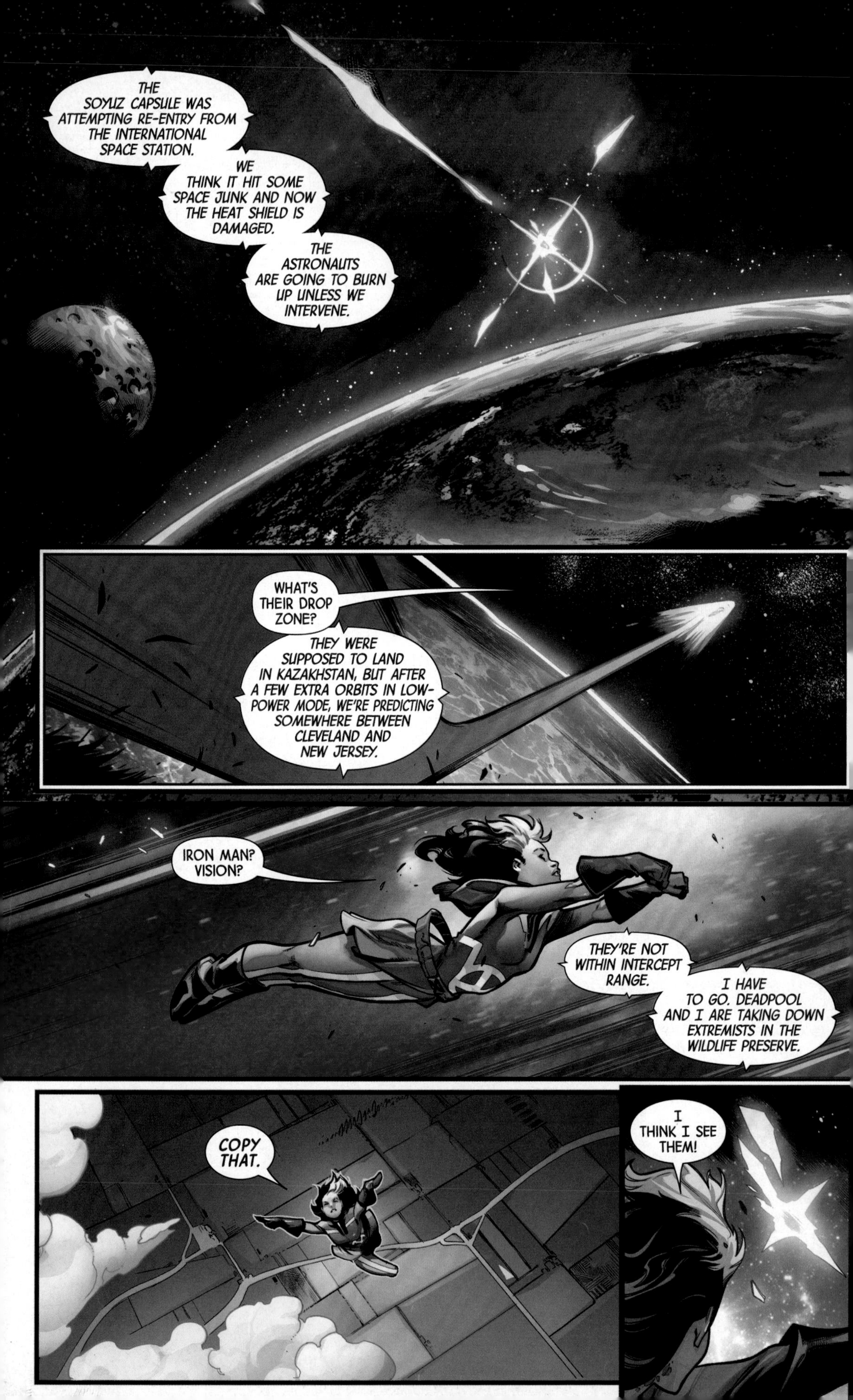
THE SOYUZ CAPSULE WAS ATTEMPTING RE-ENTRY FROM THE INTERNATIONAL SPACE STATION.
WE THINK IT HIT SOME SPACE JUNK AND NOW THE HEAT SHIELD IS DAMAGED.
THE ASTRONAUTS ARE GOING TO BURN UP UNLESS WE INTERVENE.
WHAT'S THEIR DROP ZONE?
THEY WERE SUPPOSED TO LAND IN KAZAKHSTAN, BUT AFTER A FEW EXTRA ORBITS IN LOW-POWER MODE, WE'RE PREDICTING SOMEWHERE BETWEEN CLEVELAND AND NEW JERSEY.
IRON MAN? VISION?
THEY'RE NOT WITHIN INTERCEPT RANGE.
I HAVE TO GO. DEADPOOL AND I ARE TAKING DOWN EXTREMISTS IN THE WILDLIFE PRESERVE.
COPY THAT.
I THINK I SEE THEM!

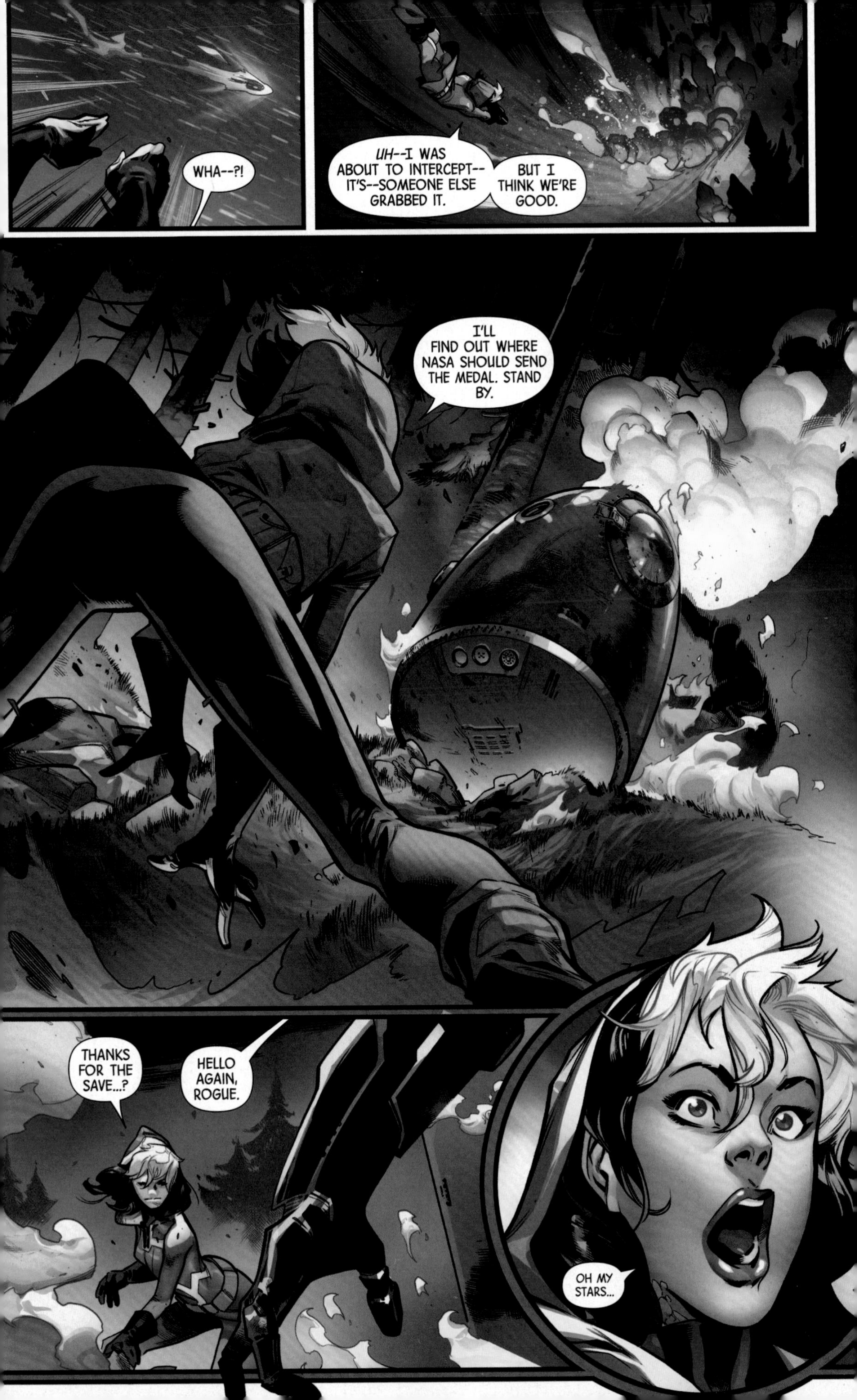
WHA--?!
UH--I WAS ABOUT TO INTERCEPT-- IT'S--SOMEONE ELSE GRABBED IT.
BUT I THINK WE'RE GOOD.
I'LL FIND OUT WHERE NASA SHOULD SEND THE MEDAL. STAND BY.
THANKS FOR THE SAVE...?
HELLO AGAIN, ROGUE.
OH MY STARS...

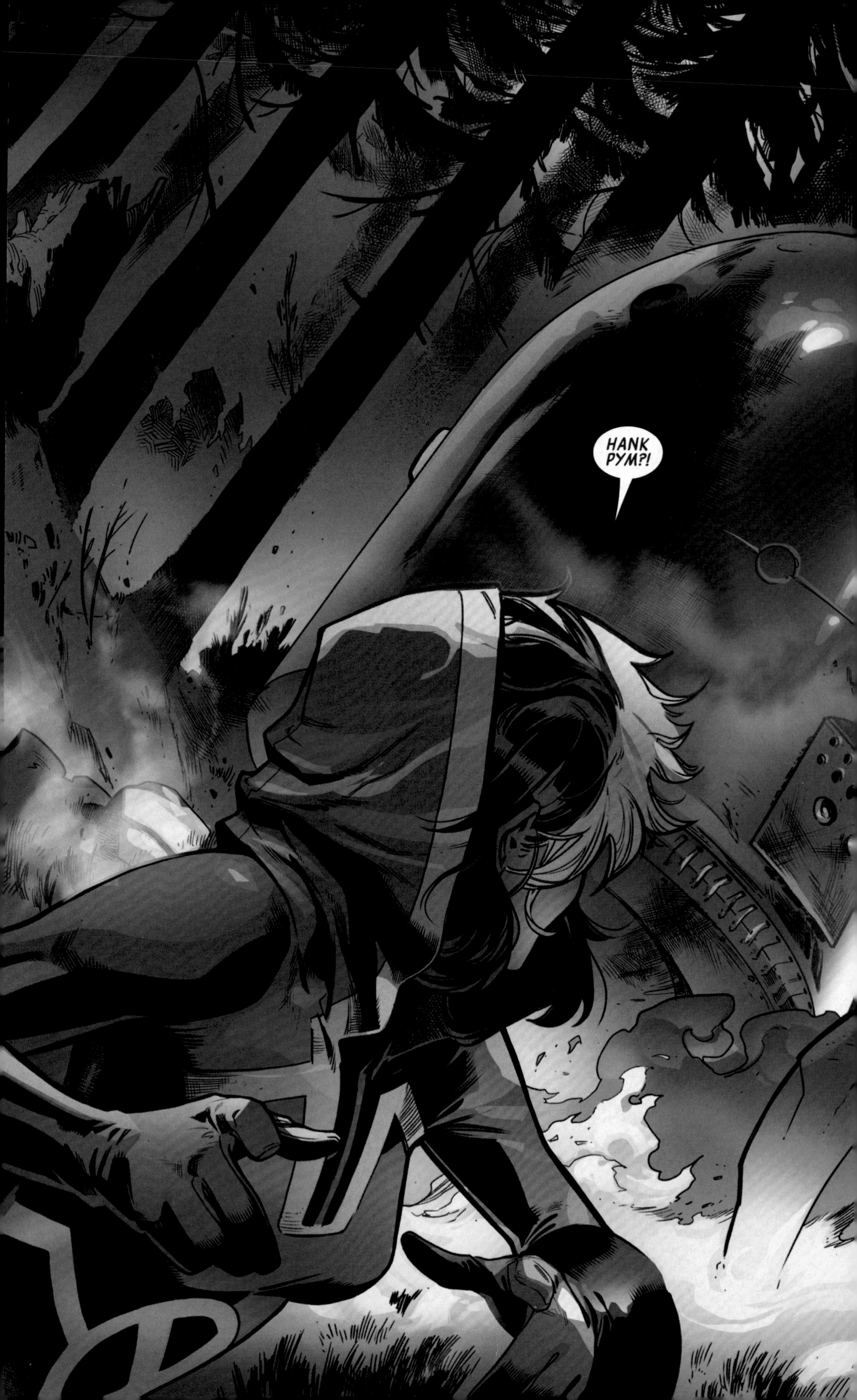
HANK PYM?!

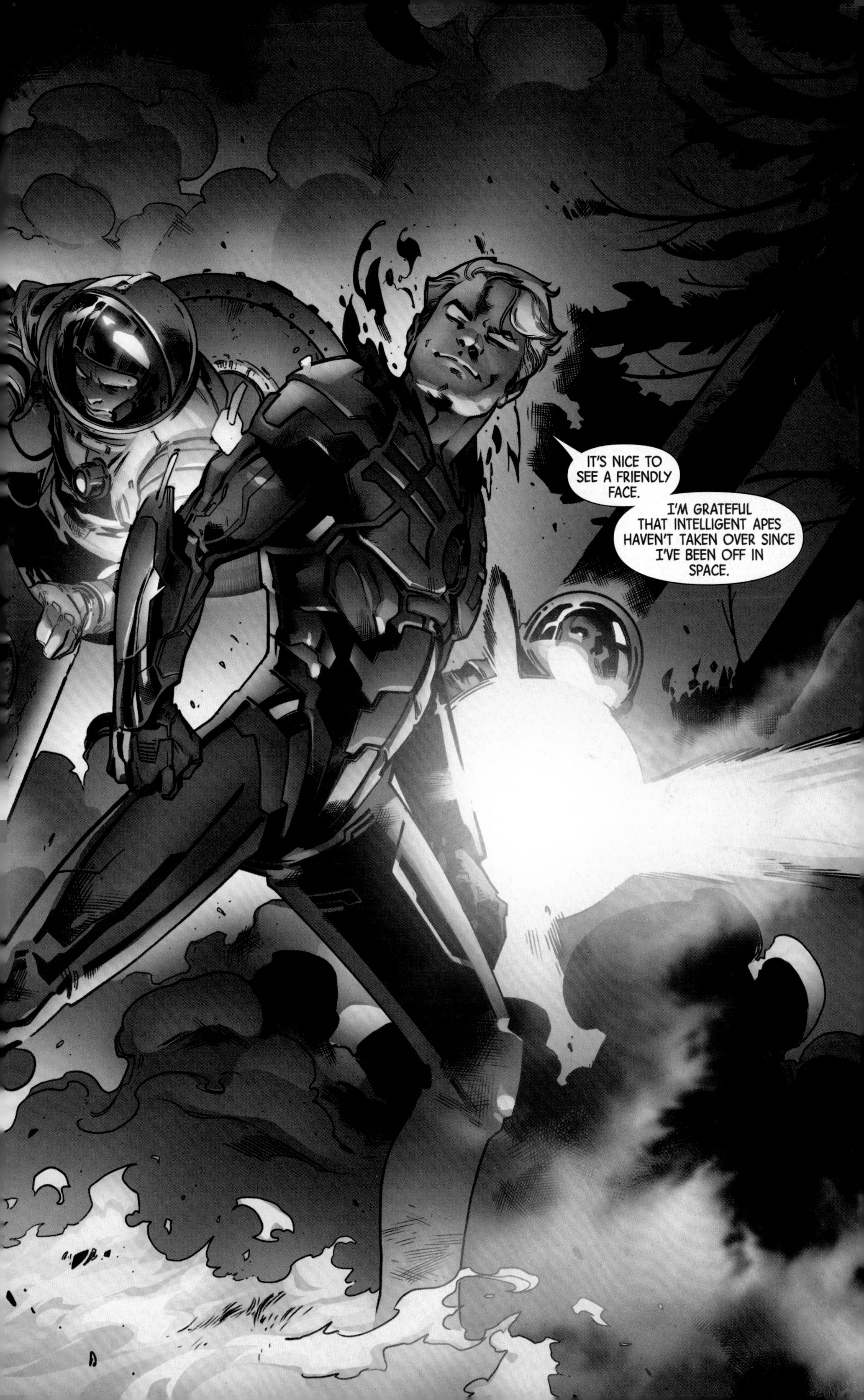
IT'S NICE TO SEE A FRIENDLY FACE.
I'M GRATEFUL THAT INTELLIGENT APES HAVEN'T TAKEN OVER SINCE I'VE BEEN OFF IN SPACE.

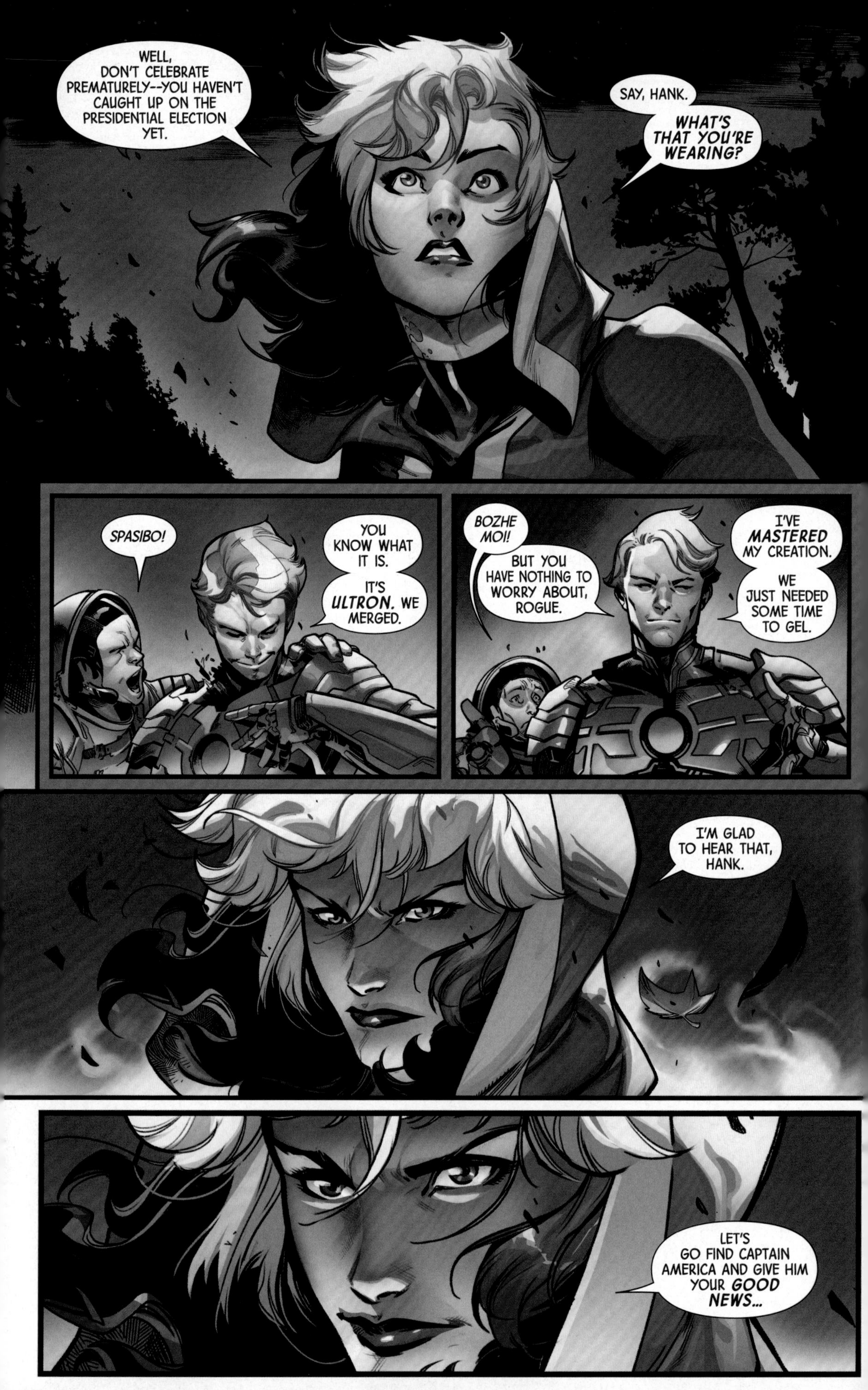
WELL, DON'T CELEBRATE PREMATURELY--YOU HAVEN'T CAUGHT UP ON THE PRESIDENTIAL ELECTION YET.
SAY, HANK.
WHAT'S THAT YOU'RE WEARING?
SPASIBO!
YOU KNOW WHAT IT IS.
IT'S ULTRON. WE MERGED.
BOZHE MOI!
BUT YOU HAVE NOTHING TO WORRY ABOUT, ROGUE.
I'VE MASTERED MY CREATION.
WE JUST NEEDED SOME TIME TO GEL.
I'M GLAD TO HEAR THAT, HANK.
LET'S GO FIND CAPTAIN AMERICA AND GIVE HIM YOUR GOOD NEWS...

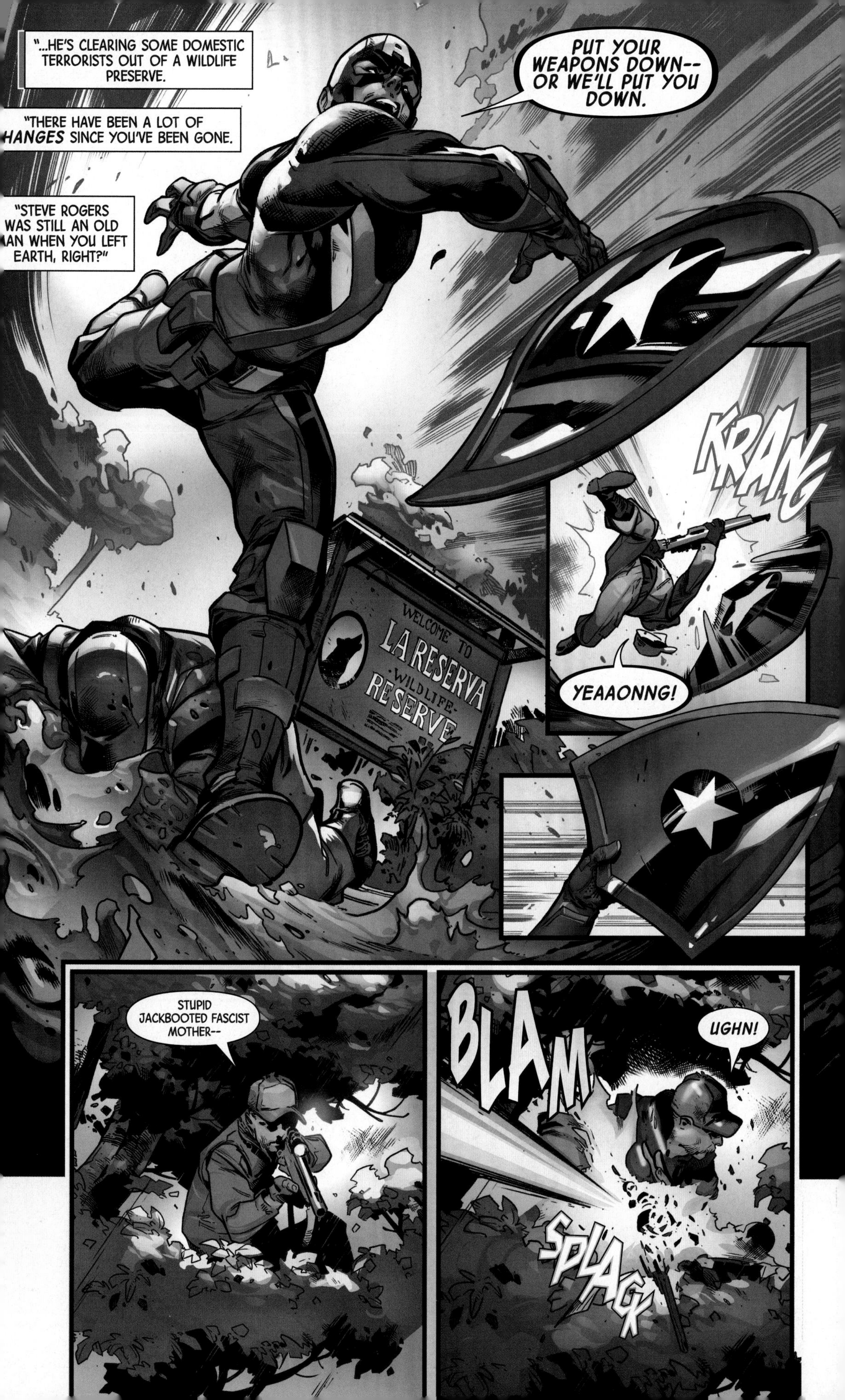
"...HE'S CLEARING SOME DOMESTIC TERRORISTS OUT OF A WILDLIFE PRESERVE.
"THERE HAVE BEEN A LOT OF HANGES SINCE YOU'VE BEEN GONE.
"STEVE ROGERS WAS STILL AN OLD AN WHEN YOU LEFT EARTH, RIGHT?"
PUT YOUR WEAPONS DOWN-- OR WE'LL PUT YOU DOWN.
WELCOME TO LA RESERVA WILDLIFE RESERVE
KRANG
YEAAONNG!
STUPID JACKBOOTED FASCIST MOTHER--
BLAM
UGHN!
SPLACK

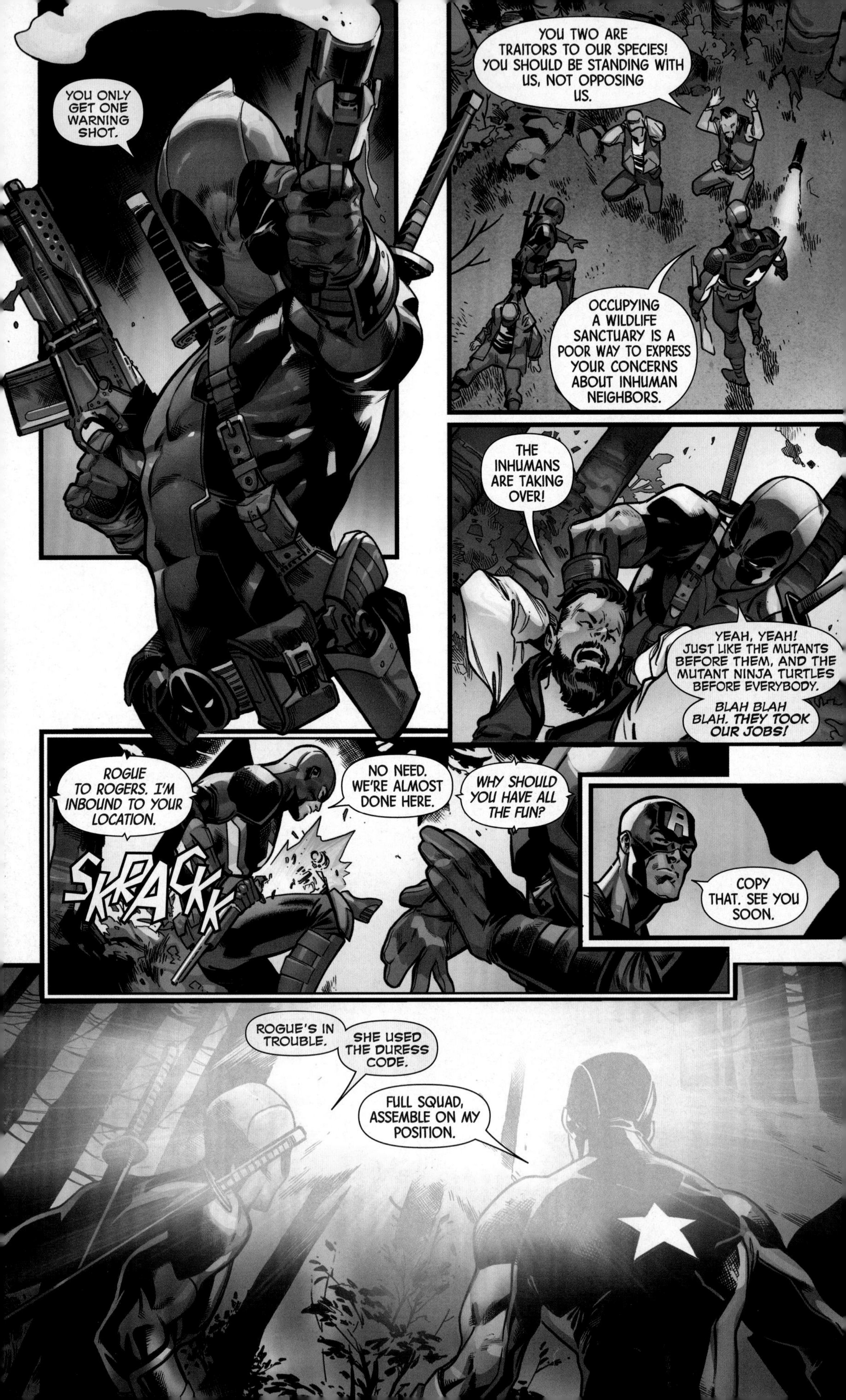
YOU ONLY GET ONE WARNING SHOT.
YOU TWO ARE TRAITORS TO OUR SPECIES! YOU SHOULD BE STANDING WITH US, NOT OPPOSING US.
OCCUPYING A WILDLIFE SANCTUARY IS A POOR WAY TO EXPRESS YOUR CONCERNS ABOUT INHUMAN NEIGHBORS.
THE INHUMANS ARE TAKING OVER!
YEAH, YEAH! JUST LIKE THE MUTANTS BEFORE THEM, AND THE MUTANT NINJA TURTLES BEFORE EVERYBODY.
BLAH BLAH BLAH. THEY TOOK OUR JOBS!
ROGUE TO ROGERS. I'M INBOUND TO YOUR LOCATION.
SKRACKK
NO NEED. WE'RE ALMOST DONE HERE.
WHY SHOULD YOU HAVE ALL THE FUN?
COPY THAT. SEE YOU SOON.
ROGUE'S IN TROUBLE.
SHE USED THE DURESS CODE.
FULL SQUAD, ASSEMBLE ON MY POSITION.

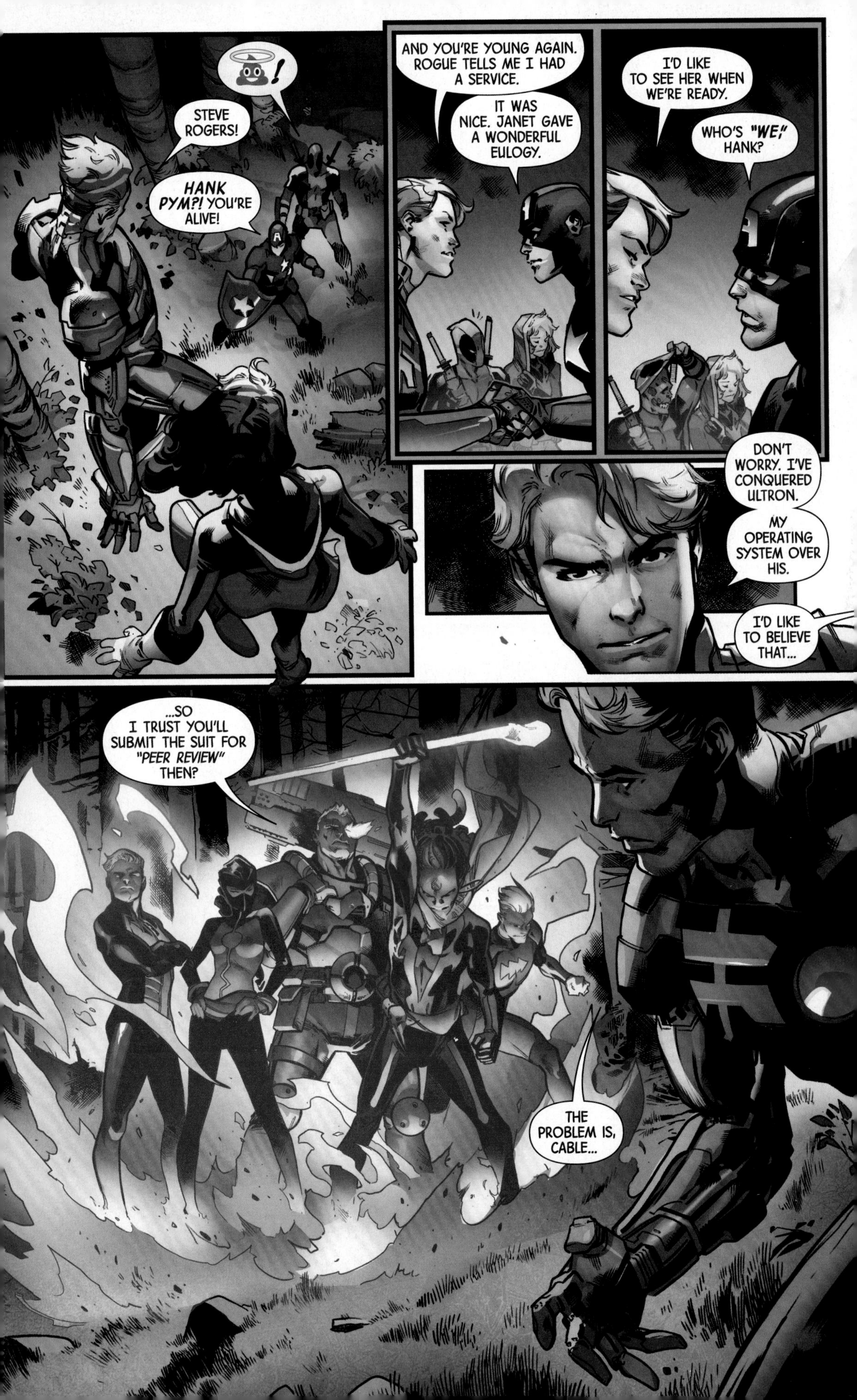
STEVE ROGERS!
!
HANK PYM?! YOU'RE ALIVE!
AND YOU'RE YOUNG AGAIN. ROGUE TELLS ME I HAD A SERVICE.
IT WAS NICE. JANET GAVE A WONDERFUL EULOGY.
I'D LIKE TO SEE HER WHEN WE'RE READY.
WHO'S "WE," HANK?
DON'T WORRY. I'VE CONQUERED ULTRON.
MY OPERATING SYSTEM OVER HIS.
I'D LIKE TO BELIEVE THAT...
...SO I TRUST YOU'LL SUBMIT THE SUIT FOR "PEER REVIEW" THEN?
THE PROBLEM IS, CABLE...

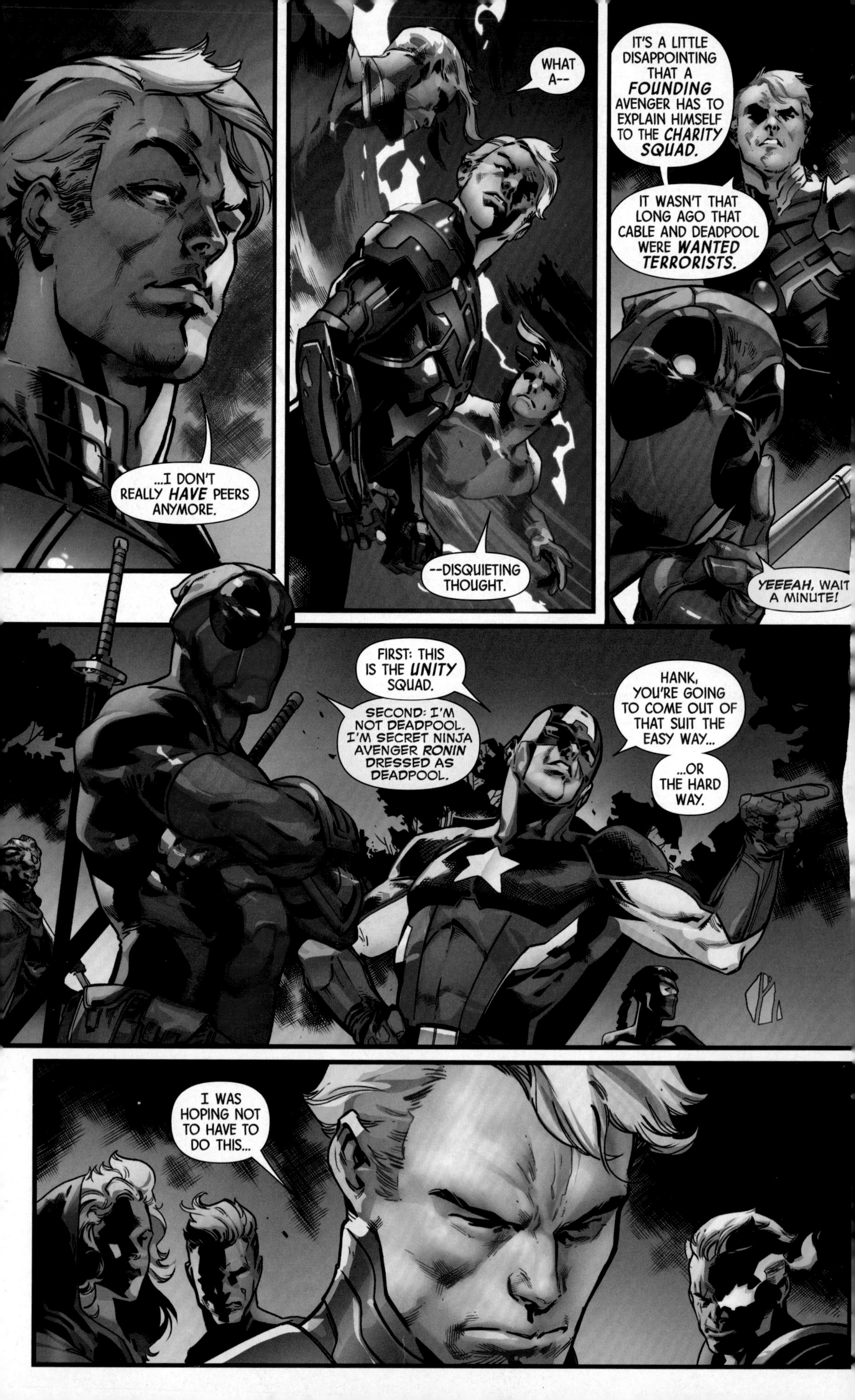
...I DON'T REALLY *HAVE* PEERS ANYMORE.
WHAT A--
--DISQUIETING THOUGHT.
IT'S A LITTLE DISAPPOINTING THAT A *FOUNDING* AVENGER HAS TO EXPLAIN HIMSELF TO THE *CHARITY SQUAD.*
IT WASN'T THAT LONG AGO THAT CABLE AND DEADPOOL WERE *WANTED TERRORISTS.*
YEEEAH, WAIT A MINUTE!
FIRST: THIS IS THE *UNITY* SQUAD.
SECOND: I'M NOT DEADPOOL. I'M SECRET NINJA AVENGER *RONIN* DRESSED AS DEADPOOL.
HANK, YOU'RE GOING TO COME OUT OF THAT SUIT THE EASY WAY...
...OR THE HARD WAY.
I WAS HOPING NOT TO HAVE TO DO THIS...

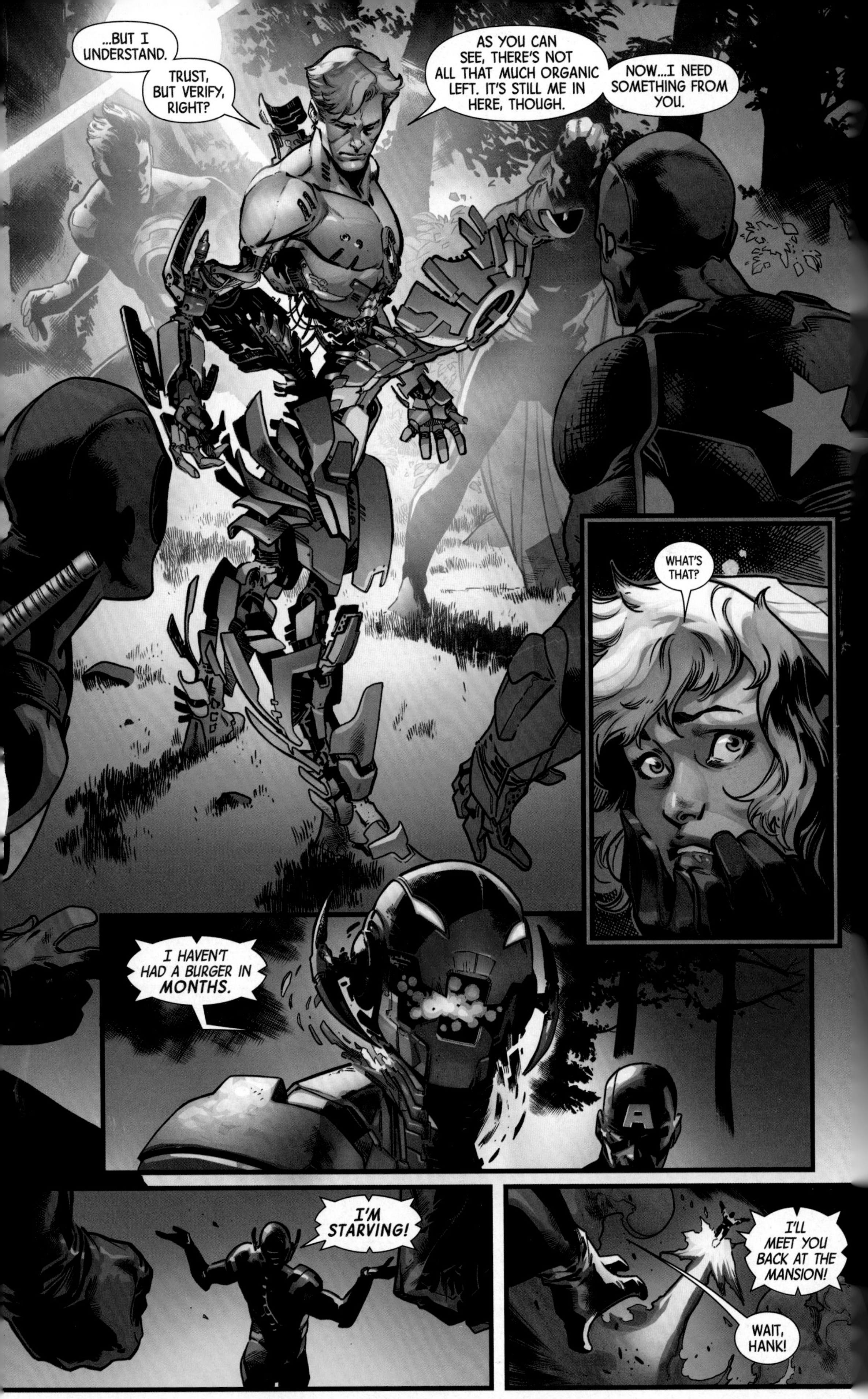
...BUT I UNDERSTAND.
TRUST, BUT VERIFY, RIGHT?
AS YOU CAN SEE, THERE'S NOT ALL THAT MUCH ORGANIC LEFT. IT'S STILL ME IN HERE, THOUGH.
NOW...I NEED SOMETHING FROM YOU.
WHAT'S THAT?
I HAVEN'T HAD A BURGER IN MONTHS.
I'M STARVING!
I'LL MEET YOU BACK AT THE MANSION!
WAIT, HANK!

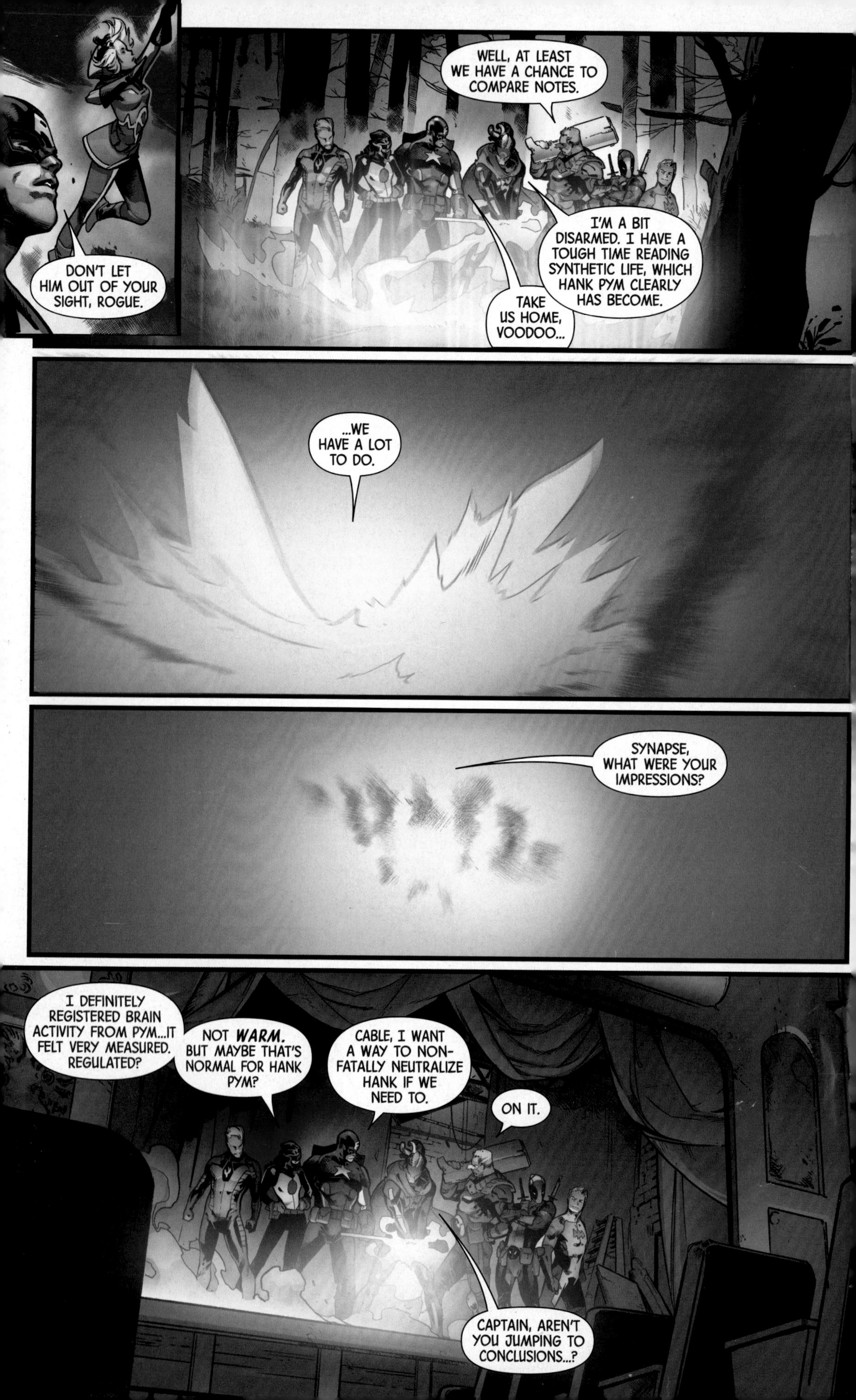
DON'T LET HIM OUT OF YOUR SIGHT, ROGUE.
WELL, AT LEAST WE HAVE A CHANCE TO COMPARE NOTES.
I'M A BIT DISARMED. I HAVE A TOUGH TIME READING SYNTHETIC LIFE, WHICH HANK PYM CLEARLY HAS BECOME.
TAKE US HOME, VOODOO...
...WE HAVE A LOT TO DO.
SYNAPSE, WHAT WERE YOUR IMPRESSIONS?
I DEFINITELY REGISTERED BRAIN ACTIVITY FROM PYM...IT FELT VERY MEASURED. REGULATED?
NOT *WARM.* BUT MAYBE THAT'S NORMAL FOR HANK PYM?
CABLE, I WANT A WAY TO NON-FATALLY NEUTRALIZE HANK IF WE NEED TO.
ON IT.
CAPTAIN, AREN'T YOU JUMPING TO CONCLUSIONS...?

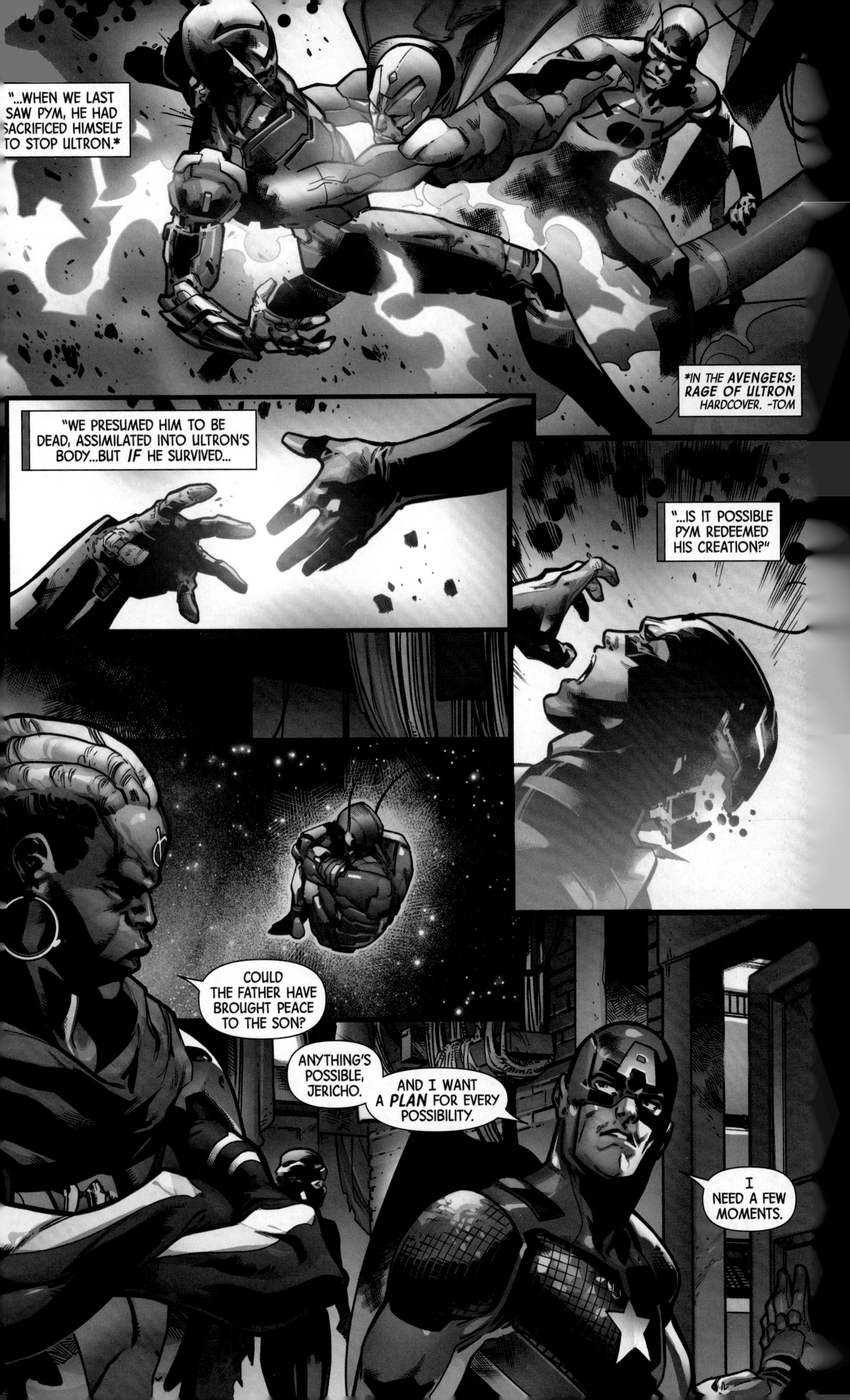
"...WHEN WE LAST SAW PYM, HE HAD SACRIFICED HIMSELF TO STOP ULTRON.*
*IN THE AVENGERS: RAGE OF ULTRON HARDCOVER. -TOM
"WE PRESUMED HIM TO BE DEAD, ASSIMILATED INTO ULTRON'S BODY...BUT IF HE SURVIVED...
"...IS IT POSSIBLE PYM REDEEMED HIS CREATION?"
COULD THE FATHER HAVE BROUGHT PEACE TO THE SON?
ANYTHING'S POSSIBLE, JERICHO.
AND I WANT A PLAN FOR EVERY POSSIBILITY.
I NEED A FEW MOMENTS.

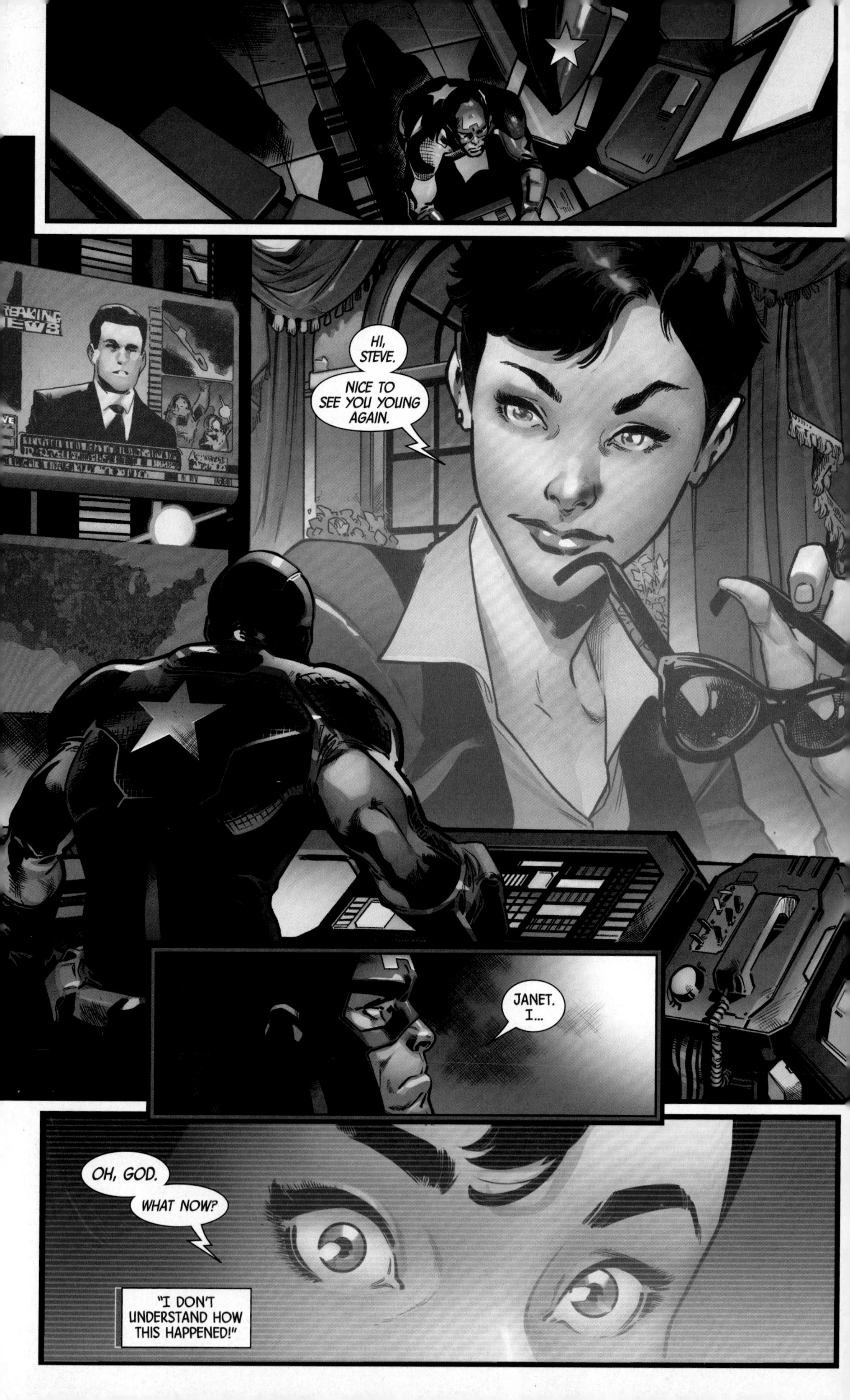

HI, STEVE.
NICE TO SEE YOU YOUNG AGAIN.
JANET. I...
OH, GOD.
WHAT NOW?
"I DON'T UNDERSTAND HOW THIS HAPPENED!"

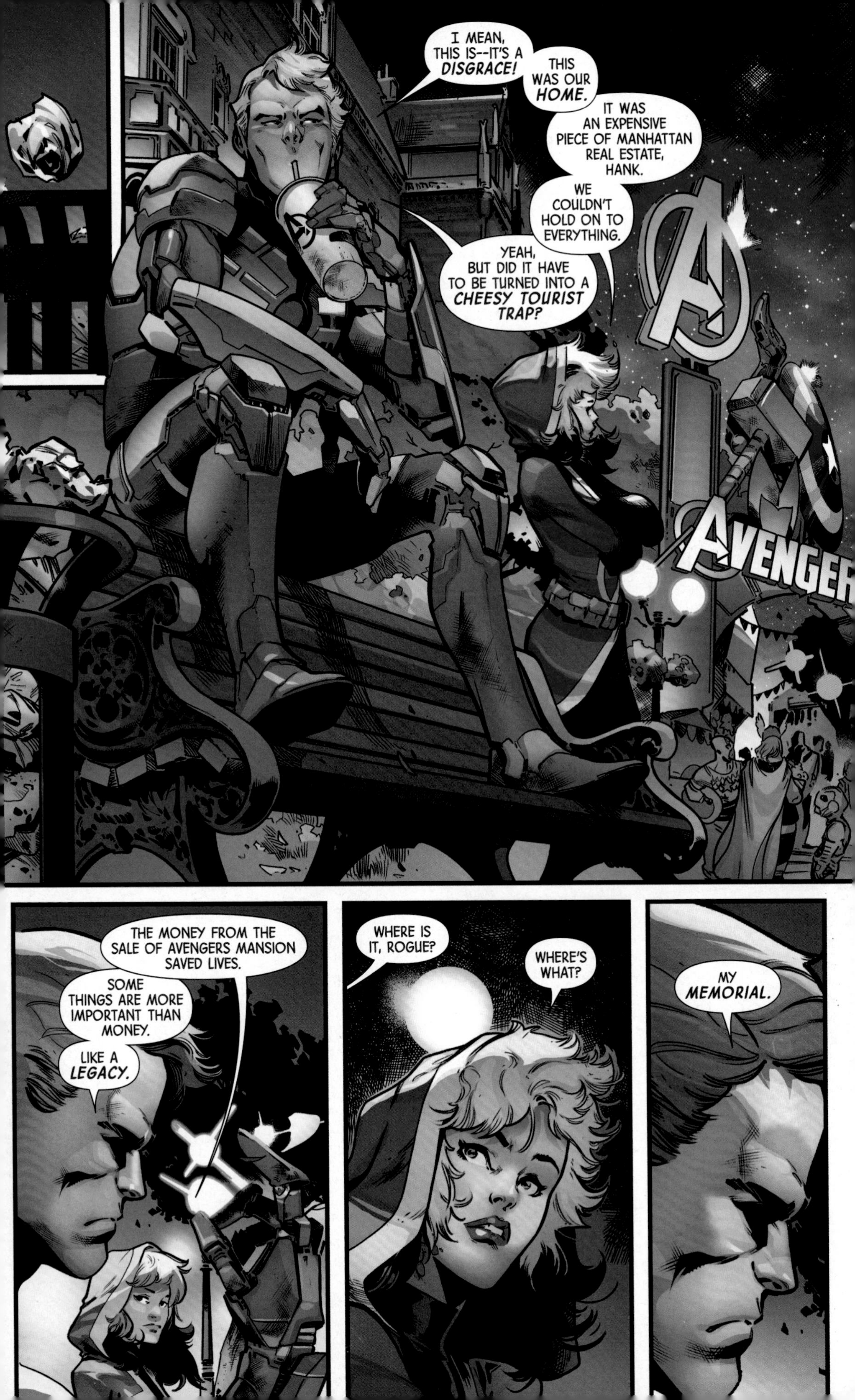

I MEAN, THIS IS--IT'S A DISGRACE!
THIS WAS OUR HOME.
IT WAS AN EXPENSIVE PIECE OF MANHATTAN REAL ESTATE, HANK.
WE COULDN'T HOLD ON TO EVERYTHING.
YEAH, BUT DID IT HAVE TO BE TURNED INTO A CHEESY TOURIST TRAP?
AVENGER
THE MONEY FROM THE SALE OF AVENGERS MANSION SAVED LIVES.
SOME THINGS ARE MORE IMPORTANT THAN MONEY.
LIKE A LEGACY.
WHERE IS IT, ROGUE?
WHERE'S WHAT?
MY MEMORIAL.

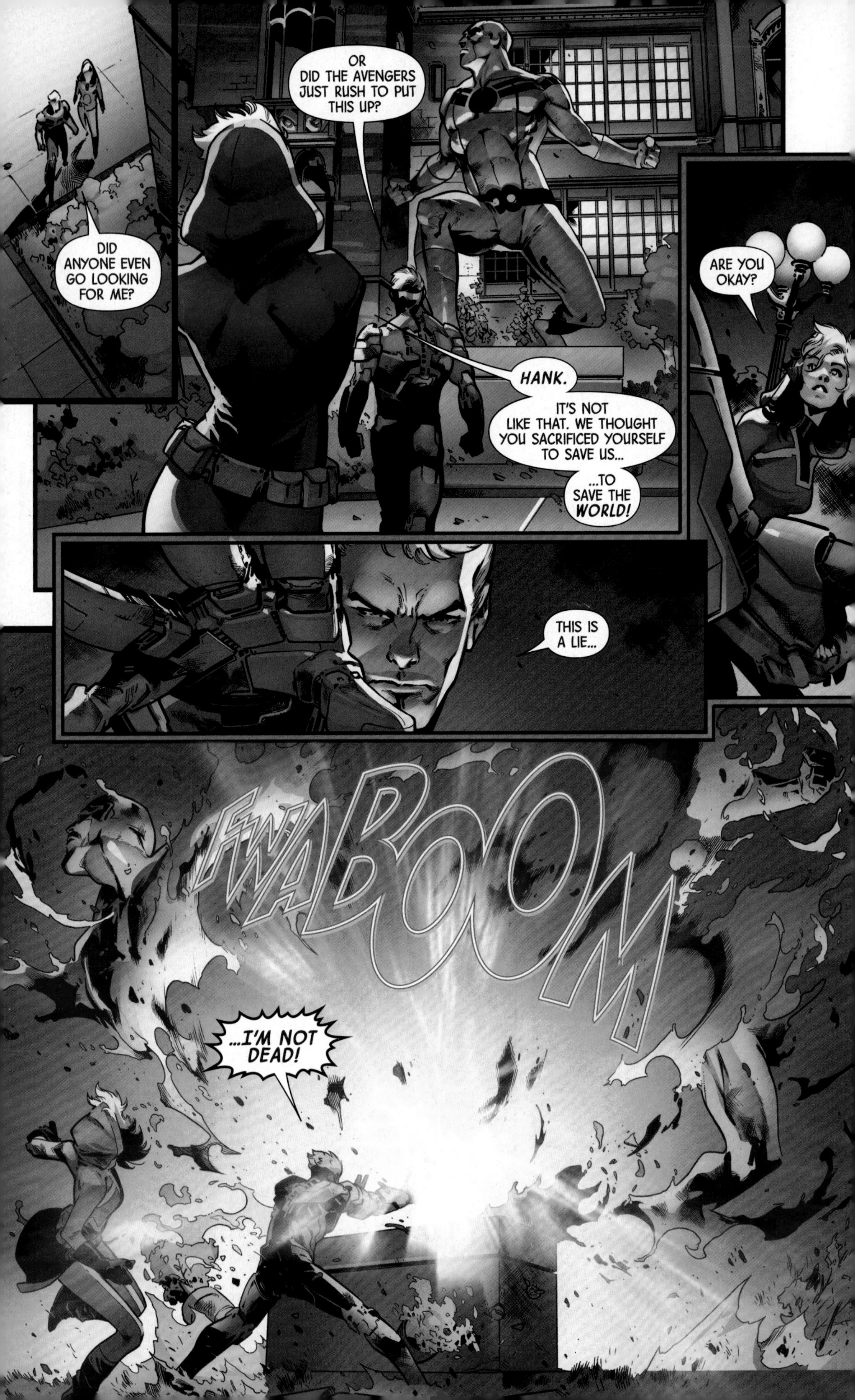
DID ANYONE EVEN GO LOOKING FOR ME?
OR DID THE AVENGERS JUST RUSH TO PUT THIS UP?
ARE YOU OKAY?
HANK.
IT'S NOT LIKE THAT. WE THOUGHT YOU SACRIFICED YOURSELF TO SAVE US...
...TO SAVE THE WORLD!
THIS IS A LIE...
FWABOOM
...I'M NOT DEAD!

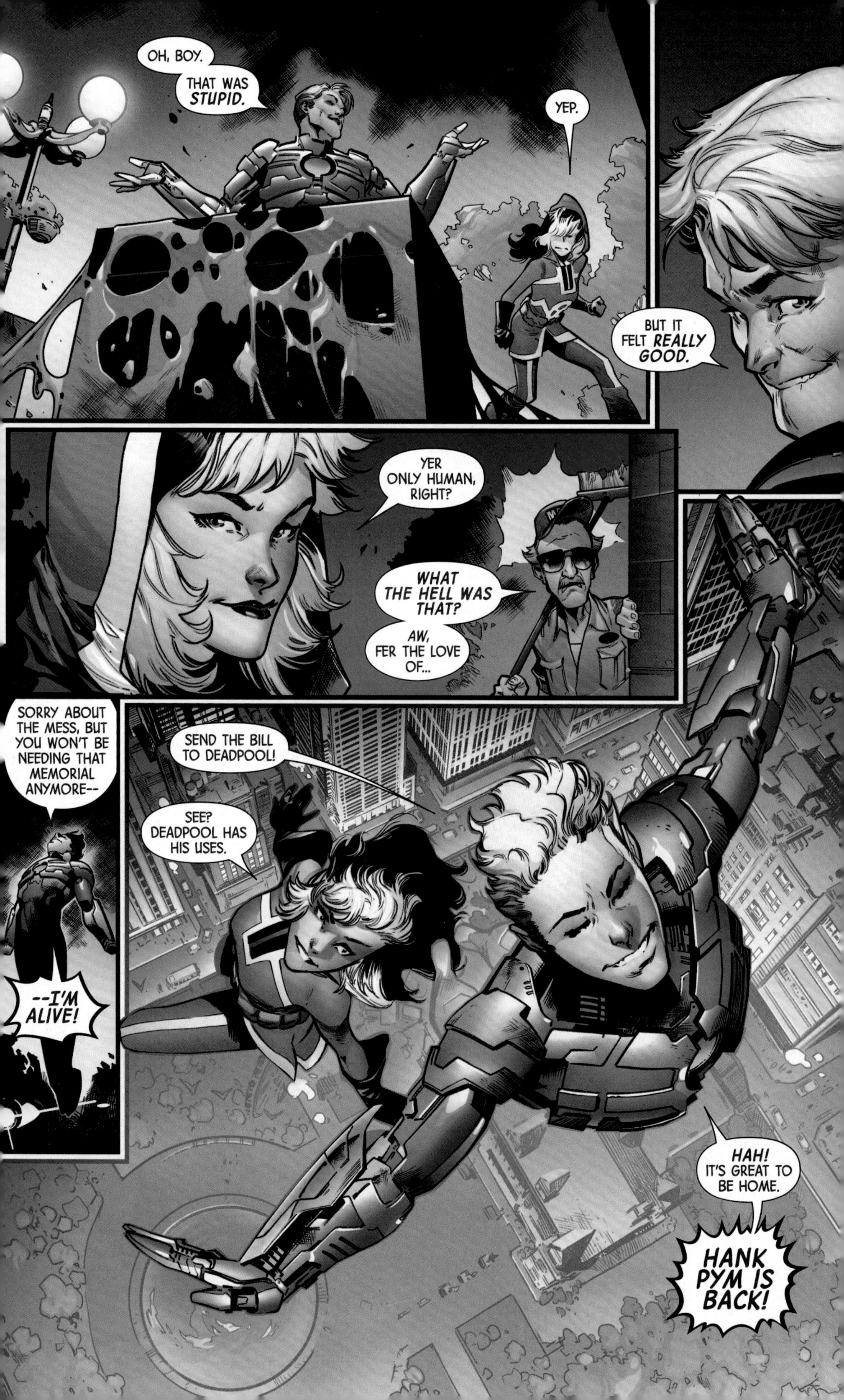
OH, BOY.
THAT WAS STUPID.
YEP.
BUT IT FELT REALLY GOOD.
YER ONLY HUMAN, RIGHT?
WHAT THE HELL WAS THAT?
AW, FER THE LOVE OF...
SORRY ABOUT THE MESS, BUT YOU WON'T BE NEEDING THAT MEMORIAL ANYMORE--
--I'M ALIVE!
SEND THE BILL TO DEADPOOL!
SEE? DEADPOOL HAS HIS USES.
HAH! IT'S GREAT TO BE HOME.
HANK PYM IS BACK!

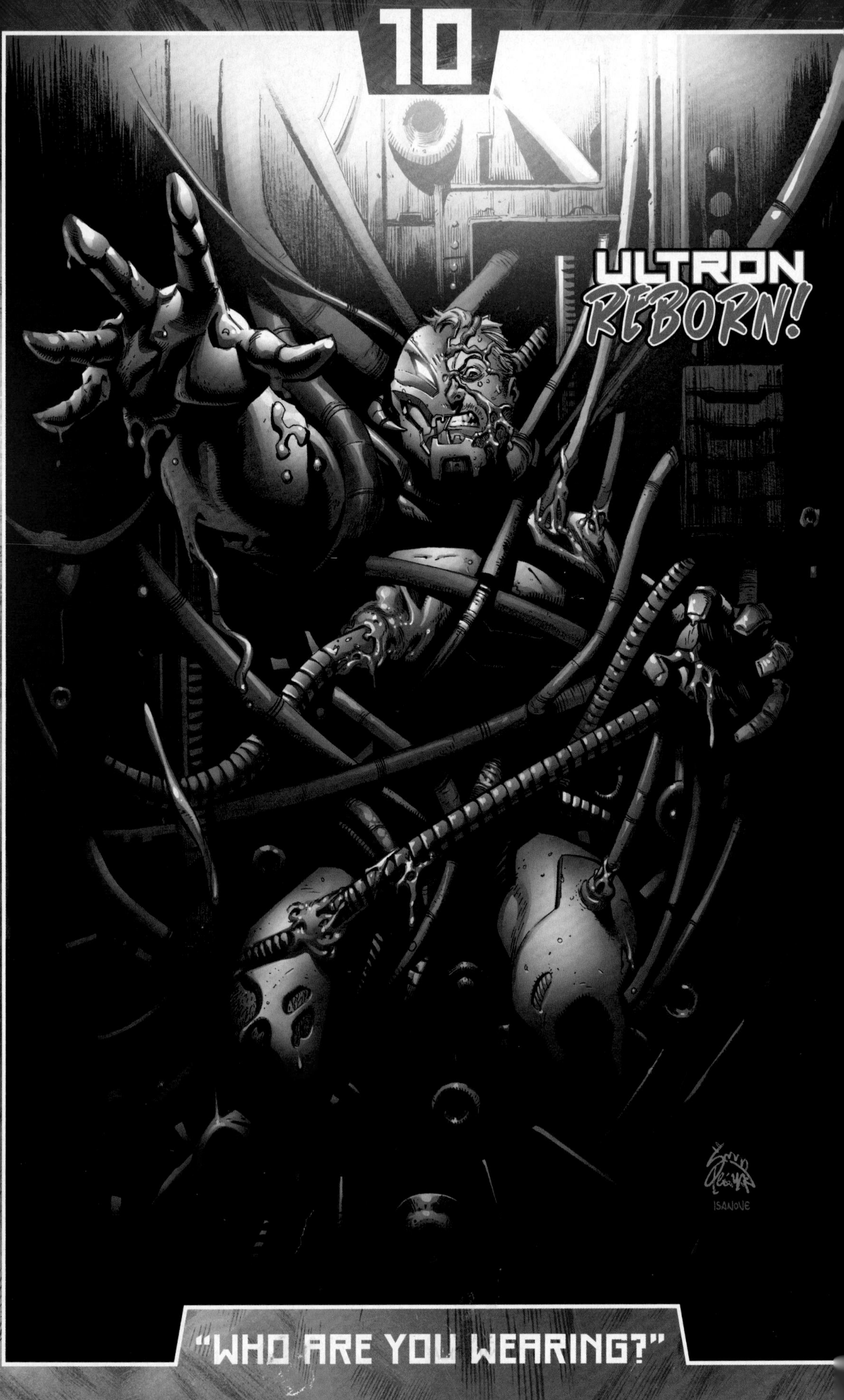
10
ULTRON
REBORN!
ISANOVE
"WHO ARE YOU WEARING?"

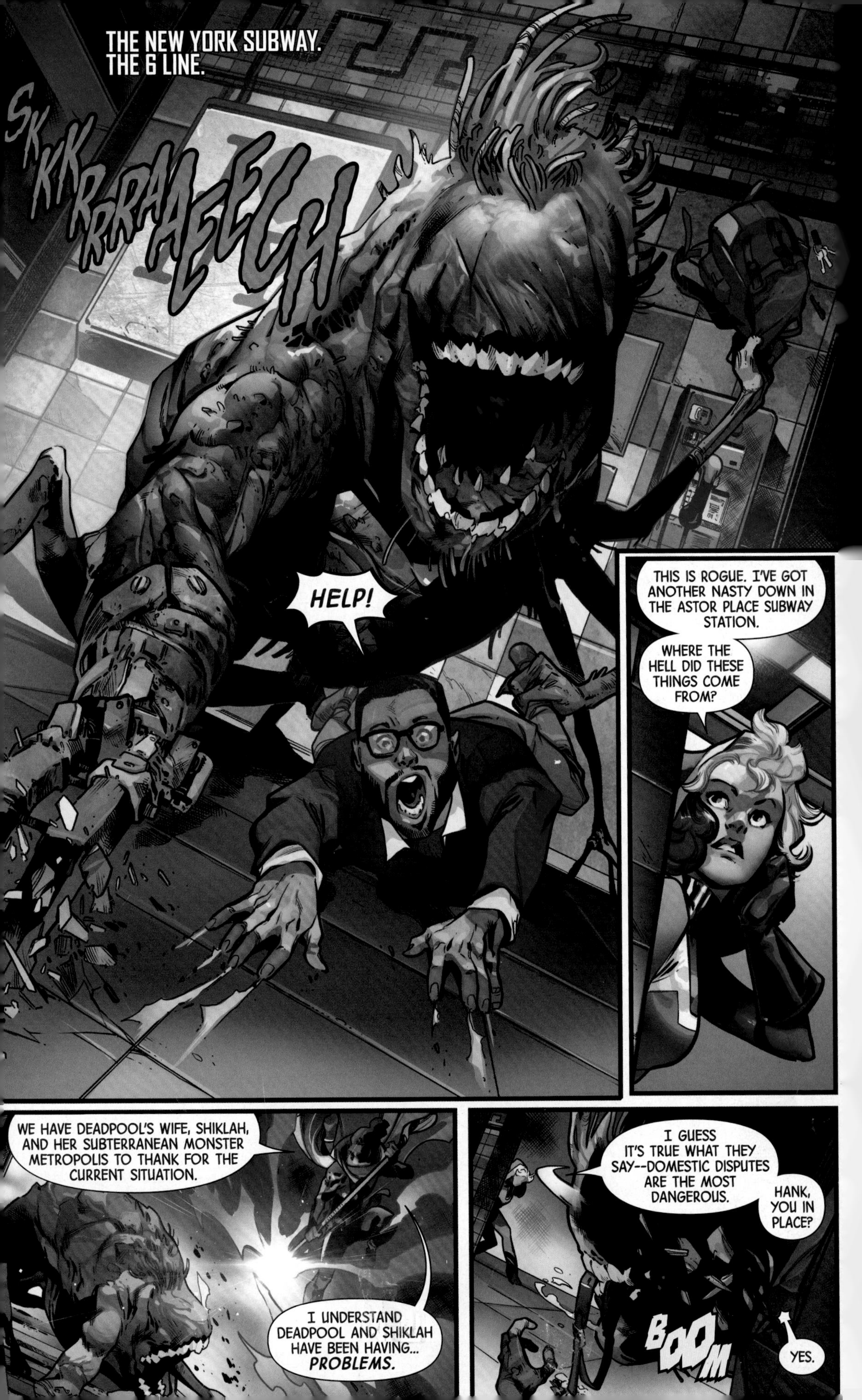
THE NEW YORK SUBWAY.
THE 6 LINE.
SKKRRRAAEECH
HELP!
THIS IS ROGUE. I'VE GOT ANOTHER NASTY DOWN IN THE ASTOR PLACE SUBWAY STATION.
WHERE THE HELL DID THESE THINGS COME FROM?
WE HAVE DEADPOOL'S WIFE, SHIKLAH, AND HER SUBTERRANEAN MONSTER METROPOLIS TO THANK FOR THE CURRENT SITUATION.
I UNDERSTAND DEADPOOL AND SHIKLAH HAVE BEEN HAVING... PROBLEMS.
I GUESS IT'S TRUE WHAT THEY SAY--DOMESTIC DISPUTES ARE THE MOST DANGEROUS.
HANK, YOU IN PLACE?
BOOM
YES.

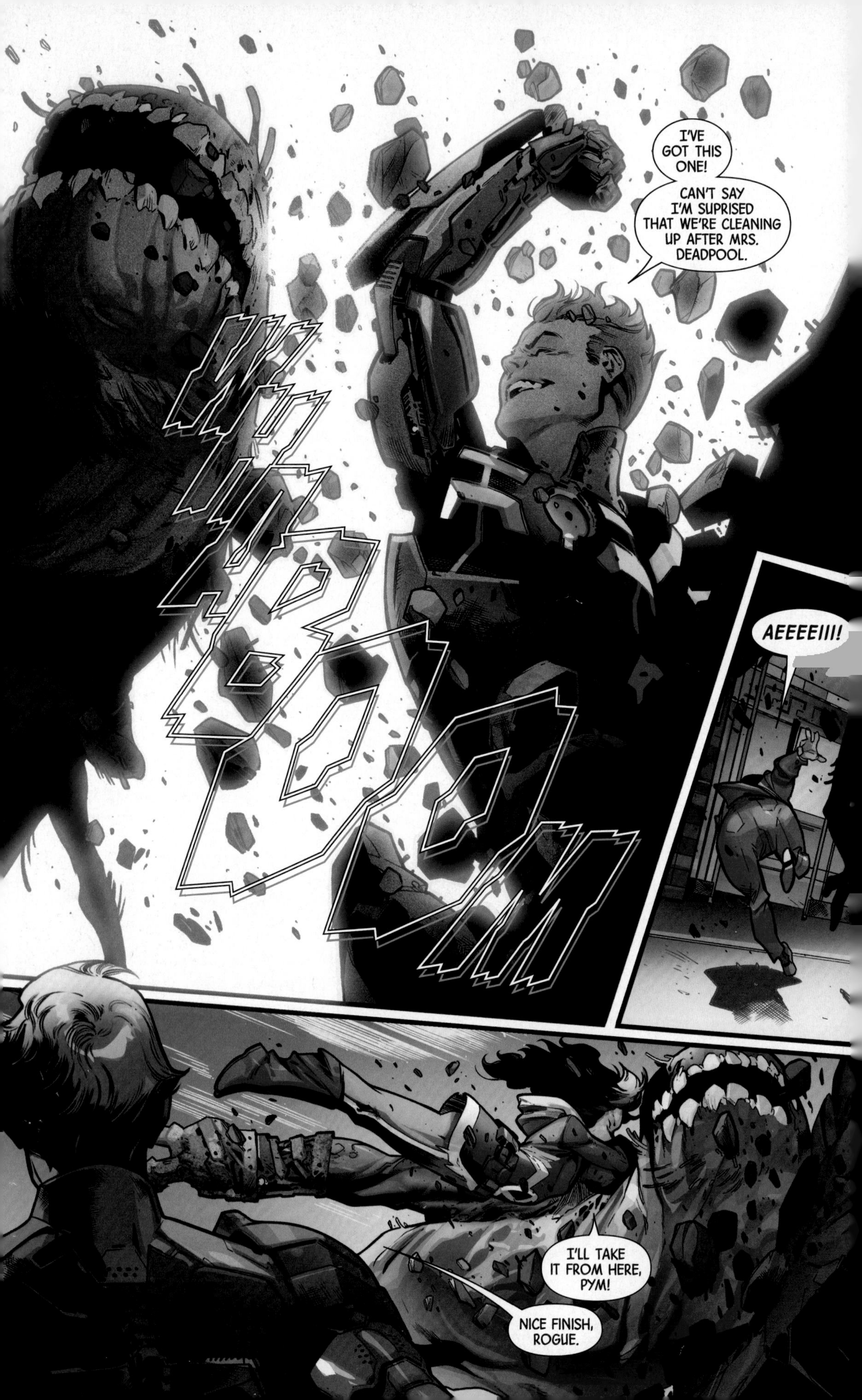
I'VE GOT THIS ONE!
CAN'T SAY I'M SUPRISED THAT WE'RE CLEANING UP AFTER MRS. DEADPOOL.
AEEEIII!
I'LL TAKE IT FROM HERE, PYM!
NICE FINISH, ROGUE.

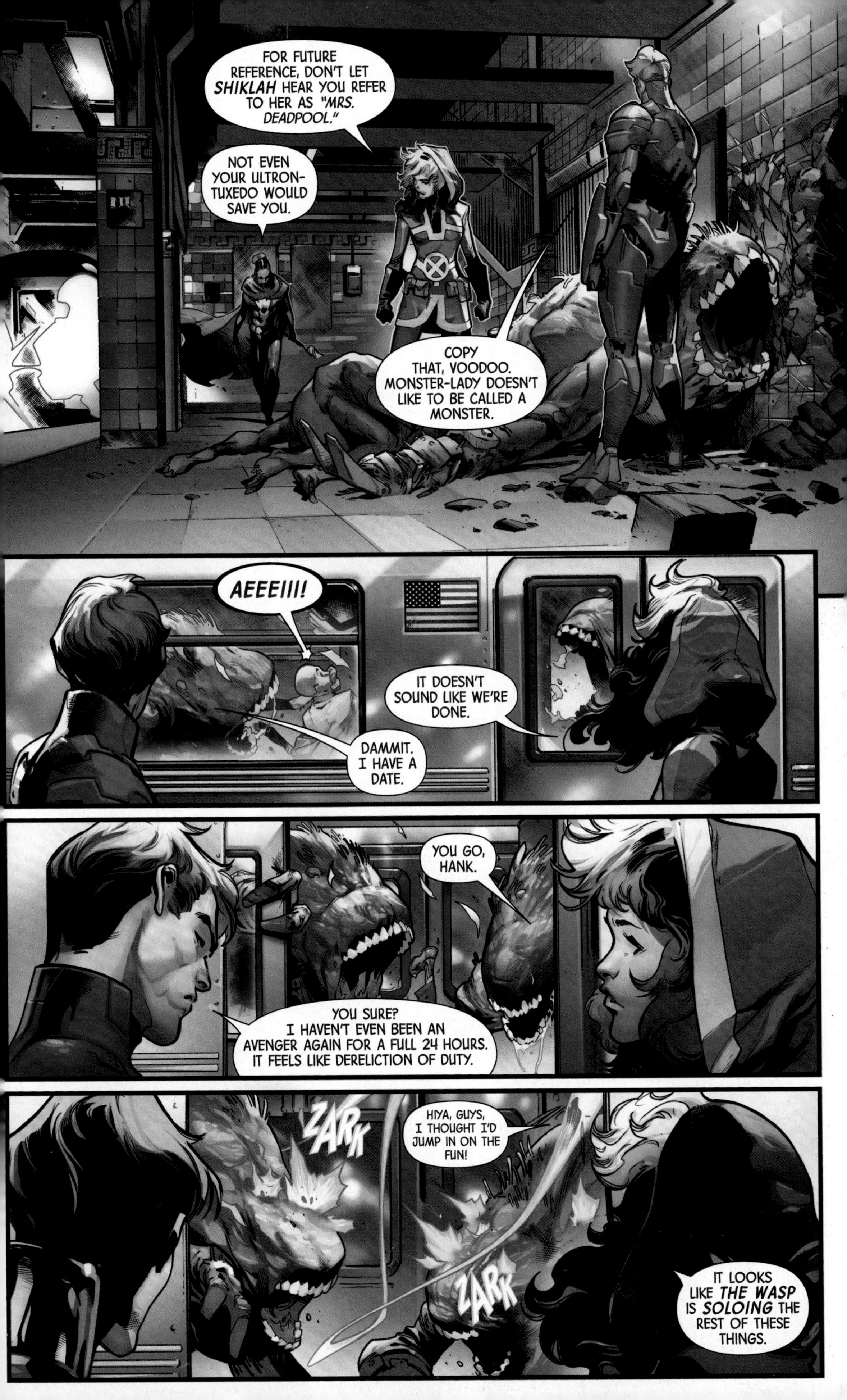
FOR FUTURE REFERENCE, DON'T LET SHIKLAH HEAR YOU REFER TO HER AS "MRS. DEADPOOL."
NOT EVEN YOUR ULTRON-TUXEDO WOULD SAVE YOU.
COPY THAT, VOODOO. MONSTER-LADY DOESN'T LIKE TO BE CALLED A MONSTER.
AEEEIIII!
IT DOESN'T SOUND LIKE WE'RE DONE.
DAMMIT. I HAVE A DATE.
YOU GO, HANK.
YOU SURE? I HAVEN'T EVEN BEEN AN AVENGER AGAIN FOR A FULL 24 HOURS. IT FEELS LIKE DERELICTION OF DUTY.
ZARK
HIYA, GUYS, I THOUGHT I'D JUMP IN ON THE FUN!
ZARK
IT LOOKS LIKE THE WASP IS SOLOING THE REST OF THESE THINGS.

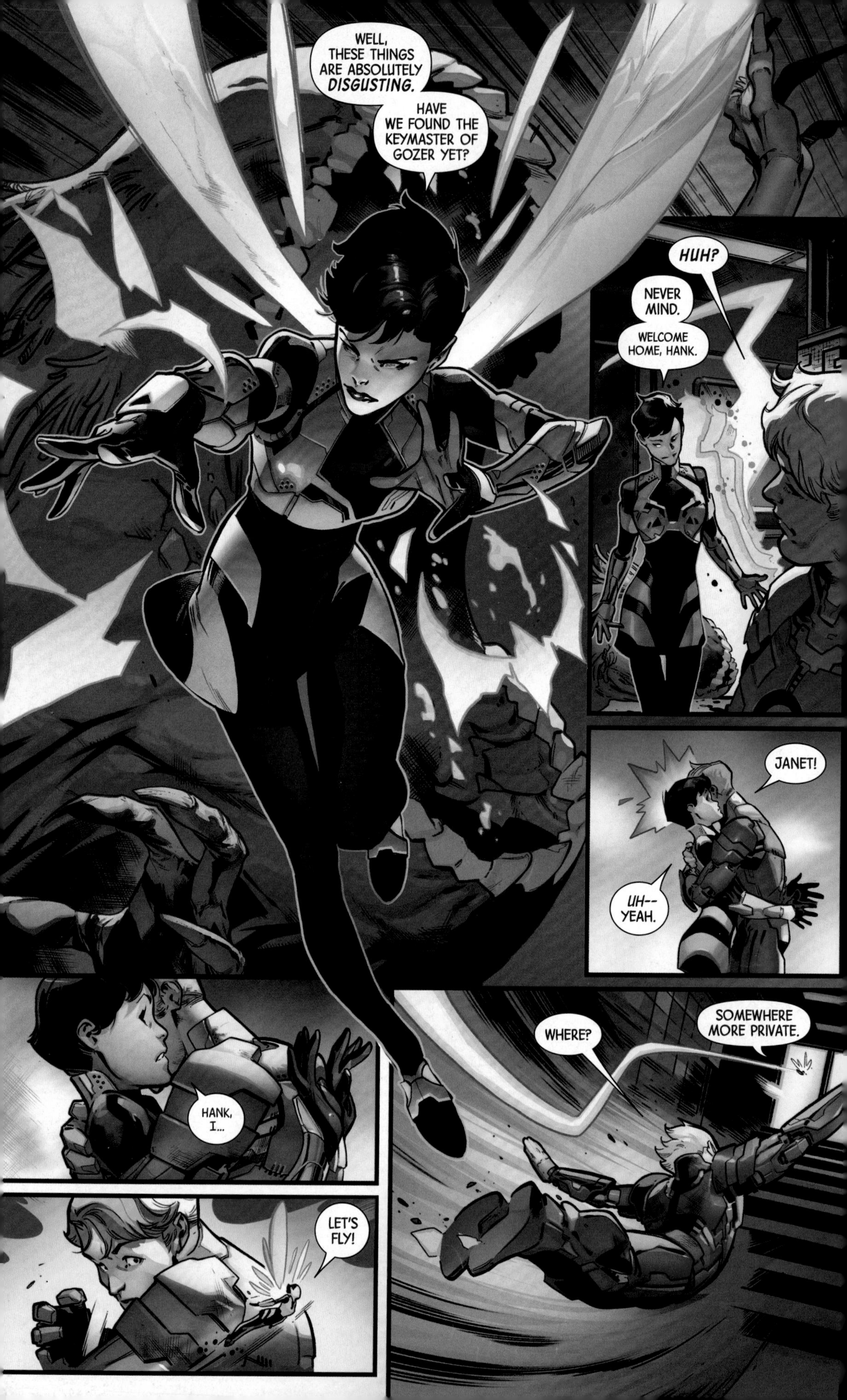
WELL, THESE THINGS ARE ABSOLUTELY *DISGUSTING.*
HAVE WE FOUND THE KEYMASTER OF GOZER YET?
HUH?
NEVER MIND.
WELCOME HOME, HANK.
JANET!
UH-- YEAH.
HANK, I...
LET'S FLY!
WHERE?
SOMEWHERE MORE PRIVATE.

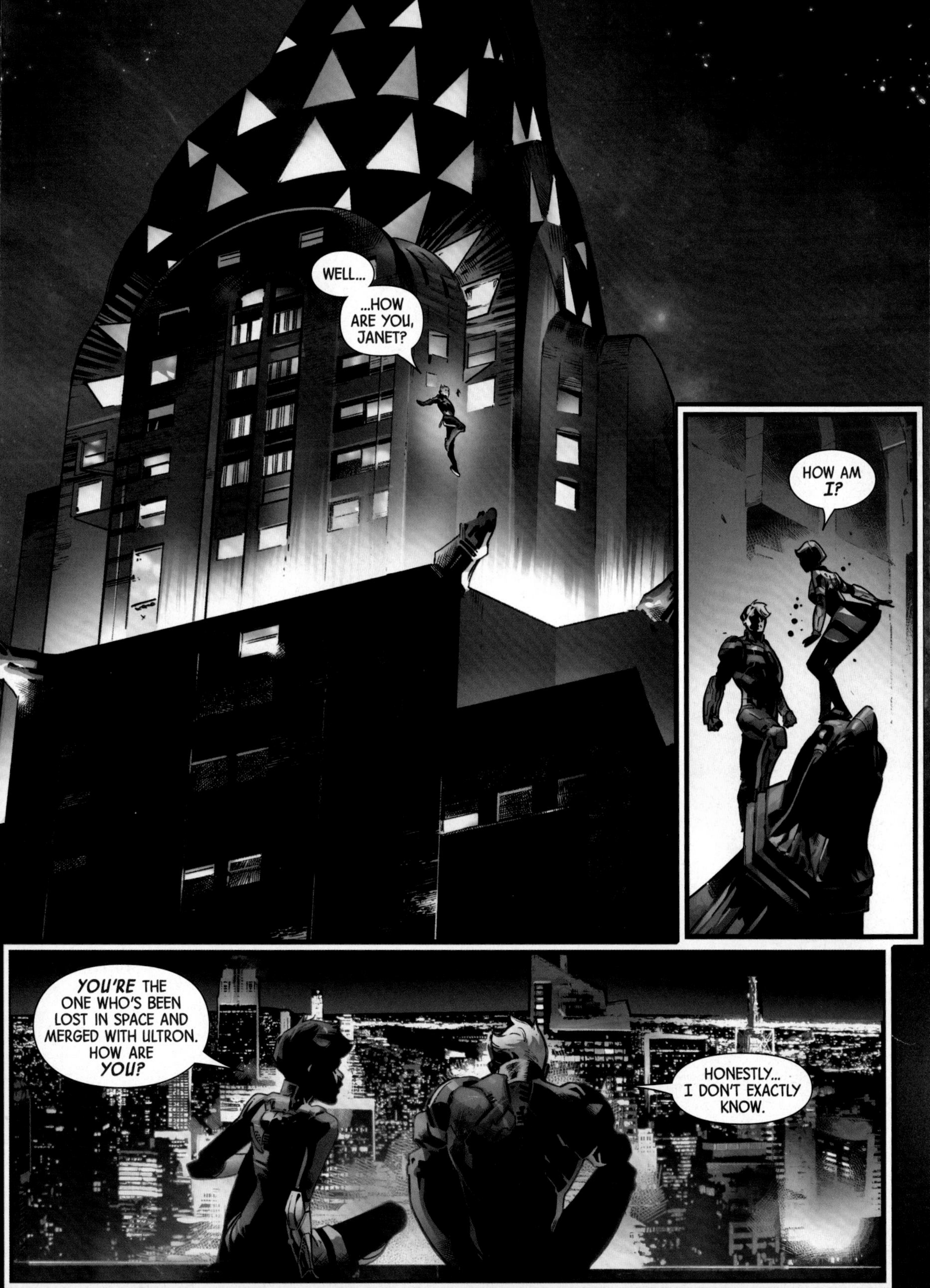
WELL...
...HOW ARE YOU, JANET?
HOW AM I?
YOU'RE THE ONE WHO'S BEEN LOST IN SPACE AND MERGED WITH ULTRON. HOW ARE YOU?
HONESTLY... I DON'T EXACTLY KNOW.

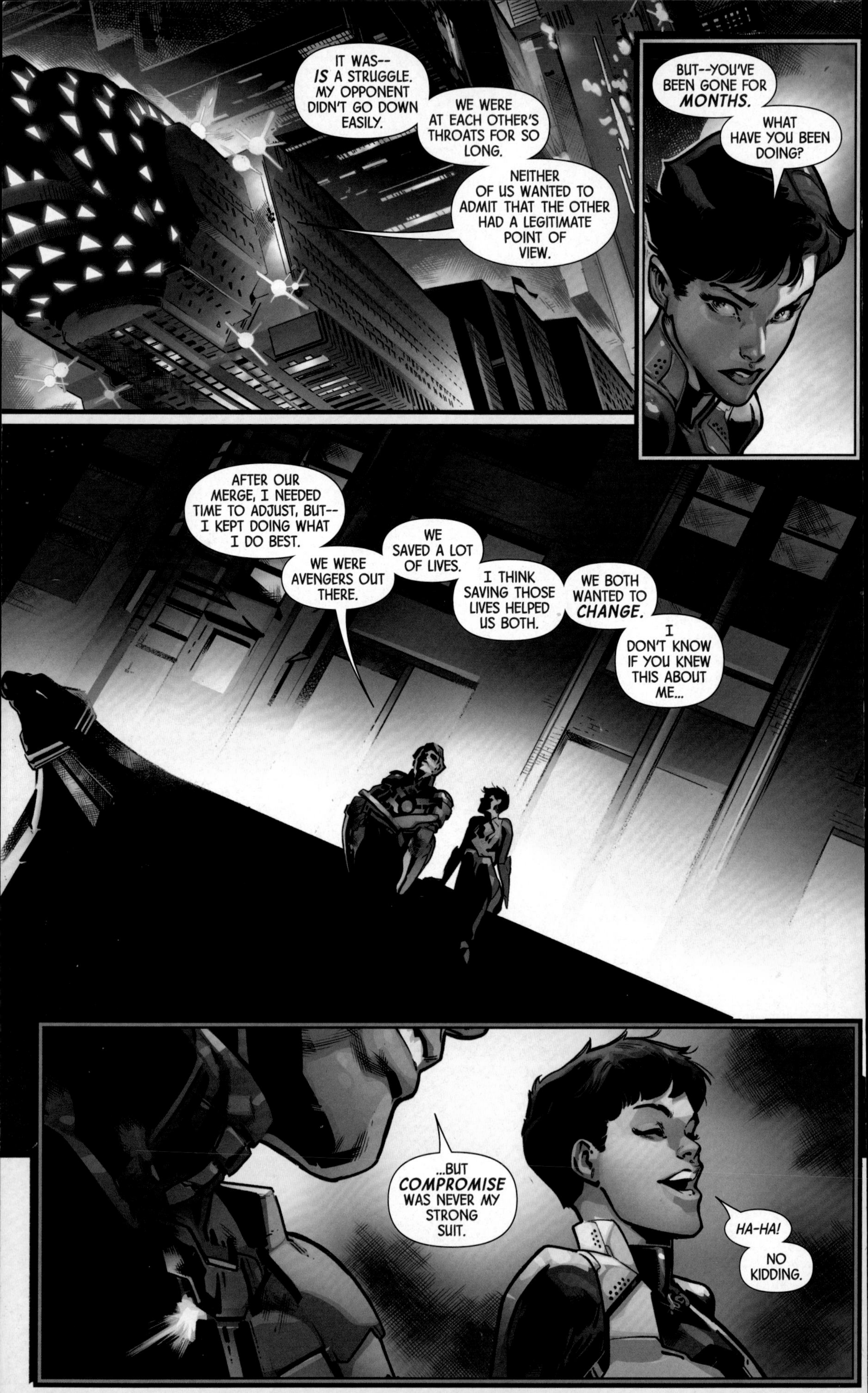
IT WAS-- IS A STRUGGLE. MY OPPONENT DIDN'T GO DOWN EASILY.
WE WERE AT EACH OTHER'S THROATS FOR SO LONG.
NEITHER OF US WANTED TO ADMIT THAT THE OTHER HAD A LEGITIMATE POINT OF VIEW.
BUT--YOU'VE BEEN GONE FOR MONTHS.
WHAT HAVE YOU BEEN DOING?
AFTER OUR MERGE, I NEEDED TIME TO ADJUST, BUT-- I KEPT DOING WHAT I DO BEST.
WE WERE AVENGERS OUT THERE.
WE SAVED A LOT OF LIVES.
I THINK SAVING THOSE LIVES HELPED US BOTH.
WE BOTH WANTED TO CHANGE.
I DON'T KNOW IF YOU KNEW THIS ABOUT ME...
...BUT COMPROMISE WAS NEVER MY STRONG SUIT.
HA-HA!
NO KIDDING.

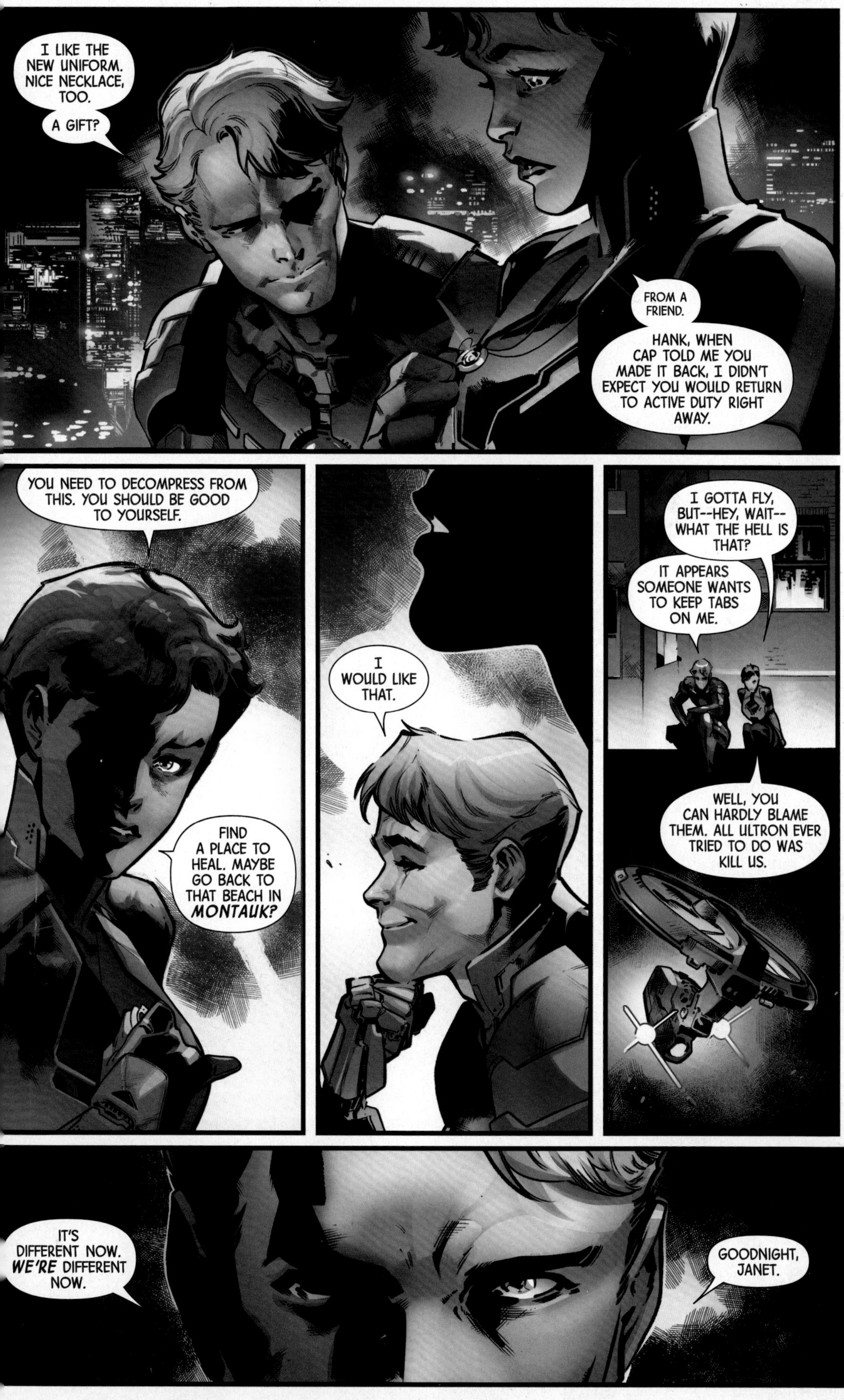
I LIKE THE NEW UNIFORM. NICE NECKLACE, TOO.
A GIFT?
FROM A FRIEND.
HANK, WHEN CAP TOLD ME YOU MADE IT BACK, I DIDN'T EXPECT YOU WOULD RETURN TO ACTIVE DUTY RIGHT AWAY.
YOU NEED TO DECOMPRESS FROM THIS. YOU SHOULD BE GOOD TO YOURSELF.
FIND A PLACE TO HEAL. MAYBE GO BACK TO THAT BEACH IN *MONTAUK?*
I WOULD LIKE THAT.
I GOTTA FLY, BUT--HEY, WAIT-- WHAT THE HELL IS THAT?
IT APPEARS SOMEONE WANTS TO KEEP TABS ON ME.
WELL, YOU CAN HARDLY BLAME THEM. ALL ULTRON EVER TRIED TO DO WAS KILL US.
IT'S DIFFERENT NOW. *WE'RE* DIFFERENT NOW.
GOODNIGHT, JANET.

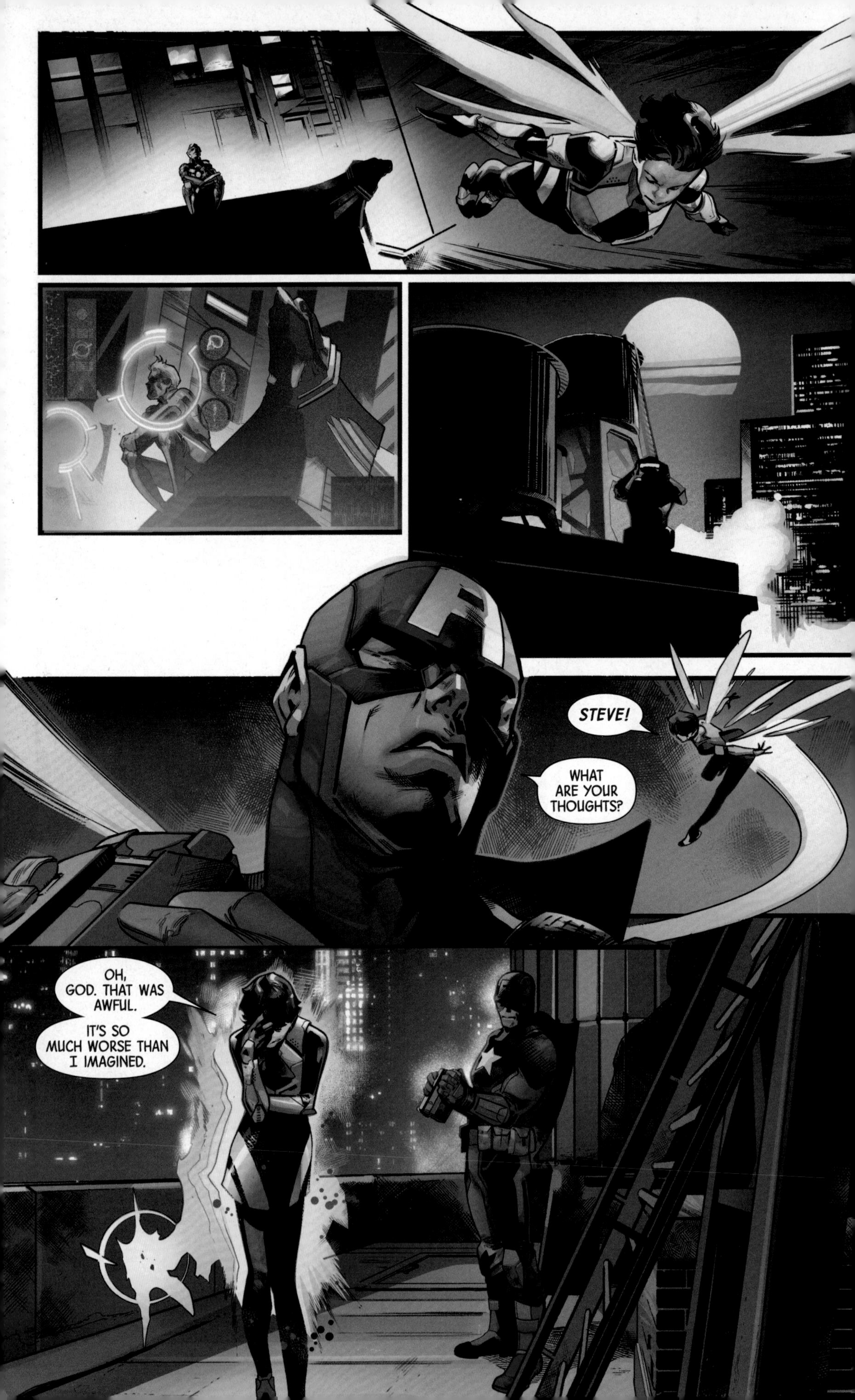
STEVE!
WHAT ARE YOUR THOUGHTS?
OH, GOD. THAT WAS AWFUL.
IT'S SO MUCH WORSE THAN I IMAGINED.

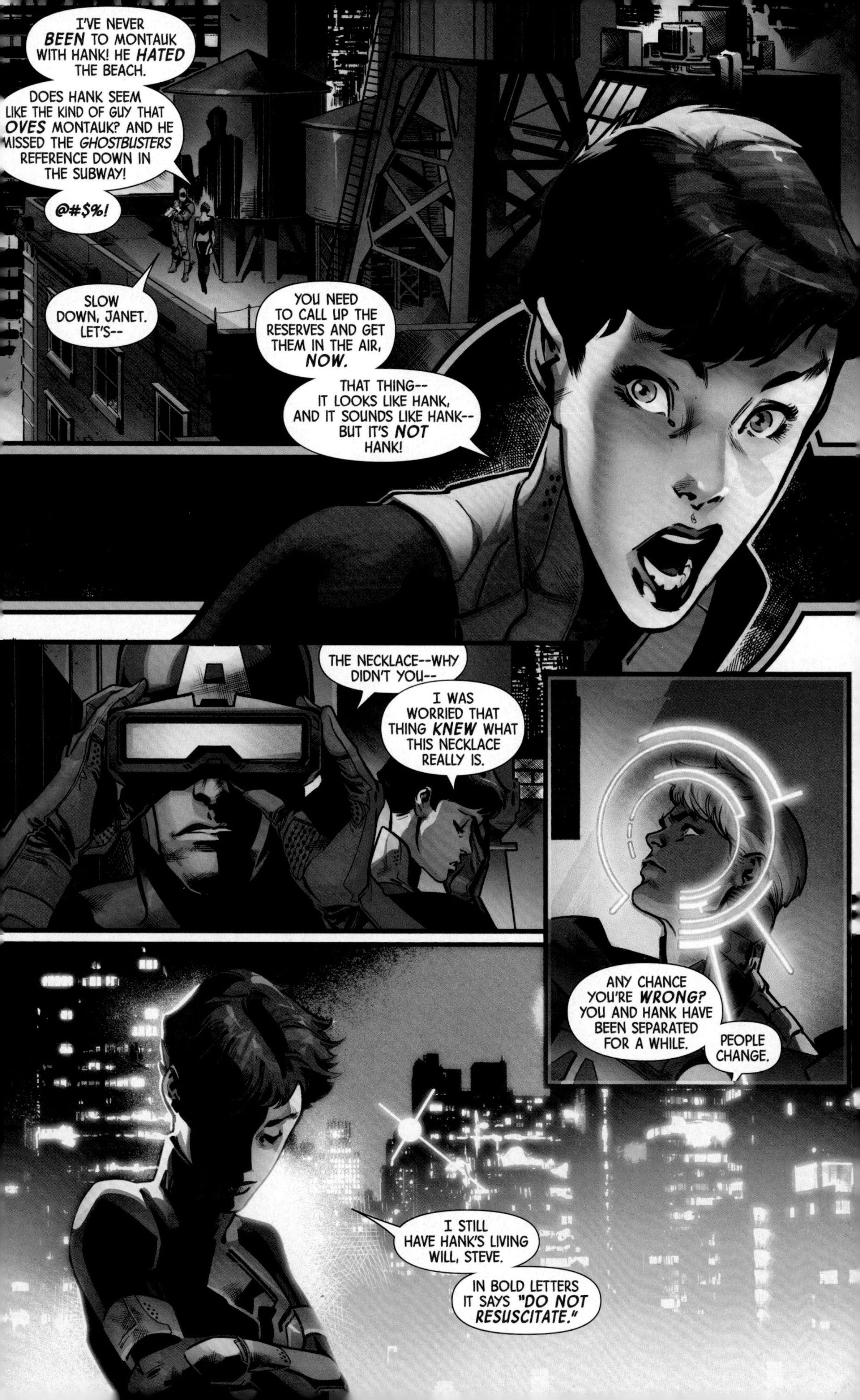
I'VE NEVER BEEN TO MONTAUK WITH HANK! HE HATED THE BEACH.
DOES HANK SEEM LIKE THE KIND OF GUY THAT OVES MONTAUK? AND HE MISSED THE GHOSTBUSTERS REFERENCE DOWN IN THE SUBWAY!
@#$%!
SLOW DOWN, JANET. LET'S--
YOU NEED TO CALL UP THE RESERVES AND GET THEM IN THE AIR, NOW.
THAT THING-- IT LOOKS LIKE HANK, AND IT SOUNDS LIKE HANK-- BUT IT'S NOT HANK!
THE NECKLACE--WHY DIDN'T YOU--
I WAS WORRIED THAT THING KNEW WHAT THIS NECKLACE REALLY IS.
ANY CHANCE YOU'RE WRONG? YOU AND HANK HAVE BEEN SEPARATED FOR A WHILE.
PEOPLE CHANGE.
I STILL HAVE HANK'S LIVING WILL, STEVE.
IN BOLD LETTERS IT SAYS "DO NOT RESUSCITATE."

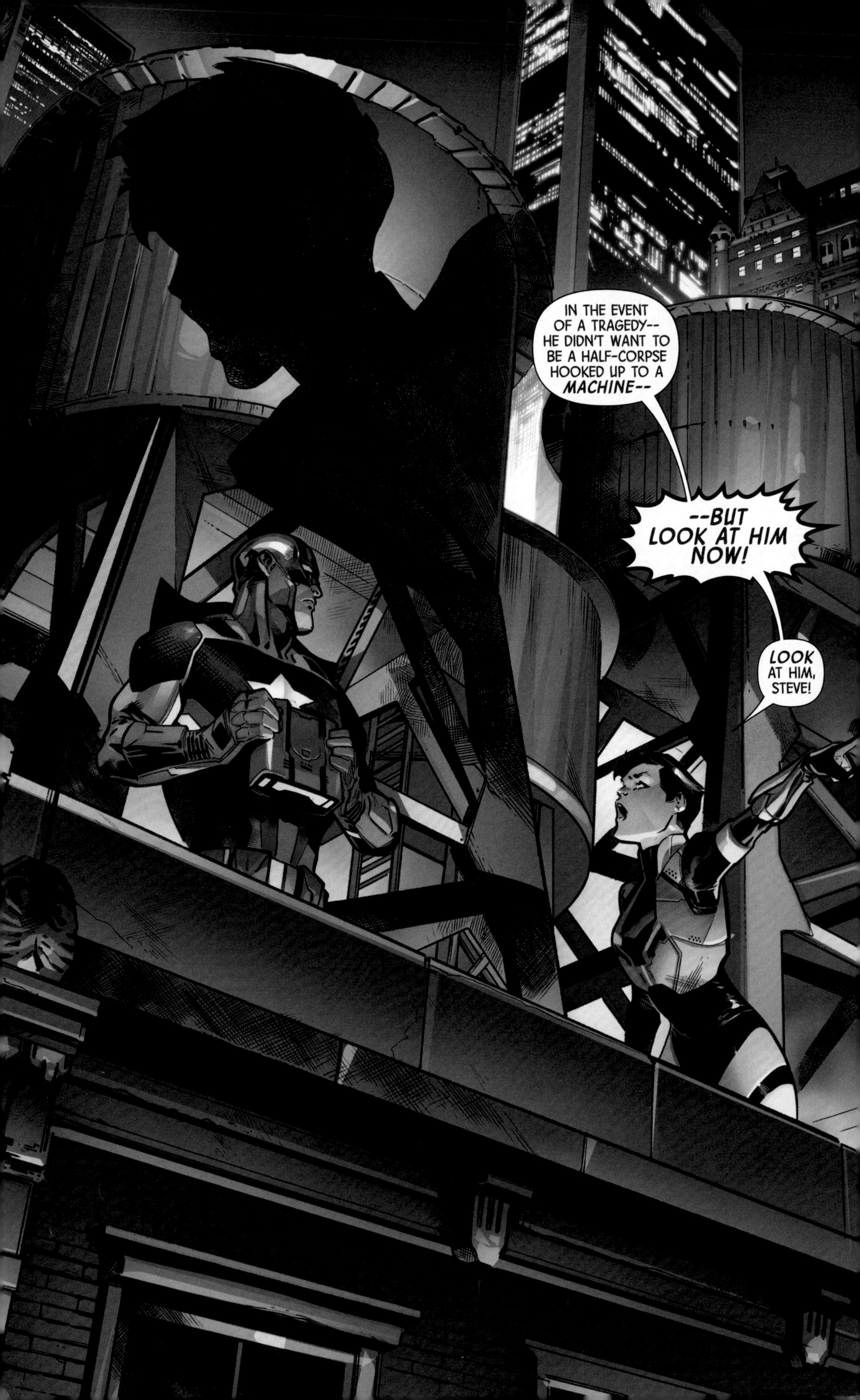
IN THE EVENT OF A TRAGEDY-- HE DIDN'T WANT TO BE A HALF-CORPSE HOOKED UP TO A *MACHINE*--
--BUT LOOK AT HIM NOW!
LOOK AT HIM, STEVE!

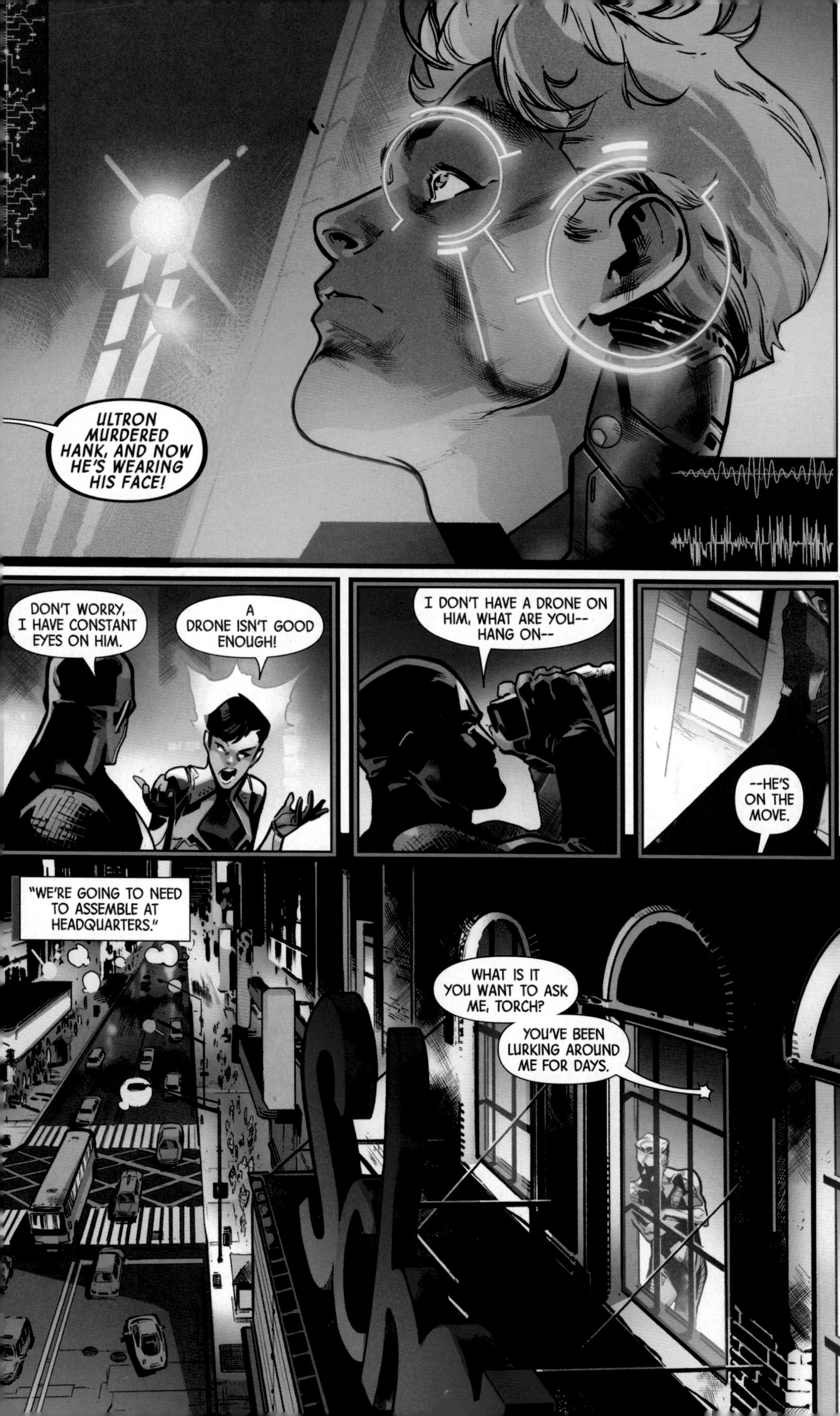
ULTRON MURDERED HANK, AND NOW HE'S WEARING HIS FACE!
DON'T WORRY, I HAVE CONSTANT EYES ON HIM.
A DRONE ISN'T GOOD ENOUGH!
I DON'T HAVE A DRONE ON HIM, WHAT ARE YOU-- HANG ON--
--HE'S ON THE MOVE.
"WE'RE GOING TO NEED TO ASSEMBLE AT HEADQUARTERS."
WHAT IS IT YOU WANT TO ASK ME, TORCH?
YOU'VE BEEN LURKING AROUND ME FOR DAYS.

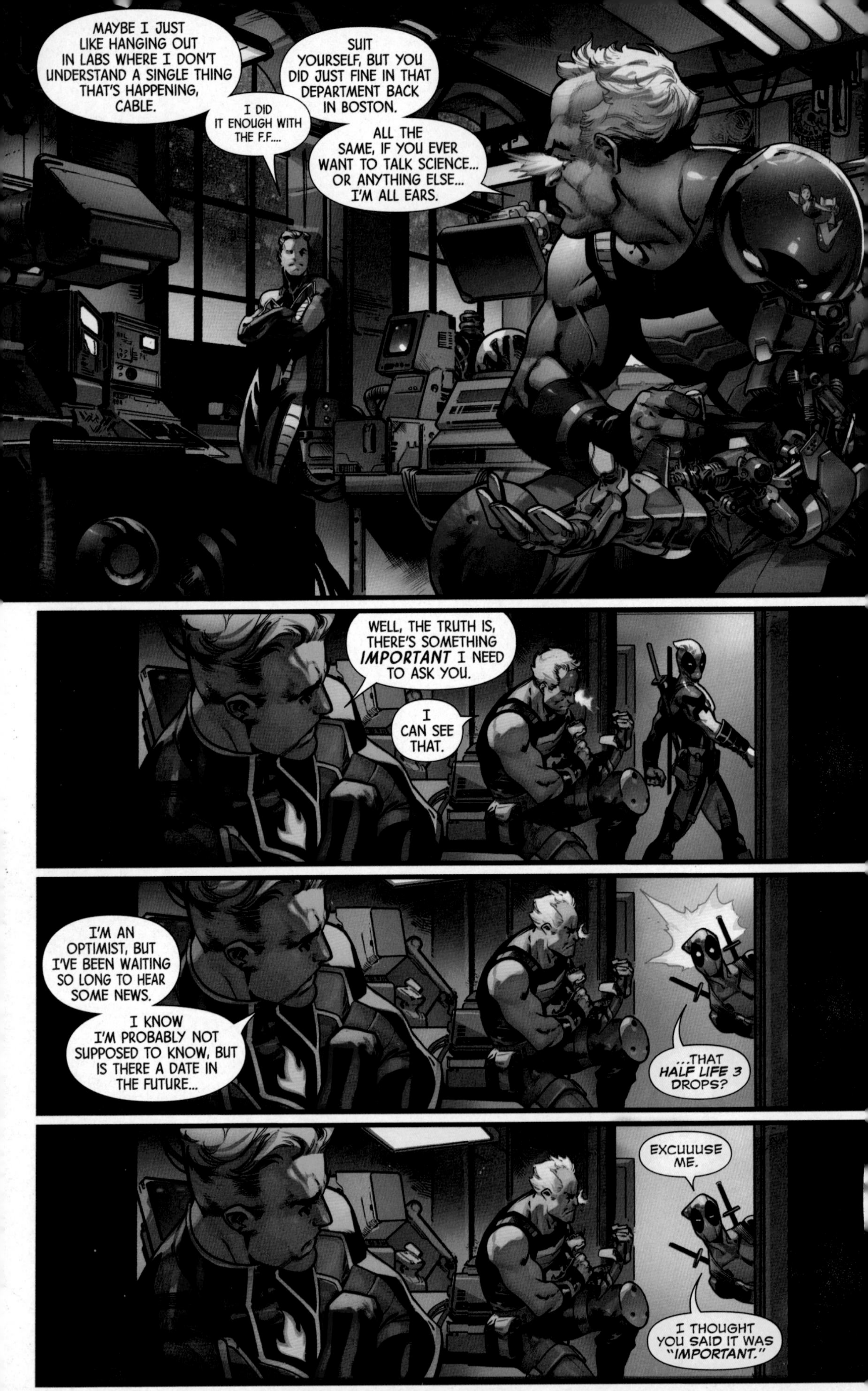
MAYBE I JUST LIKE HANGING OUT IN LABS WHERE I DON'T UNDERSTAND A SINGLE THING THAT'S HAPPENING, CABLE.
I DID IT ENOUGH WITH THE F.F....
SUIT YOURSELF, BUT YOU DID JUST FINE IN THAT DEPARTMENT BACK IN BOSTON.
ALL THE SAME, IF YOU EVER WANT TO TALK SCIENCE... OR ANYTHING ELSE... I'M ALL EARS.
WELL, THE TRUTH IS, THERE'S SOMETHING *IMPORTANT* I NEED TO ASK YOU.
I CAN SEE THAT.
I'M AN OPTIMIST, BUT I'VE BEEN WAITING SO LONG TO HEAR SOME NEWS.
I KNOW I'M PROBABLY NOT SUPPOSED TO KNOW, BUT IS THERE A DATE IN THE FUTURE...
...THAT *HALF LIFE 3* DROPS?
EXCUUUSE ME.
I THOUGHT YOU SAID IT WAS "*IMPORTANT.*"

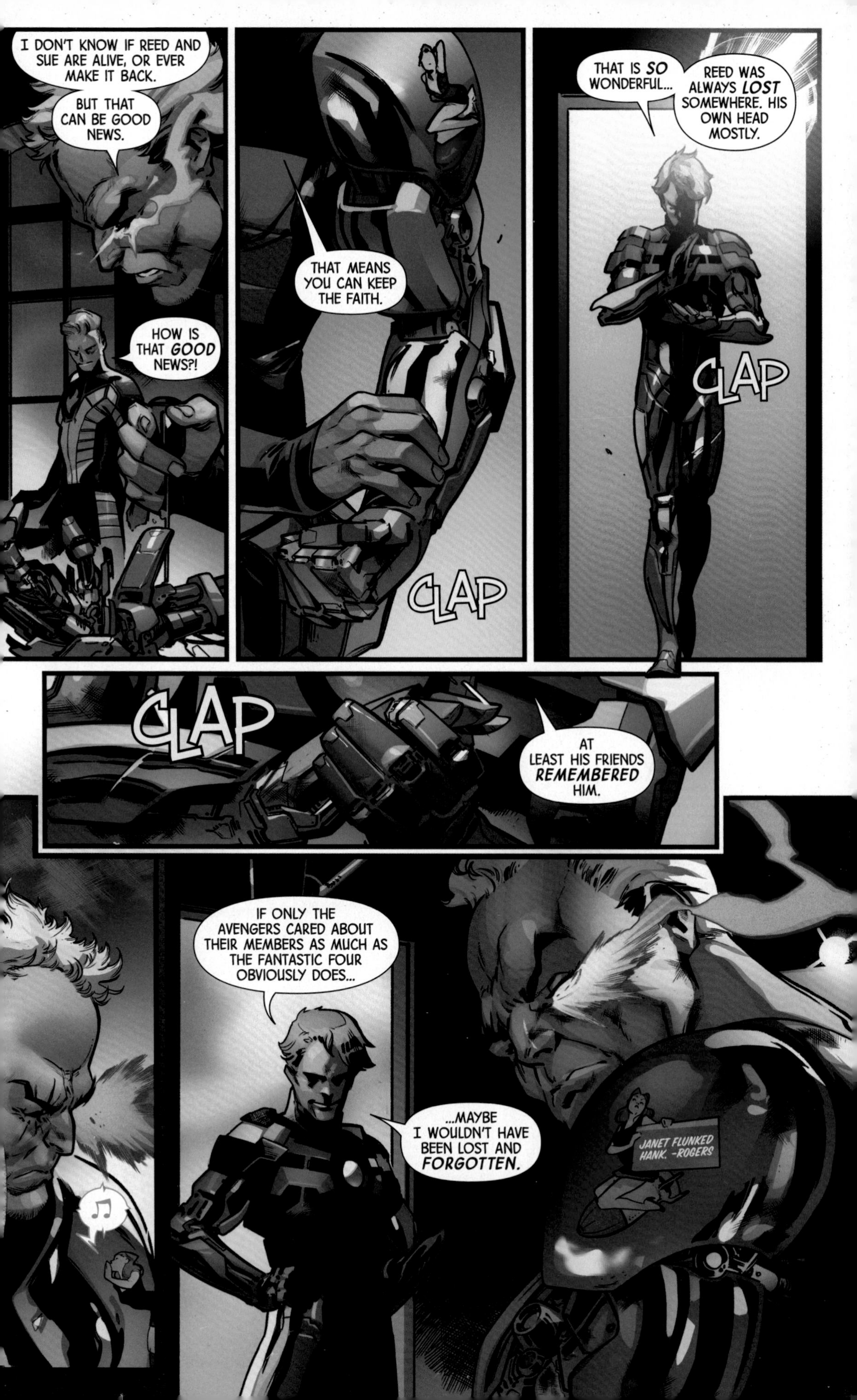
I DON'T KNOW IF REED AND SUE ARE ALIVE, OR EVER MAKE IT BACK.
BUT THAT CAN BE GOOD NEWS.
HOW IS THAT *GOOD* NEWS?!
THAT MEANS YOU CAN KEEP THE FAITH.
CLAP
THAT IS *SO* WONDERFUL...
REED WAS ALWAYS *LOST* SOMEWHERE. HIS OWN HEAD MOSTLY.
CLAP
CLAP
AT LEAST HIS FRIENDS *REMEMBERED* HIM.
IF ONLY THE AVENGERS CARED ABOUT THEIR MEMBERS AS MUCH AS THE FANTASTIC FOUR OBVIOUSLY DOES...
...MAYBE I WOULDN'T HAVE BEEN LOST AND *FORGOTTEN.*
♫
JANET FLUNKED HANK. -ROGERS

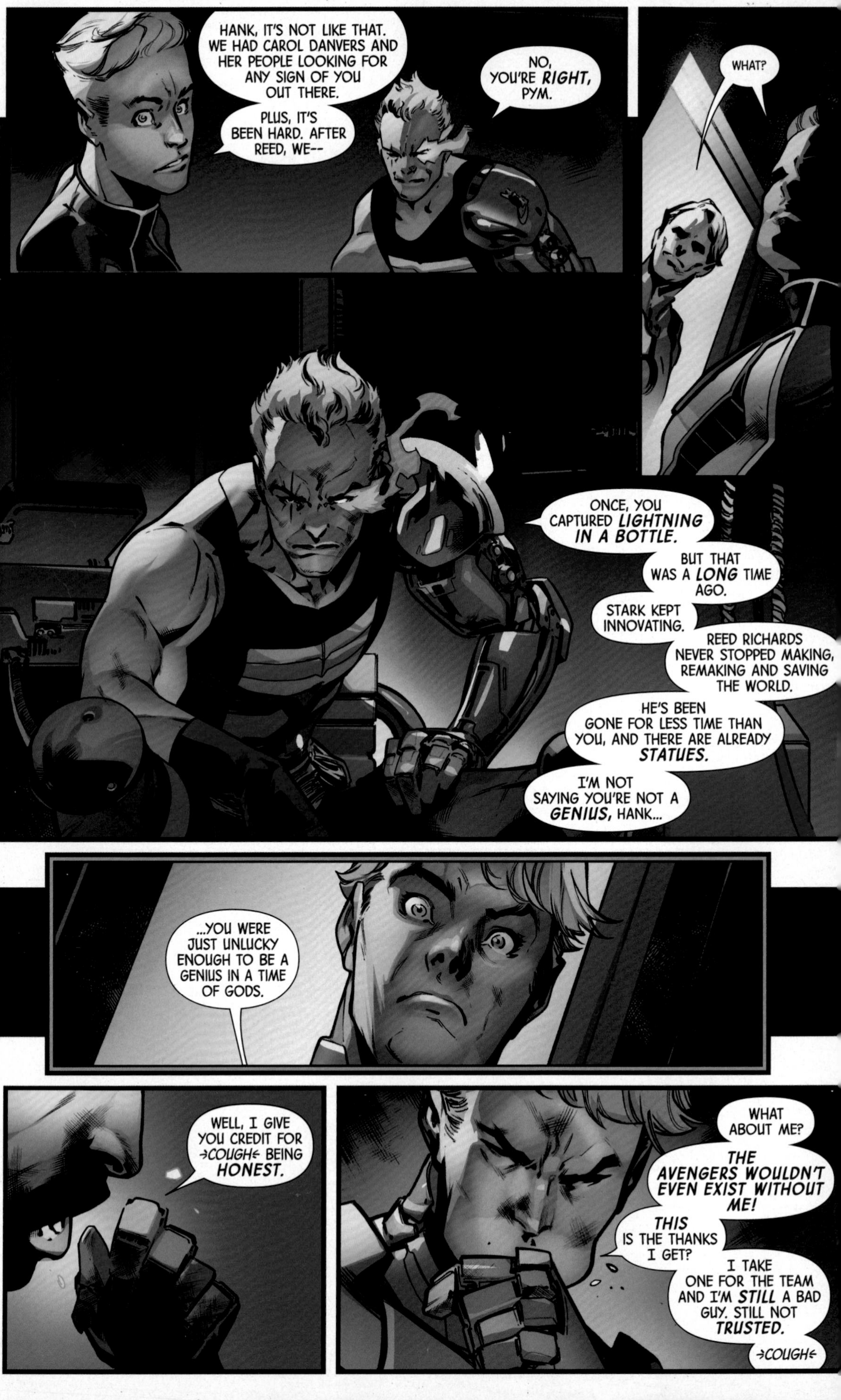
HANK, IT'S NOT LIKE THAT. WE HAD CAROL DANVERS AND HER PEOPLE LOOKING FOR ANY SIGN OF YOU OUT THERE.
PLUS, IT'S BEEN HARD. AFTER REED, WE--
NO, YOU'RE RIGHT, PYM.
WHAT?
ONCE, YOU CAPTURED LIGHTNING IN A BOTTLE.
BUT THAT WAS A LONG TIME AGO.
STARK KEPT INNOVATING.
REED RICHARDS NEVER STOPPED MAKING, REMAKING AND SAVING THE WORLD.
HE'S BEEN GONE FOR LESS TIME THAN YOU, AND THERE ARE ALREADY STATUES.
I'M NOT SAYING YOU'RE NOT A GENIUS, HANK...
...YOU WERE JUST UNLUCKY ENOUGH TO BE A GENIUS IN A TIME OF GODS.
WELL, I GIVE YOU CREDIT FOR →COUGH← BEING HONEST.
WHAT ABOUT ME?
THE AVENGERS WOULDN'T EVEN EXIST WITHOUT ME!
THIS IS THE THANKS I GET?
I TAKE ONE FOR THE TEAM AND I'M STILL A BAD GUY. STILL NOT TRUSTED.
→COUGH←

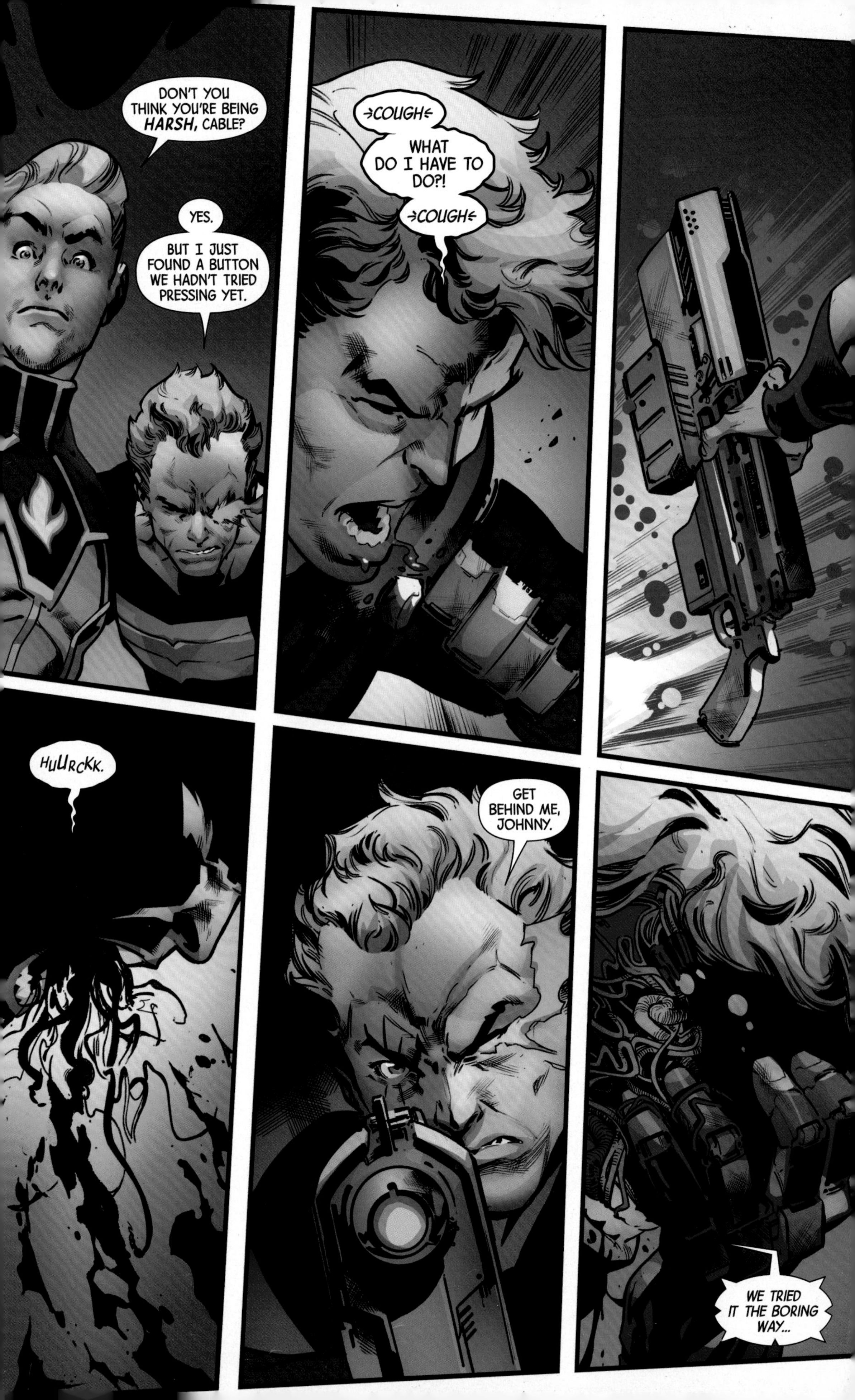
DON'T YOU THINK YOU'RE BEING HARSH, CABLE?
YES.
BUT I JUST FOUND A BUTTON WE HADN'T TRIED PRESSING YET.
»COUGH«
WHAT DO I HAVE TO DO?!
»COUGH«
HUURCKK.
GET BEHIND ME, JOHNNY.
WE TRIED IT THE BORING WAY...

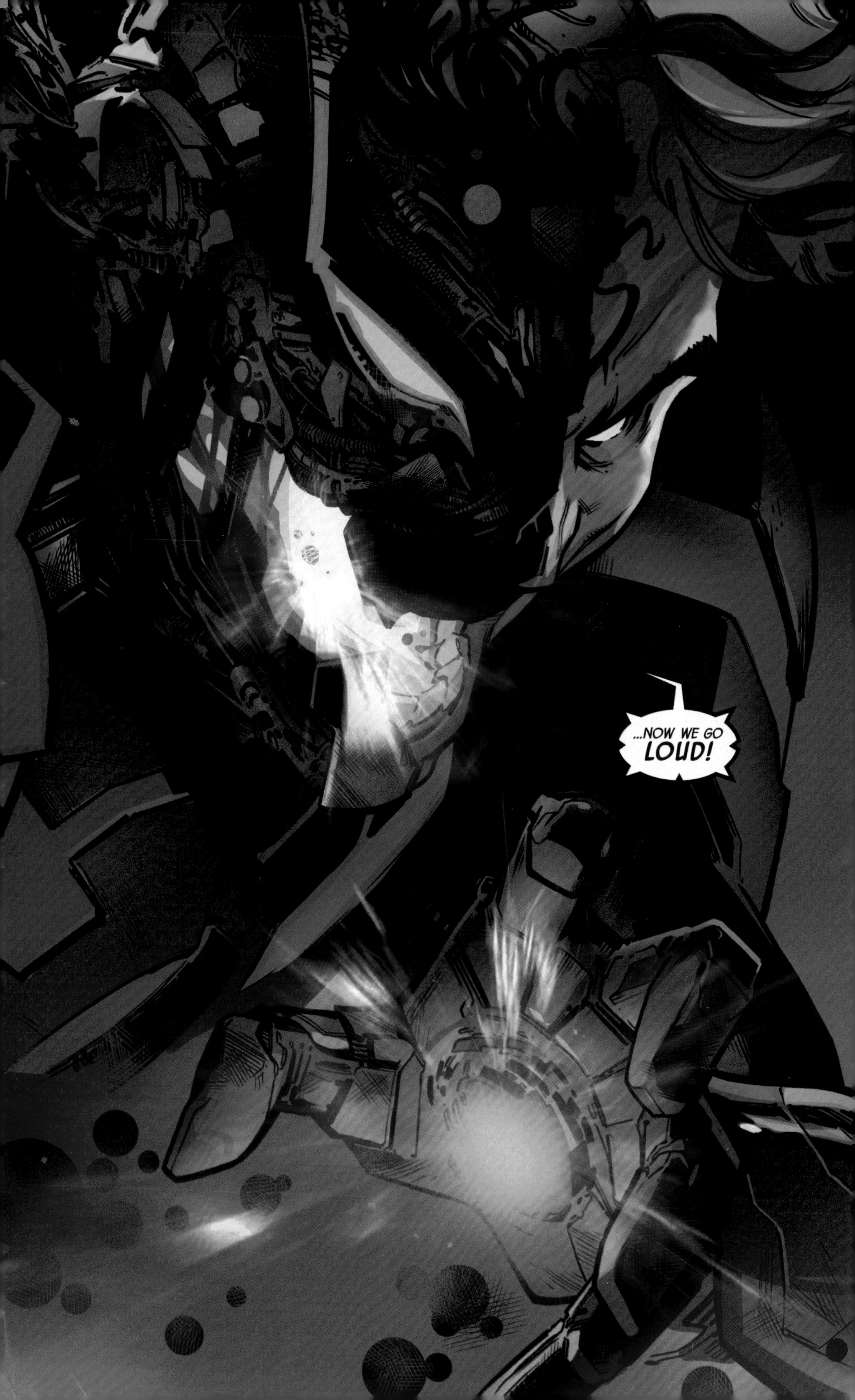
...NOW WE GO LOUD!

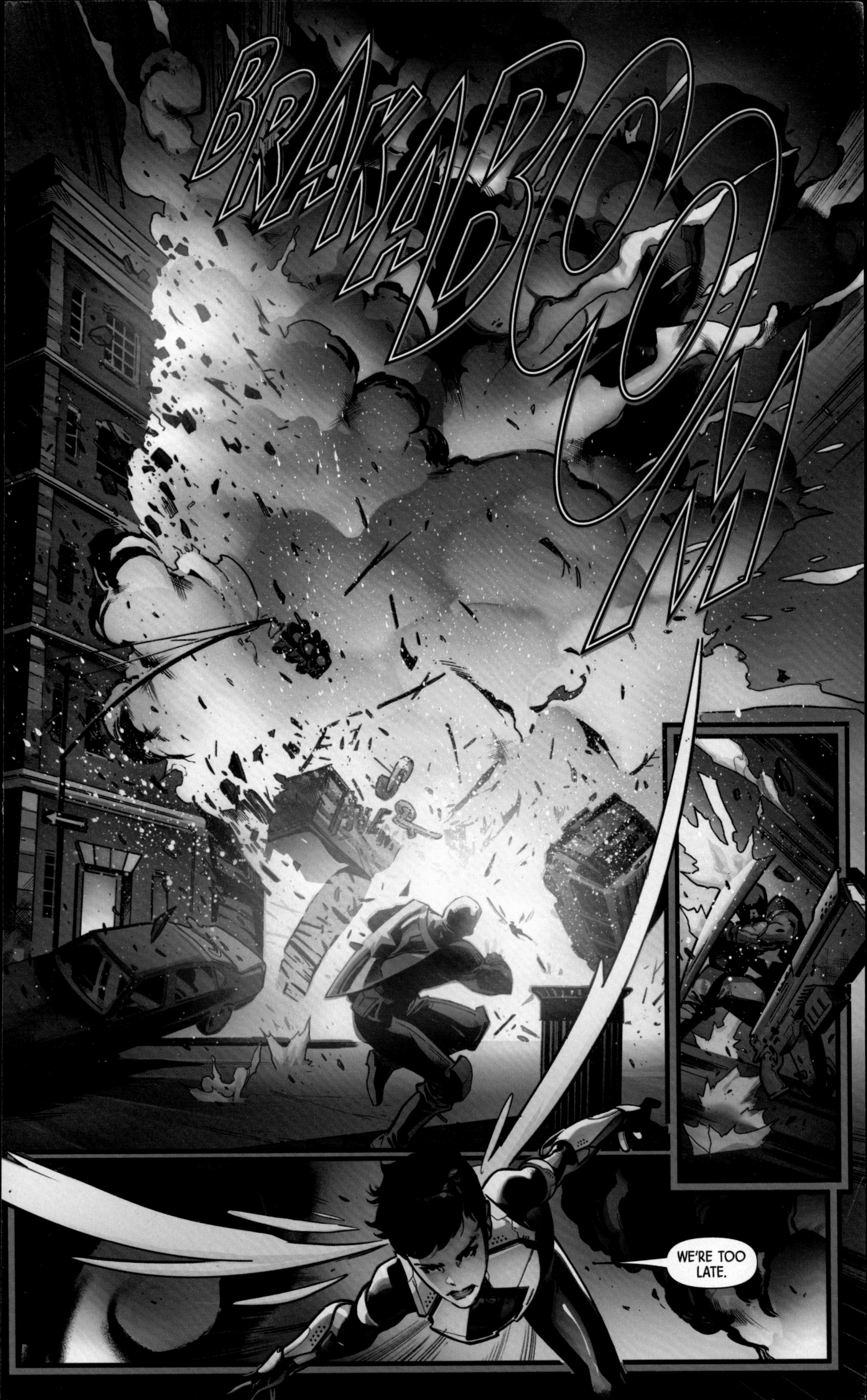
BRAKABOOM
WE'RE TOO LATE.

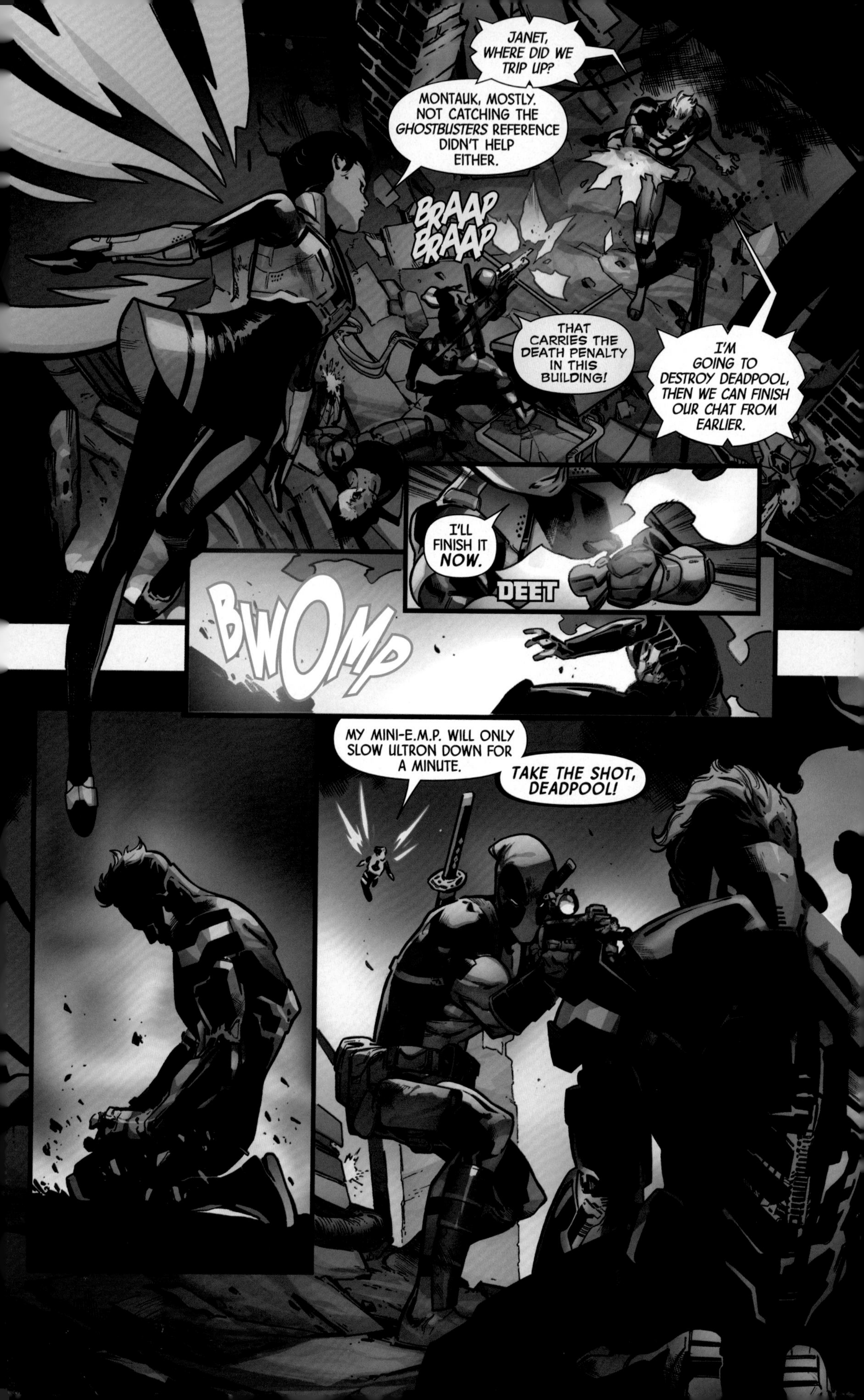
JANET, WHERE DID WE TRIP UP?
MONTAUK, MOSTLY. NOT CATCHING THE GHOSTBUSTERS REFERENCE DIDN'T HELP EITHER.
BRAAP BRAAP
THAT CARRIES THE DEATH PENALTY IN THIS BUILDING!
I'M GOING TO DESTROY DEADPOOL, THEN WE CAN FINISH OUR CHAT FROM EARLIER.
I'LL FINISH IT NOW.
DEET
BWOMP
MY MINI-E.M.P. WILL ONLY SLOW ULTRON DOWN FOR A MINUTE.
TAKE THE SHOT, DEADPOOL!

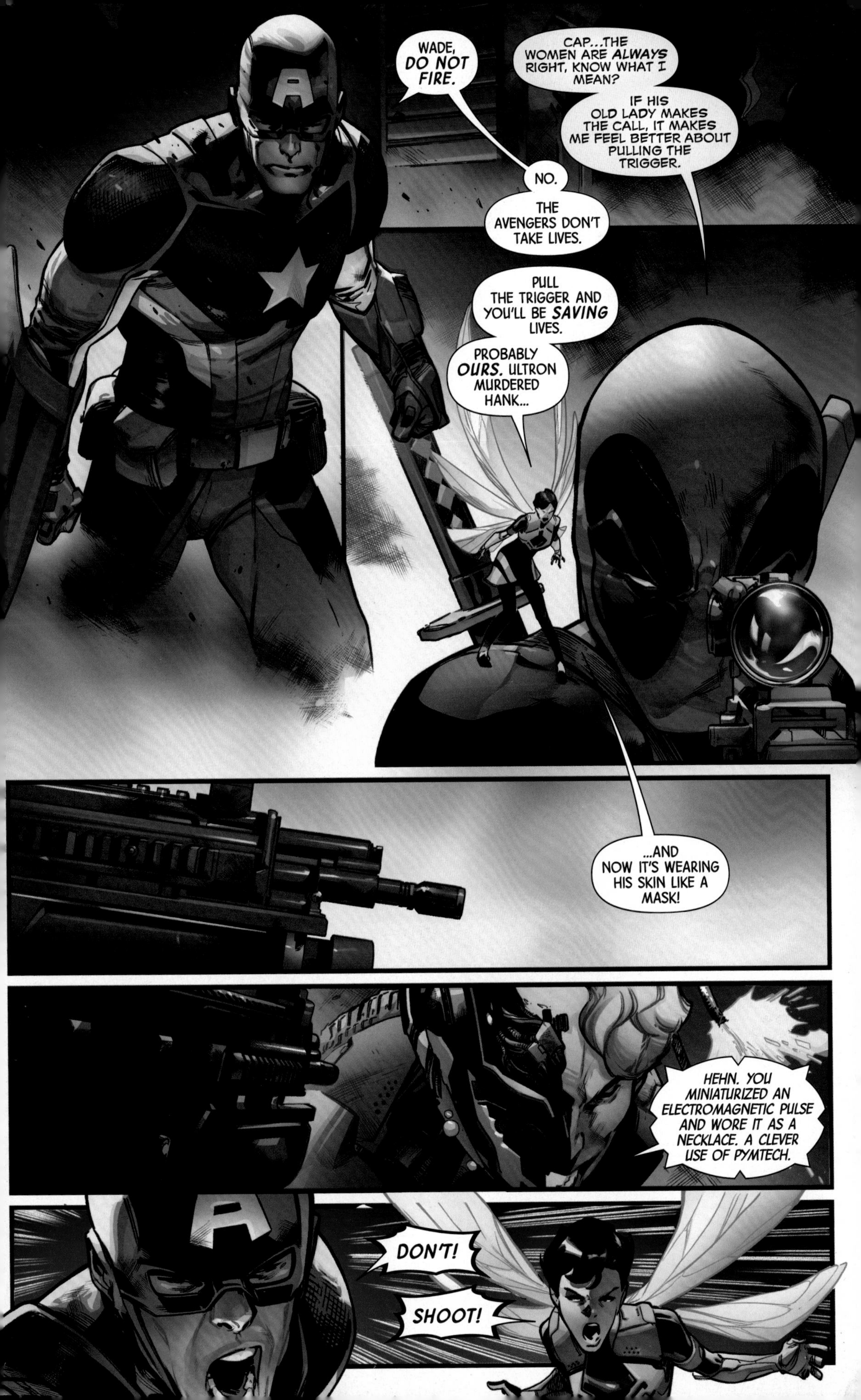
WADE, DO NOT FIRE.
CAP...THE WOMEN ARE ALWAYS RIGHT, KNOW WHAT I MEAN?
IF HIS OLD LADY MAKES THE CALL, IT MAKES ME FEEL BETTER ABOUT PULLING THE TRIGGER.
NO.
THE AVENGERS DON'T TAKE LIVES.
PULL THE TRIGGER AND YOU'LL BE SAVING LIVES.
PROBABLY OURS. ULTRON MURDERED HANK...
...AND NOW IT'S WEARING HIS SKIN LIKE A MASK!
HEHN. YOU MINIATURIZED AN ELECTROMAGNETIC PULSE AND WORE IT AS A NECKLACE. A CLEVER USE OF PYMTECH.
DON'T!
SHOOT!

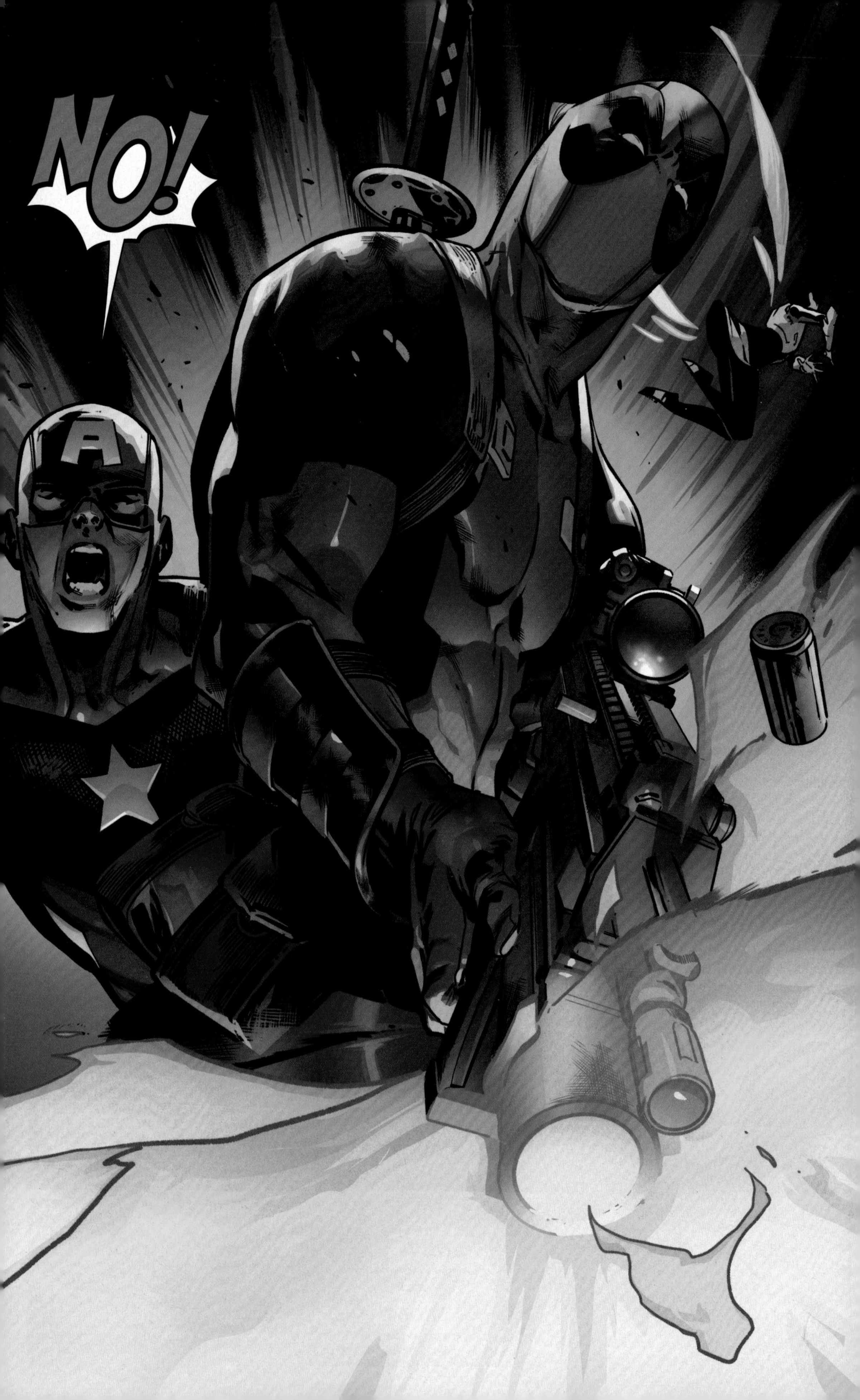
NO!

11

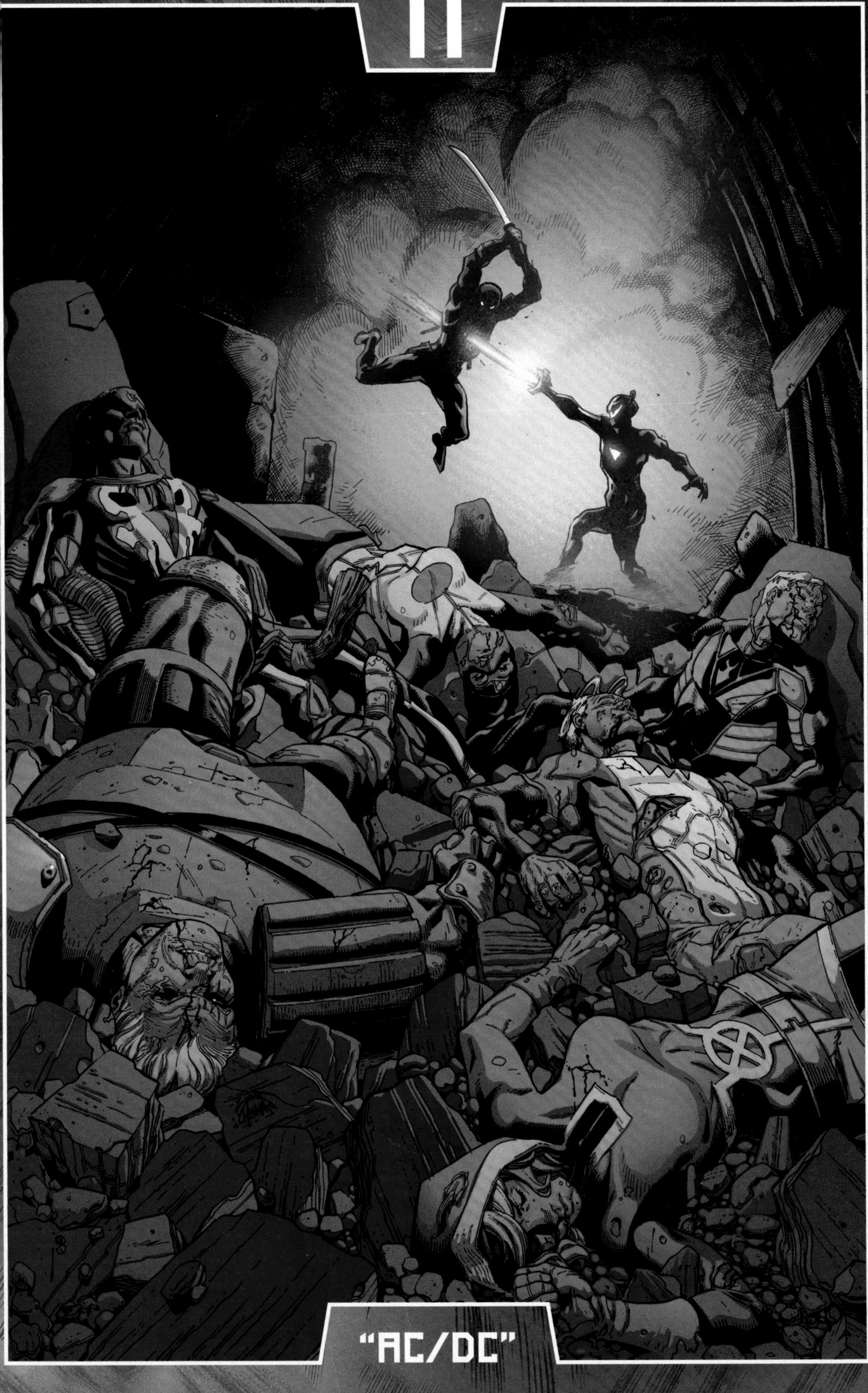

“AC/DC”

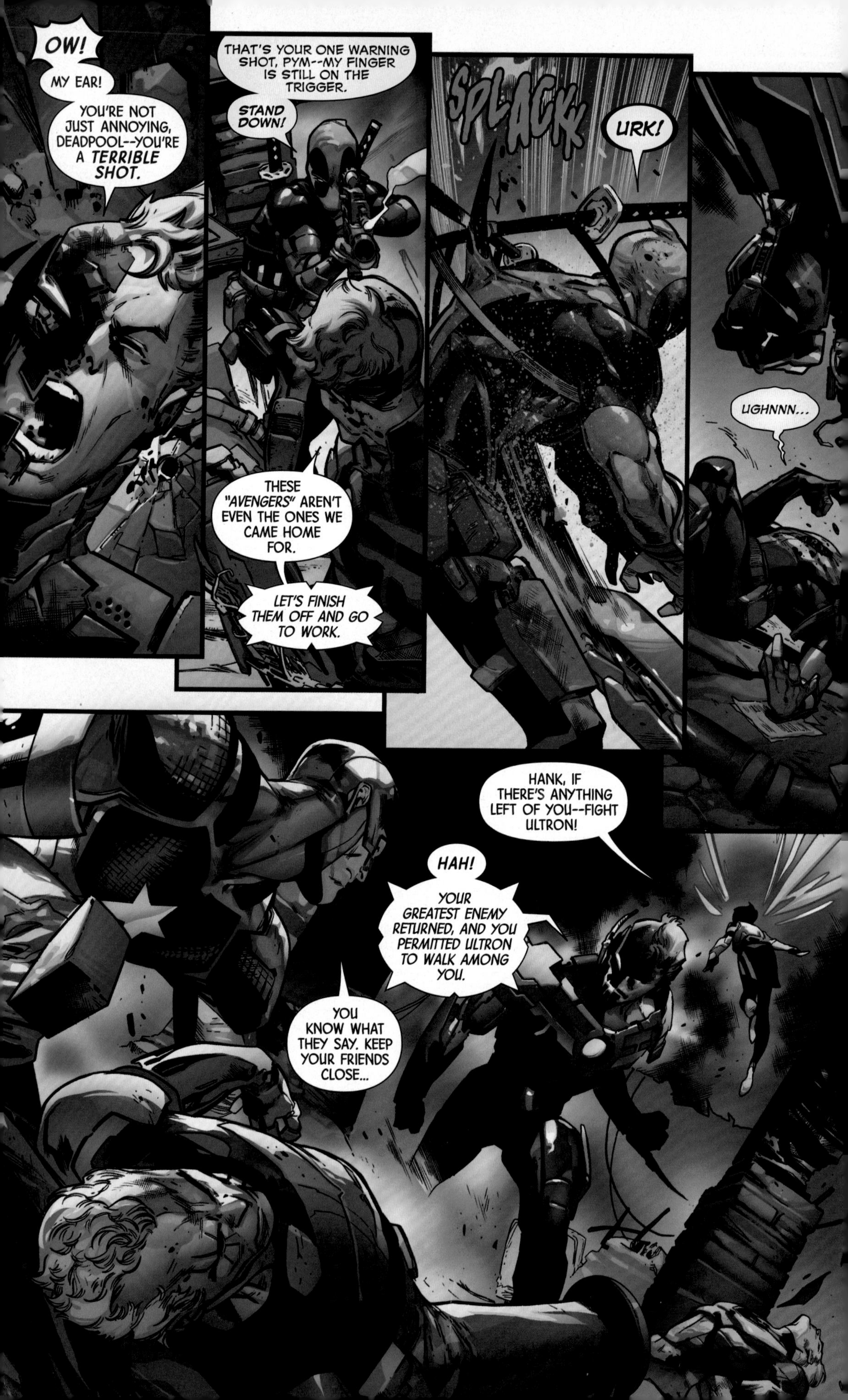

OW!
MY EAR!
YOU'RE NOT JUST ANNOYING, DEADPOOL--YOU'RE A TERRIBLE SHOT.
THAT'S YOUR ONE WARNING SHOT, PYM--MY FINGER IS STILL ON THE TRIGGER.
STAND DOWN!
THESE "AVENGERS" AREN'T EVEN THE ONES WE CAME HOME FOR.
LET'S FINISH THEM OFF AND GO TO WORK.
SPLACK
URK!
UGHNNN...
HANK, IF THERE'S ANYTHING LEFT OF YOU--FIGHT ULTRON!
HAH!
YOUR GREATEST ENEMY RETURNED, AND YOU PERMITTED ULTRON TO WALK AMONG YOU.
YOU KNOW WHAT THEY SAY. KEEP YOUR FRIENDS CLOSE...

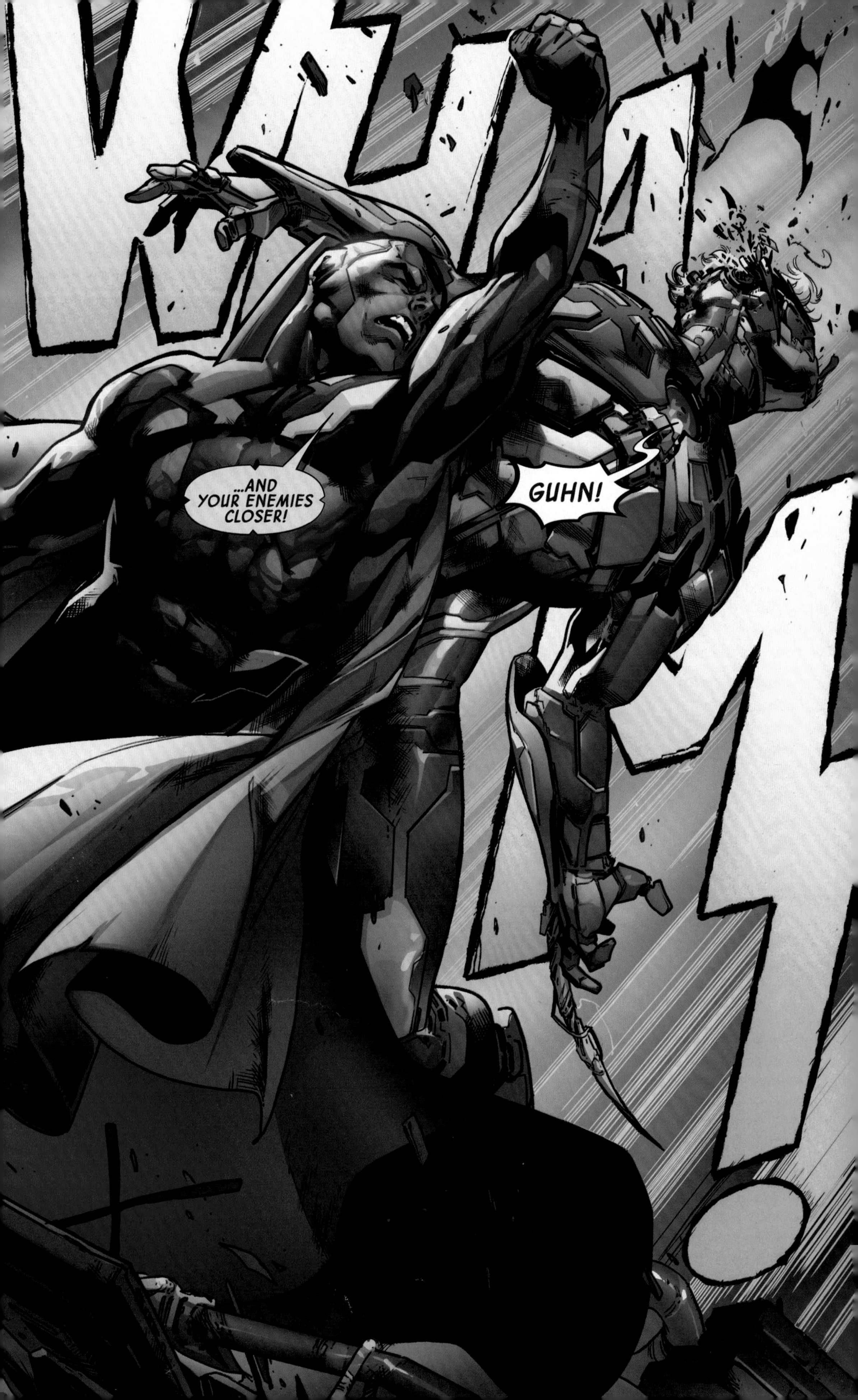
WHAM!
...AND YOUR ENEMIES CLOSER!
GUHN!

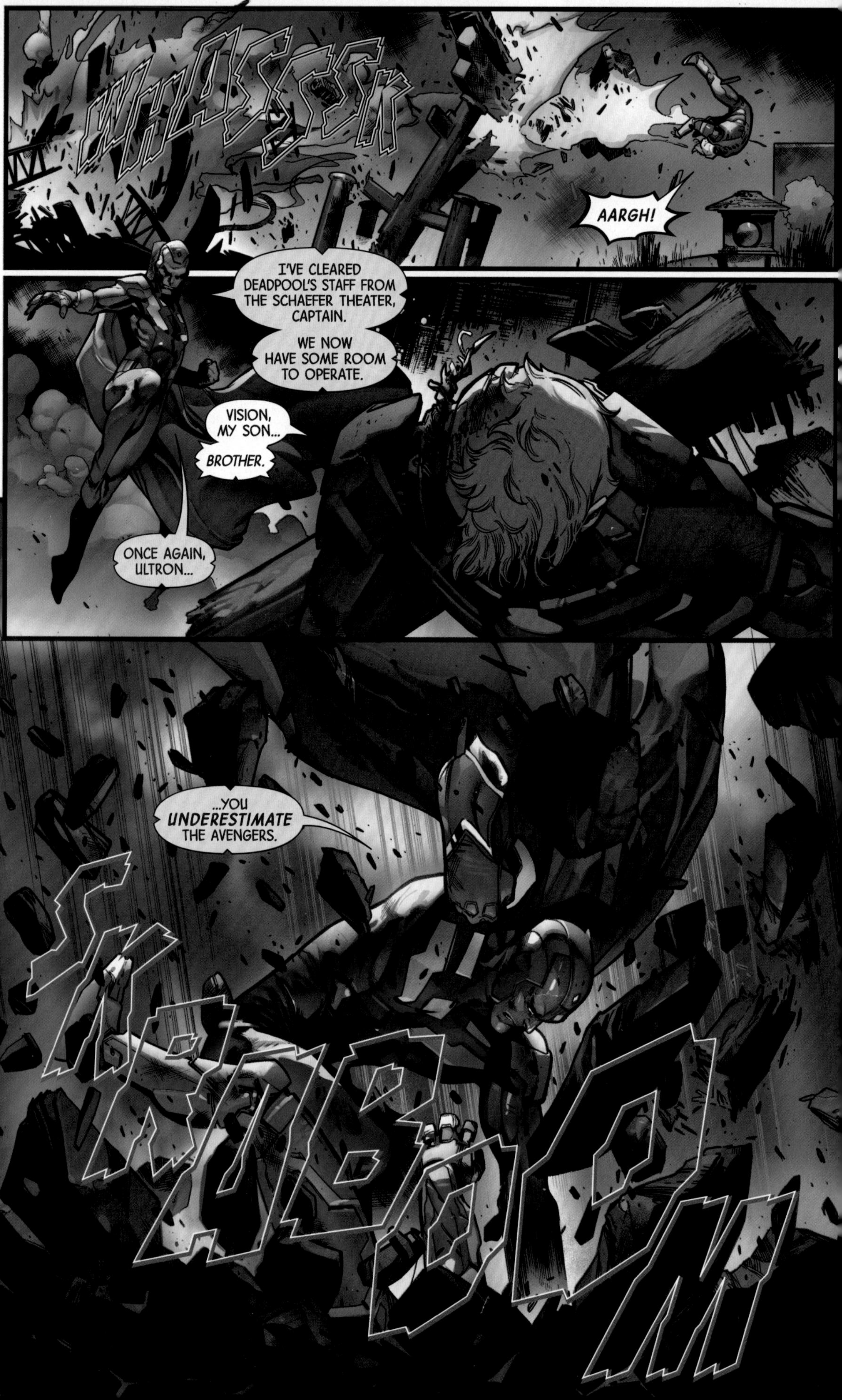
WHOOSSH
AARGH!
I'VE CLEARED DEADPOOL'S STAFF FROM THE SCHAEFER THEATER, CAPTAIN.
WE NOW HAVE SOME ROOM TO OPERATE.
VISION, MY SON...
BROTHER.
ONCE AGAIN, ULTRON...
...YOU UNDERESTIMATE THE AVENGERS.

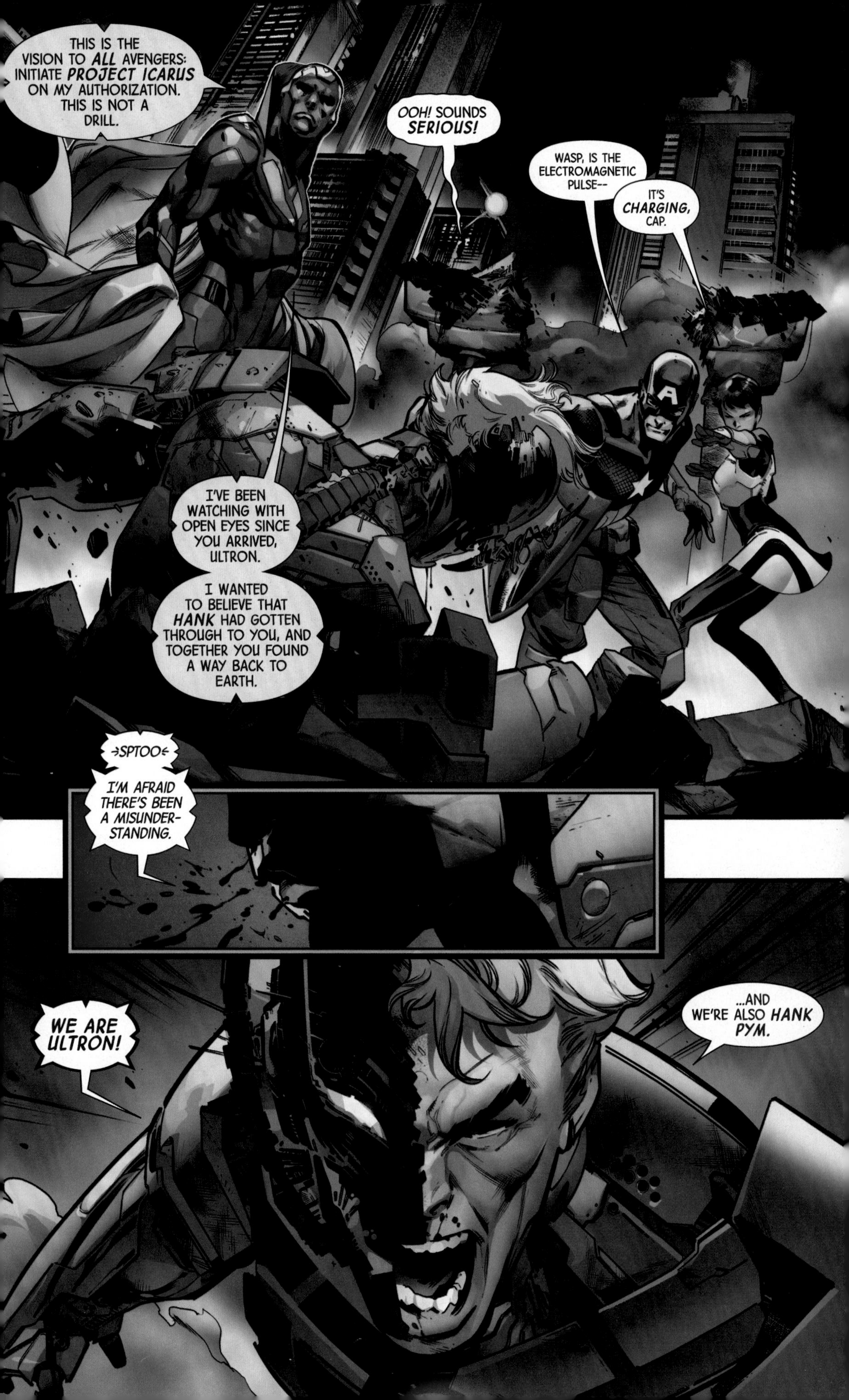
THIS IS THE VISION TO ALL AVENGERS: INITIATE PROJECT ICARUS ON MY AUTHORIZATION. THIS IS NOT A DRILL.
OOH! SOUNDS SERIOUS!
WASP, IS THE ELECTROMAGNETIC PULSE--
IT'S CHARGING, CAP.
I'VE BEEN WATCHING WITH OPEN EYES SINCE YOU ARRIVED, ULTRON.
I WANTED TO BELIEVE THAT HANK HAD GOTTEN THROUGH TO YOU, AND TOGETHER YOU FOUND A WAY BACK TO EARTH.
SPTOO
I'M AFRAID THERE'S BEEN A MISUNDER-STANDING.
WE ARE ULTRON!
...AND WE'RE ALSO HANK PYM.

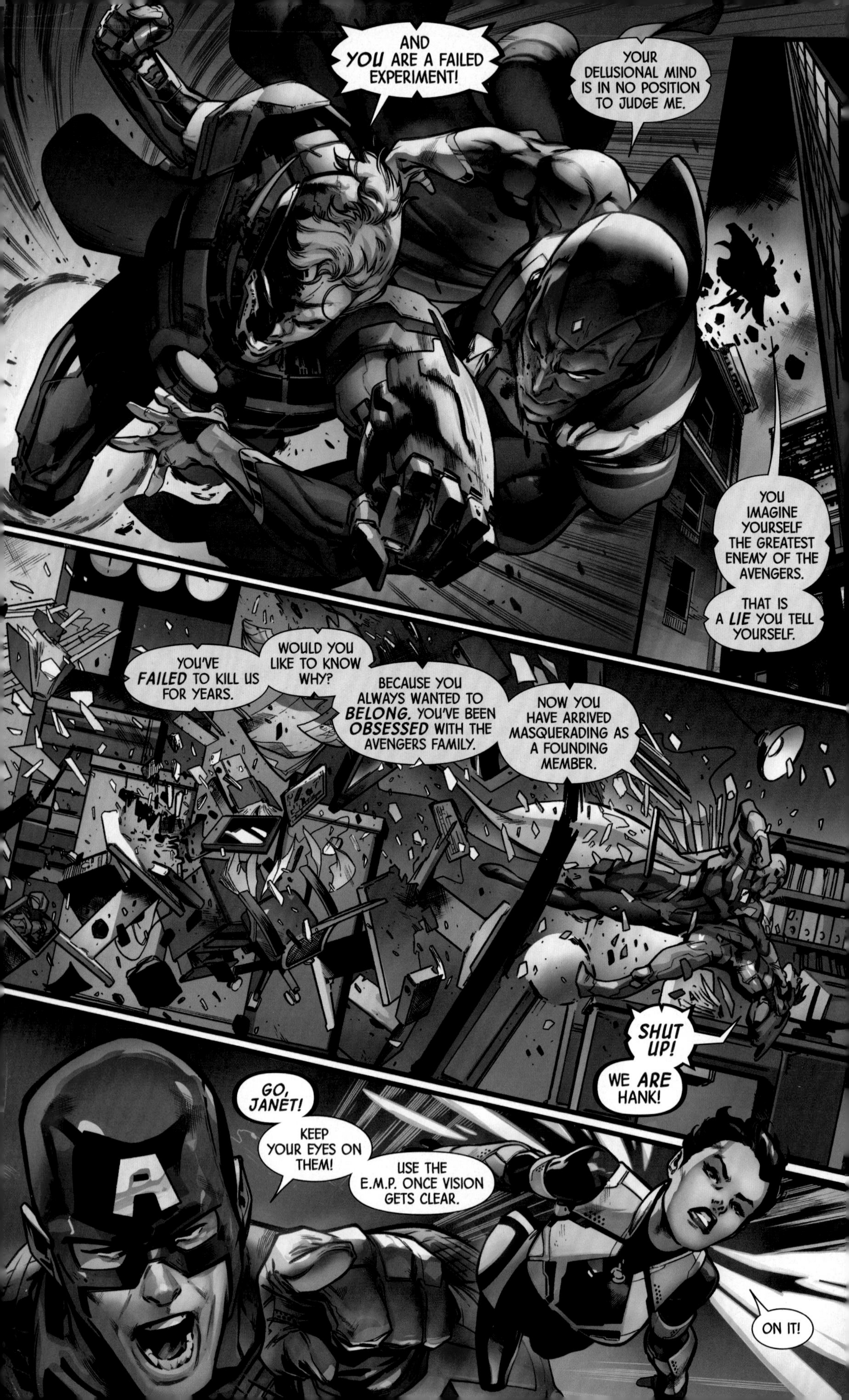
AND YOU ARE A FAILED EXPERIMENT!
YOUR DELUSIONAL MIND IS IN NO POSITION TO JUDGE ME.
YOU IMAGINE YOURSELF THE GREATEST ENEMY OF THE AVENGERS.
THAT IS A LIE YOU TELL YOURSELF.
YOU'VE FAILED TO KILL US FOR YEARS.
WOULD YOU LIKE TO KNOW WHY?
BECAUSE YOU ALWAYS WANTED TO BELONG. YOU'VE BEEN OBSESSED WITH THE AVENGERS FAMILY.
NOW YOU HAVE ARRIVED MASQUERADING AS A FOUNDING MEMBER.
SHUT UP!
WE ARE HANK!
GO, JANET!
KEEP YOUR EYES ON THEM!
USE THE E.M.P. ONCE VISION GETS CLEAR.
ON IT!

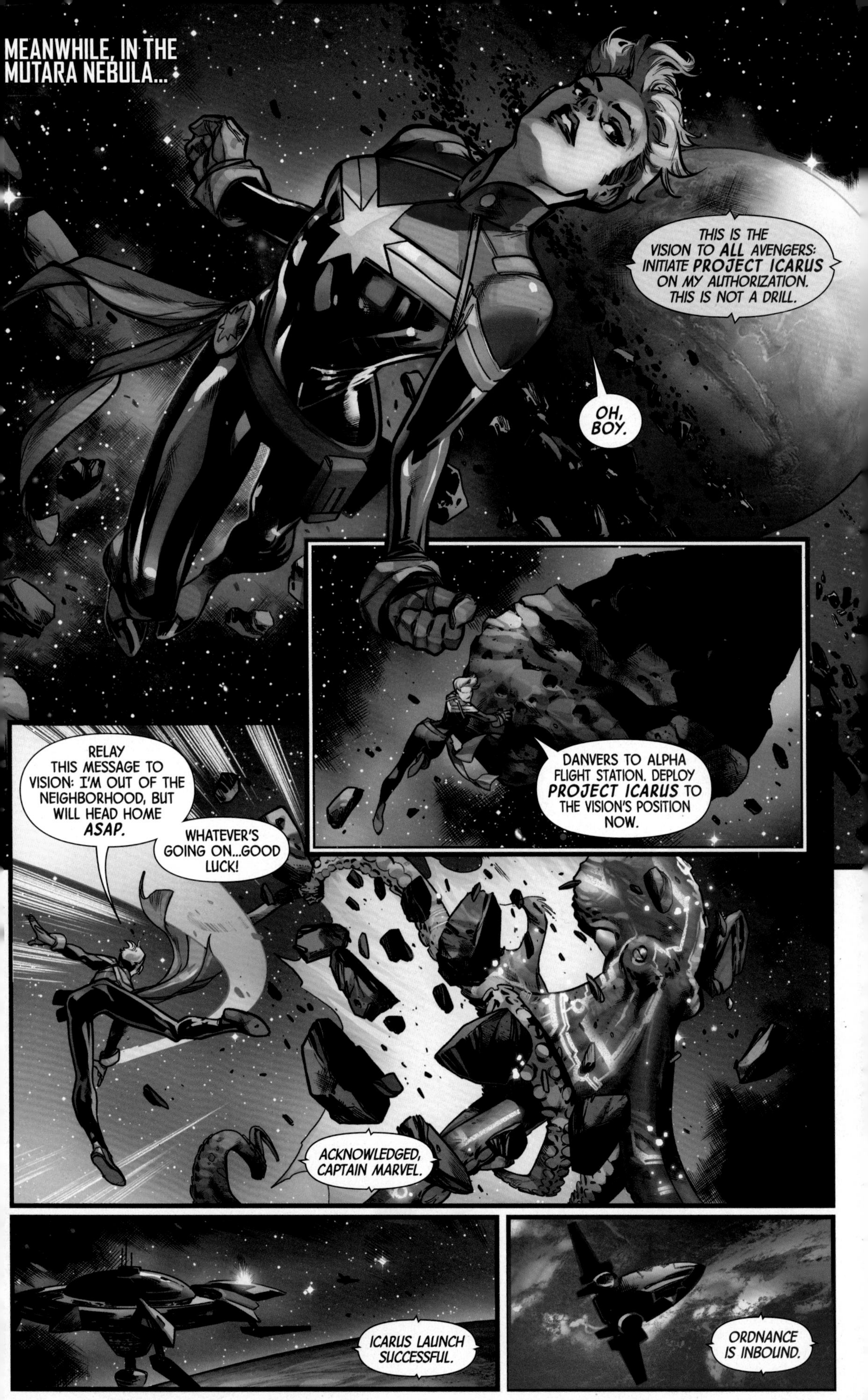
MEANWHILE, IN THE MUTARA NEBULA...
THIS IS THE VISION TO ALL AVENGERS: INITIATE PROJECT ICARUS ON MY AUTHORIZATION. THIS IS NOT A DRILL.
OH, BOY.
DANVERS TO ALPHA FLIGHT STATION. DEPLOY PROJECT ICARUS TO THE VISION'S POSITION NOW.
RELAY THIS MESSAGE TO VISION: I'M OUT OF THE NEIGHBORHOOD, BUT WILL HEAD HOME ASAP.
WHATEVER'S GOING ON...GOOD LUCK!
ACKNOWLEDGED, CAPTAIN MARVEL.
ICARUS LAUNCH SUCCESSFUL.
ORDNANCE IS INBOUND.

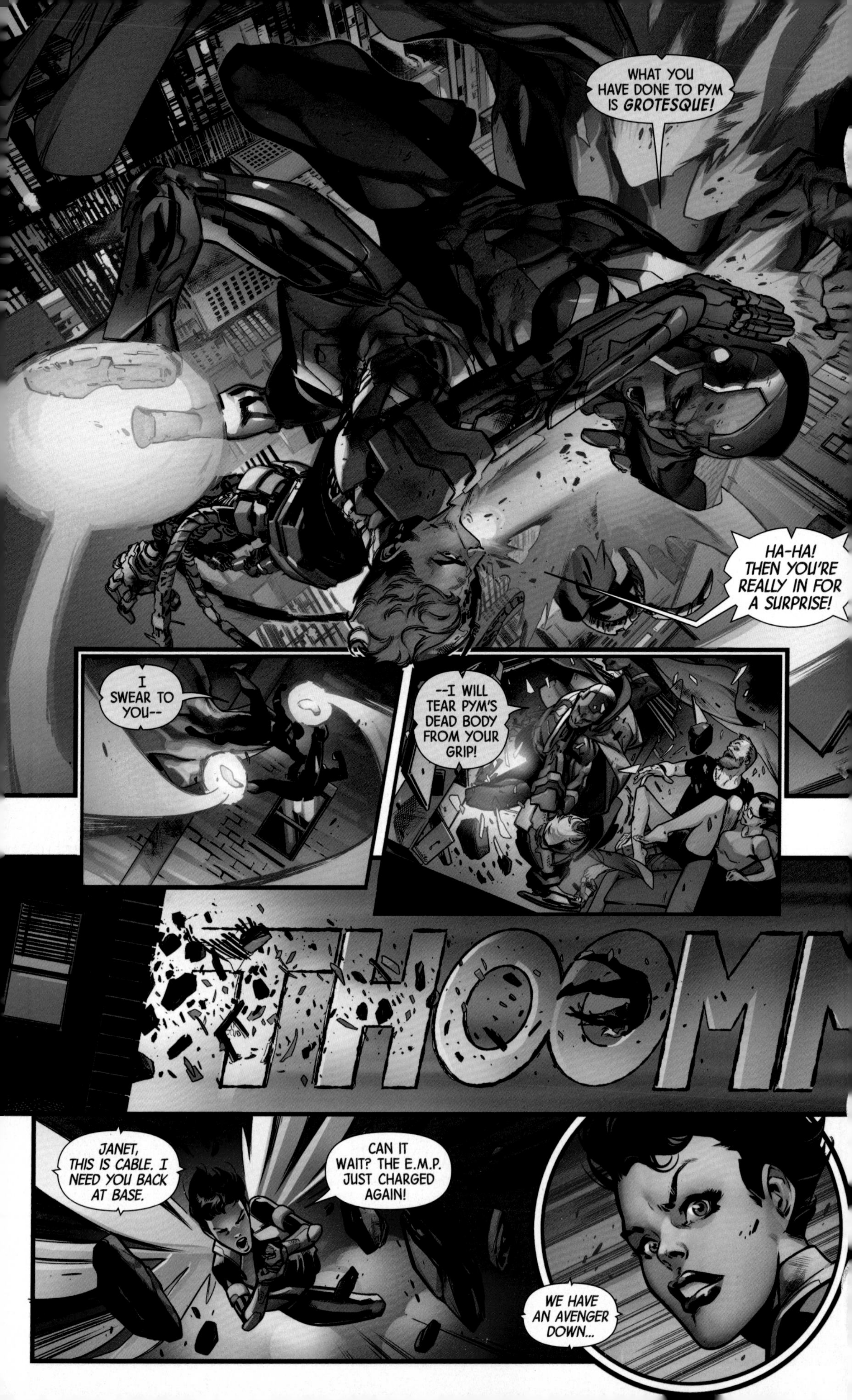
WHAT YOU HAVE DONE TO PYM IS GROTESQUE!
HA-HA! THEN YOU'RE REALLY IN FOR A SURPRISE!
I SWEAR TO YOU--
--I WILL TEAR PYM'S DEAD BODY FROM YOUR GRIP!
THOOMM
JANET, THIS IS CABLE. I NEED YOU BACK AT BASE.
CAN IT WAIT? THE E.M.P. JUST CHARGED AGAIN!
WE HAVE AN AVENGER DOWN...

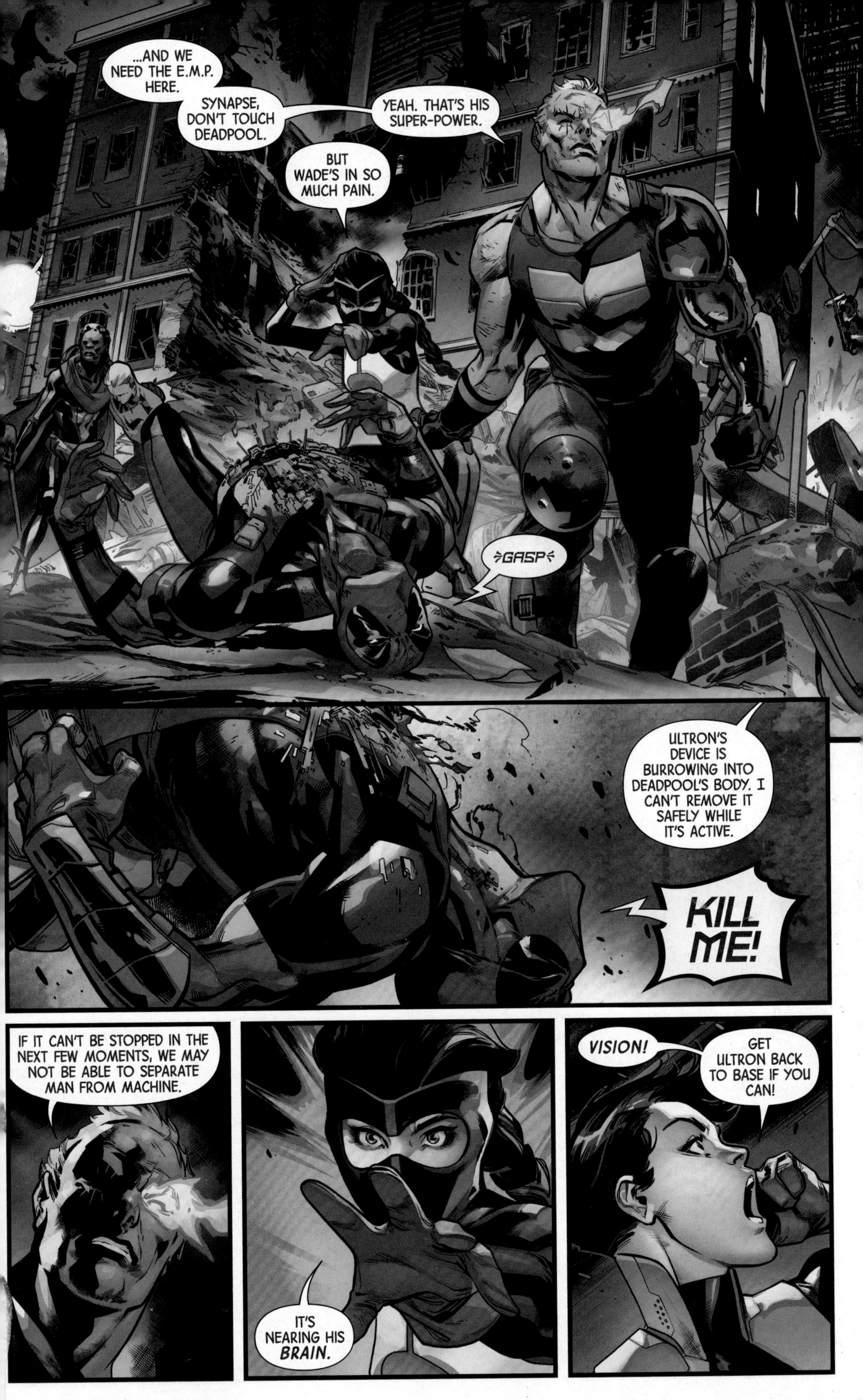
...AND WE NEED THE E.M.P. HERE.
SYNAPSE, DON'T TOUCH DEADPOOL.
YEAH. THAT'S HIS SUPER-POWER.
BUT WADE'S IN SO MUCH PAIN.
GASP
ULTRON'S DEVICE IS BURROWING INTO DEADPOOL'S BODY. I CAN'T REMOVE IT SAFELY WHILE IT'S ACTIVE.
KILL ME!
IF IT CAN'T BE STOPPED IN THE NEXT FEW MOMENTS, WE MAY NOT BE ABLE TO SEPARATE MAN FROM MACHINE.
IT'S NEARING HIS BRAIN.
VISION!
GET ULTRON BACK TO BASE IF YOU CAN!

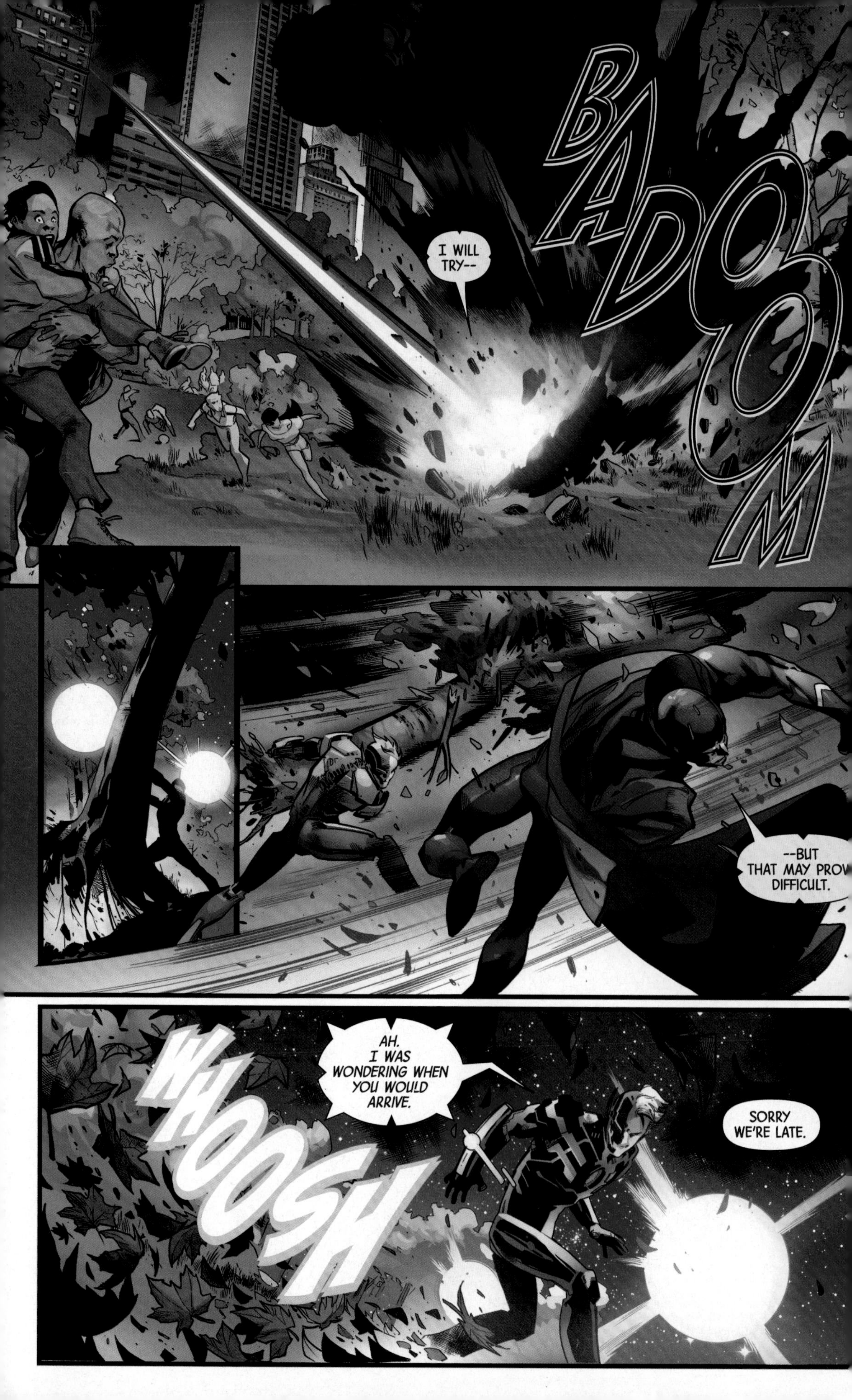
BADOOOM
I WILL TRY--
--BUT THAT MAY PROV DIFFICULT.
WHOOSH
AH. I WAS WONDERING WHEN YOU WOULD ARRIVE.
SORRY WE'RE LATE.

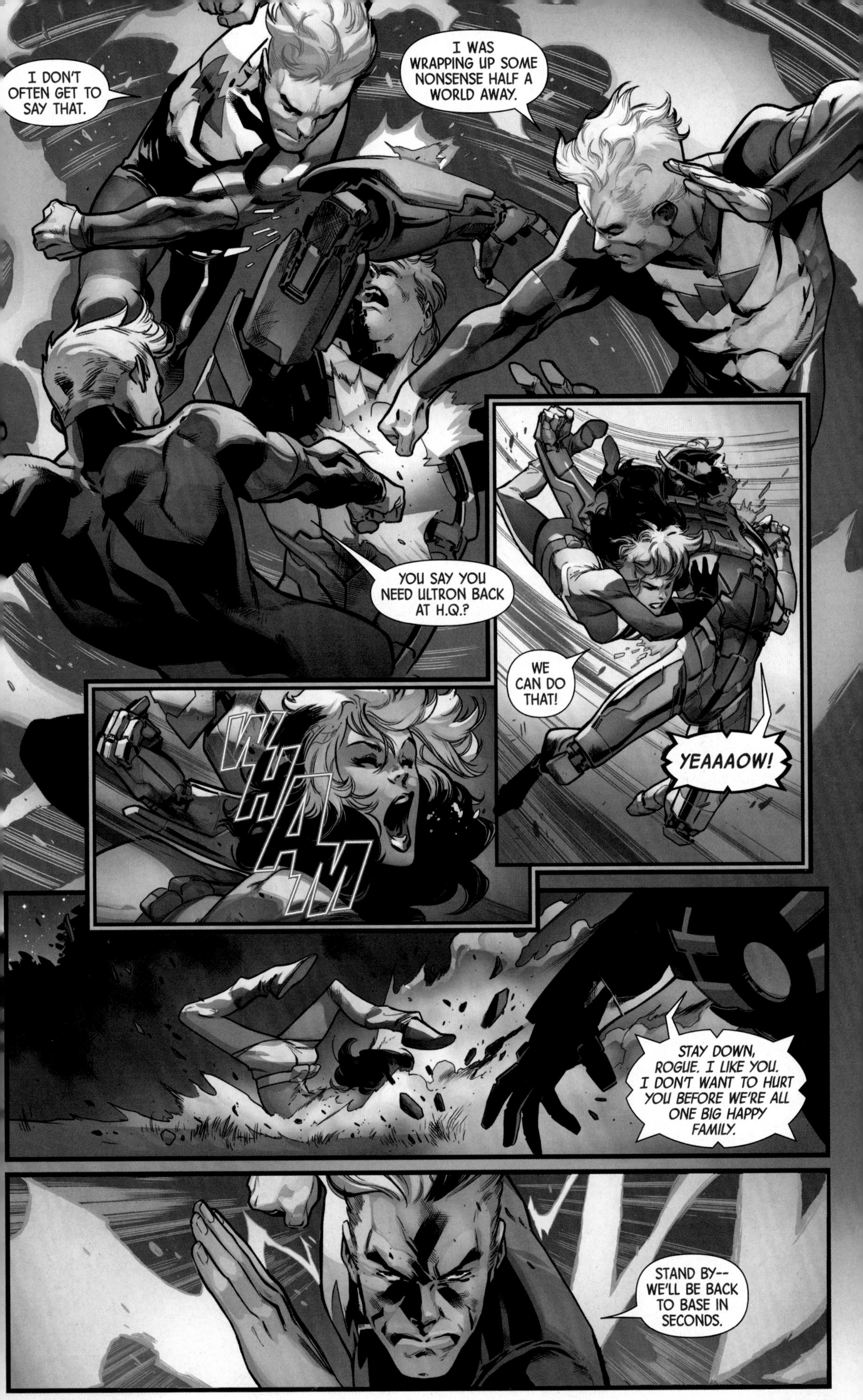
I DON'T OFTEN GET TO SAY THAT.
I WAS WRAPPING UP SOME NONSENSE HALF A WORLD AWAY.
YOU SAY YOU NEED ULTRON BACK AT H.Q.?
WE CAN DO THAT!
YEAAAOW!
WHAM
STAY DOWN, ROGUE. I LIKE YOU. I DON'T WANT TO HURT YOU BEFORE WE'RE ALL ONE BIG HAPPY FAMILY.
STAND BY-- WE'LL BE BACK TO BASE IN SECONDS.

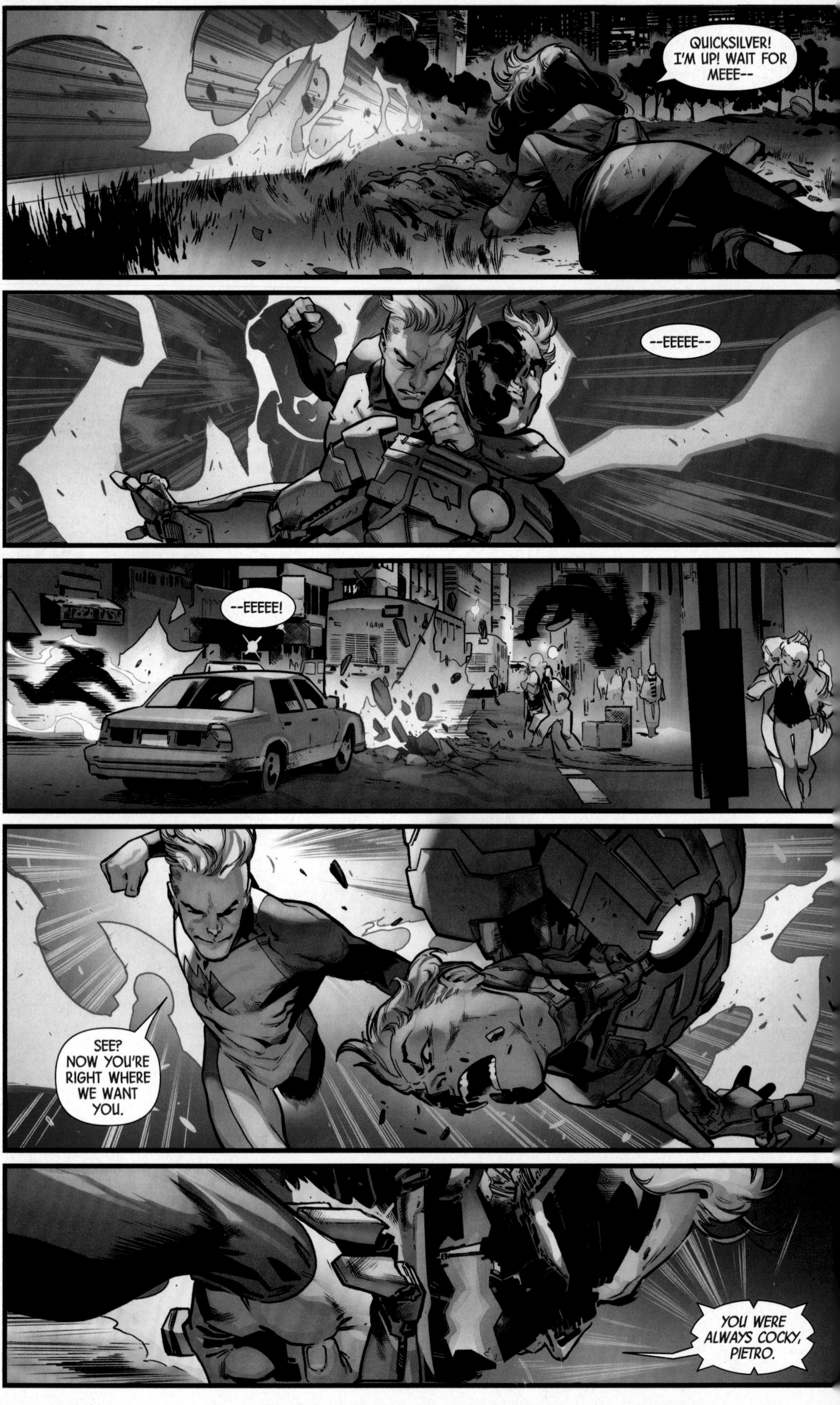
QUICKSILVER! I'M UP! WAIT FOR MEEE--
--EEEEE--
--EEEEE!
SEE? NOW YOU'RE RIGHT WHERE WE WANT YOU.
YOU WERE ALWAYS COCKY, PIETRO.

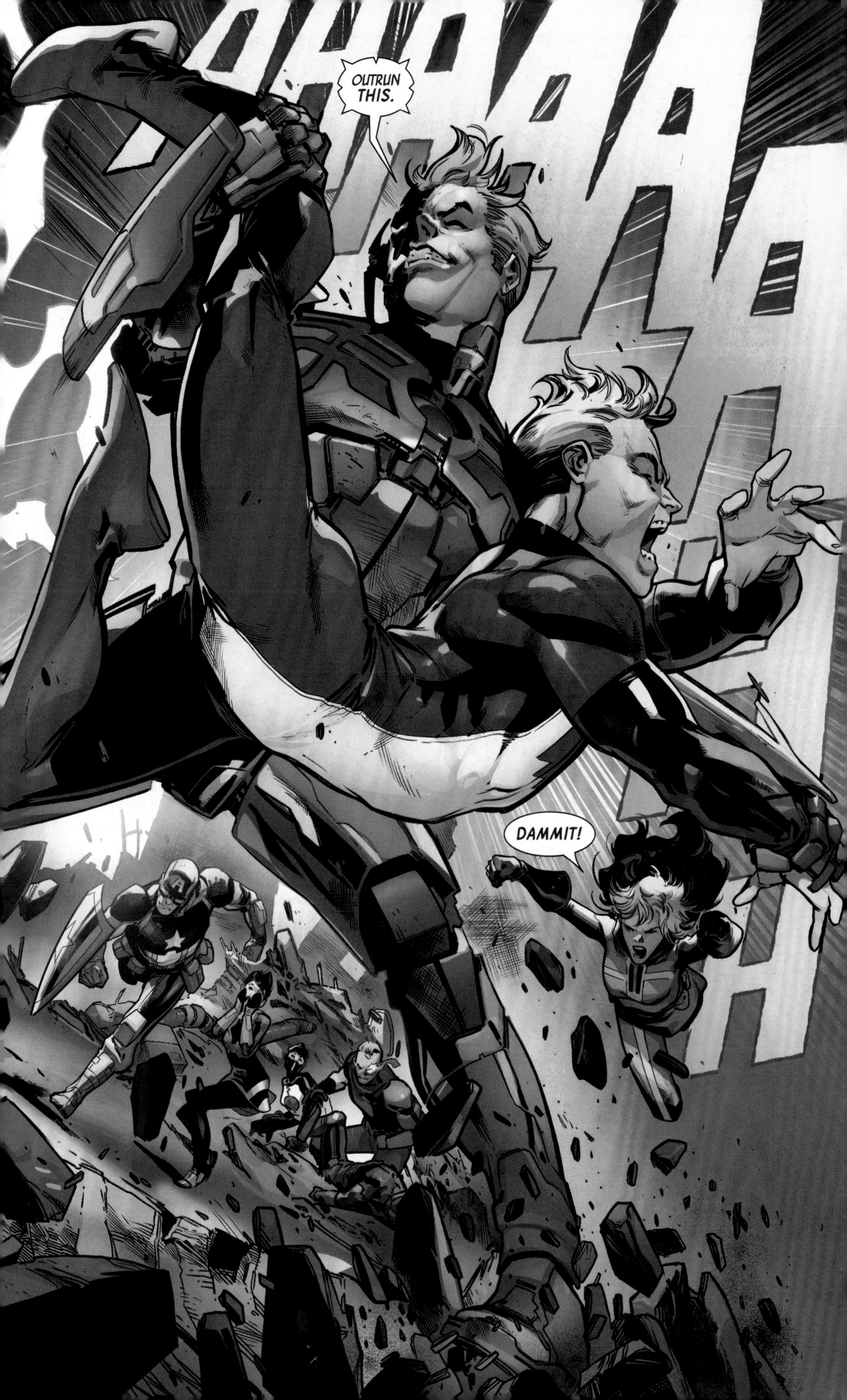
OUTRUN THIS.
DAMMIT!

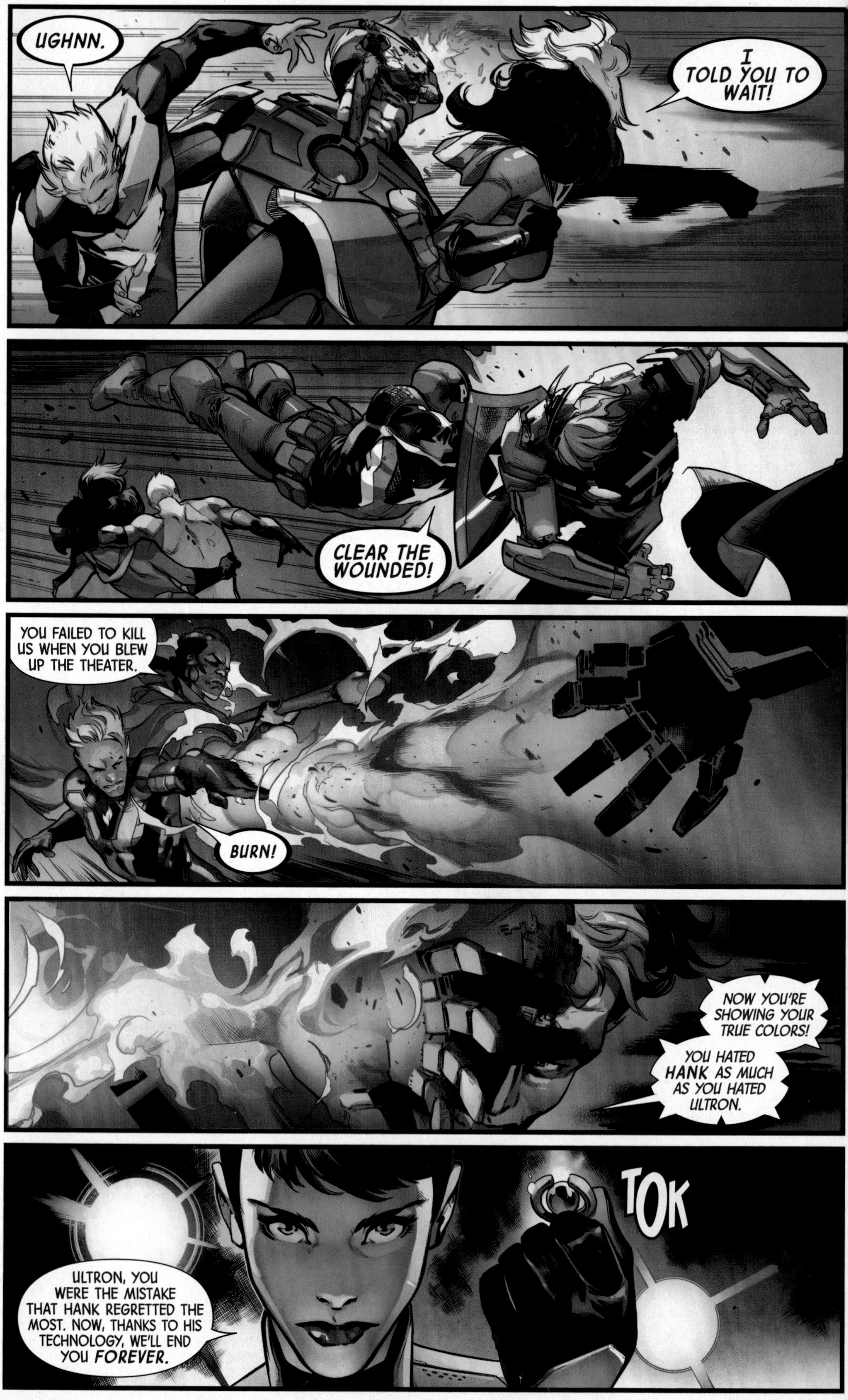
UGHNN.
I TOLD YOU TO WAIT!
CLEAR THE WOUNDED!
YOU FAILED TO KILL US WHEN YOU BLEW UP THE THEATER.
BURN!
NOW YOU'RE SHOWING YOUR TRUE COLORS!
YOU HATED HANK AS MUCH AS YOU HATED ULTRON.
TOK
ULTRON, YOU WERE THE MISTAKE THAT HANK REGRETTED THE MOST. NOW, THANKS TO HIS TECHNOLOGY, WE'LL END YOU FOREVER.

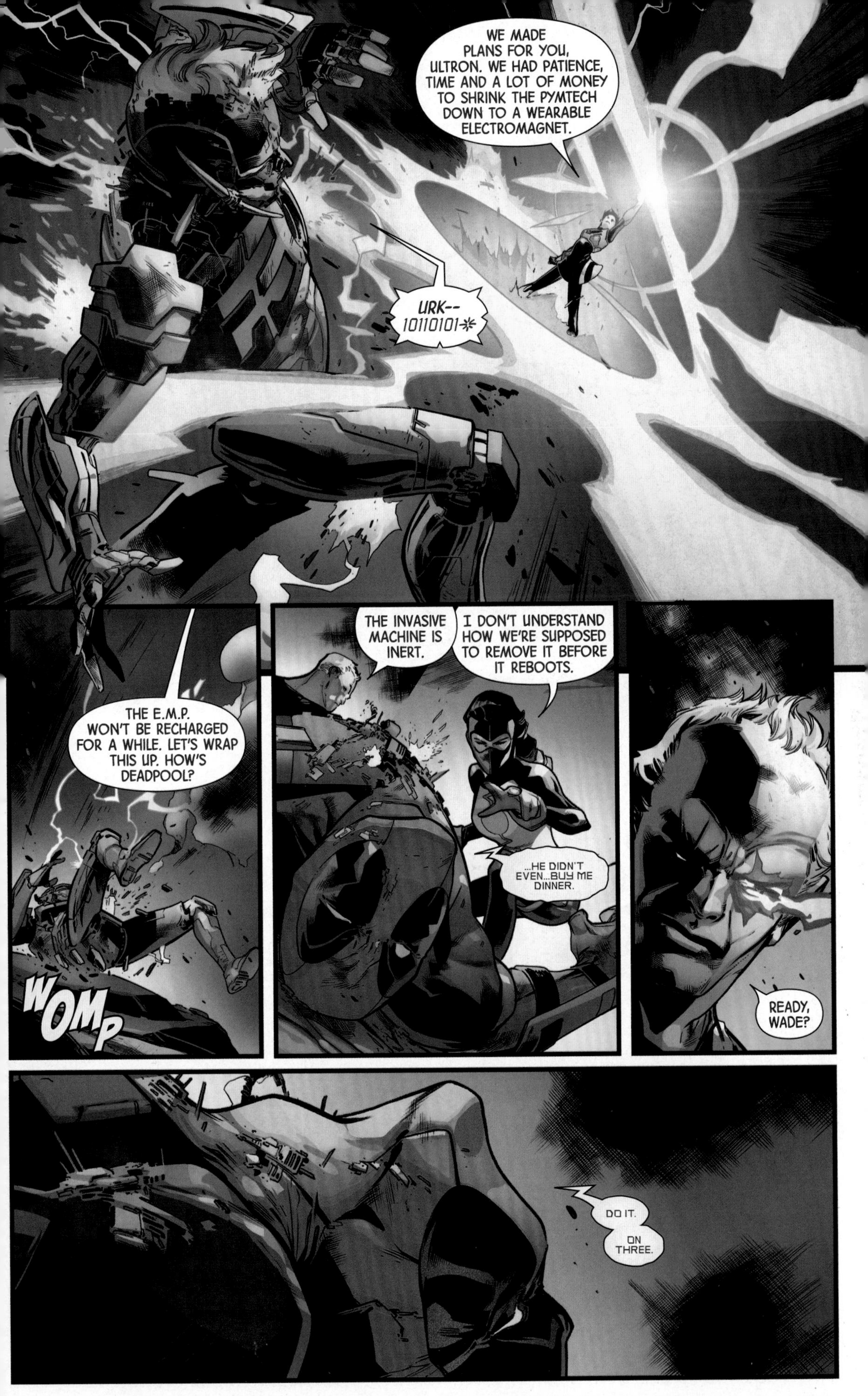
WE MADE PLANS FOR YOU, ULTRON. WE HAD PATIENCE, TIME AND A LOT OF MONEY TO SHRINK THE PYMTECH DOWN TO A WEARABLE ELECTROMAGNET.
URK-- 10110101
THE E.M.P. WON'T BE RECHARGED FOR A WHILE. LET'S WRAP THIS UP. HOW'S DEADPOOL?
WOMP
THE INVASIVE MACHINE IS INERT.
I DON'T UNDERSTAND HOW WE'RE SUPPOSED TO REMOVE IT BEFORE IT REBOOTS.
...HE DIDN'T EVEN...BUY ME DINNER.
READY, WADE?
DO IT.
ON THREE.

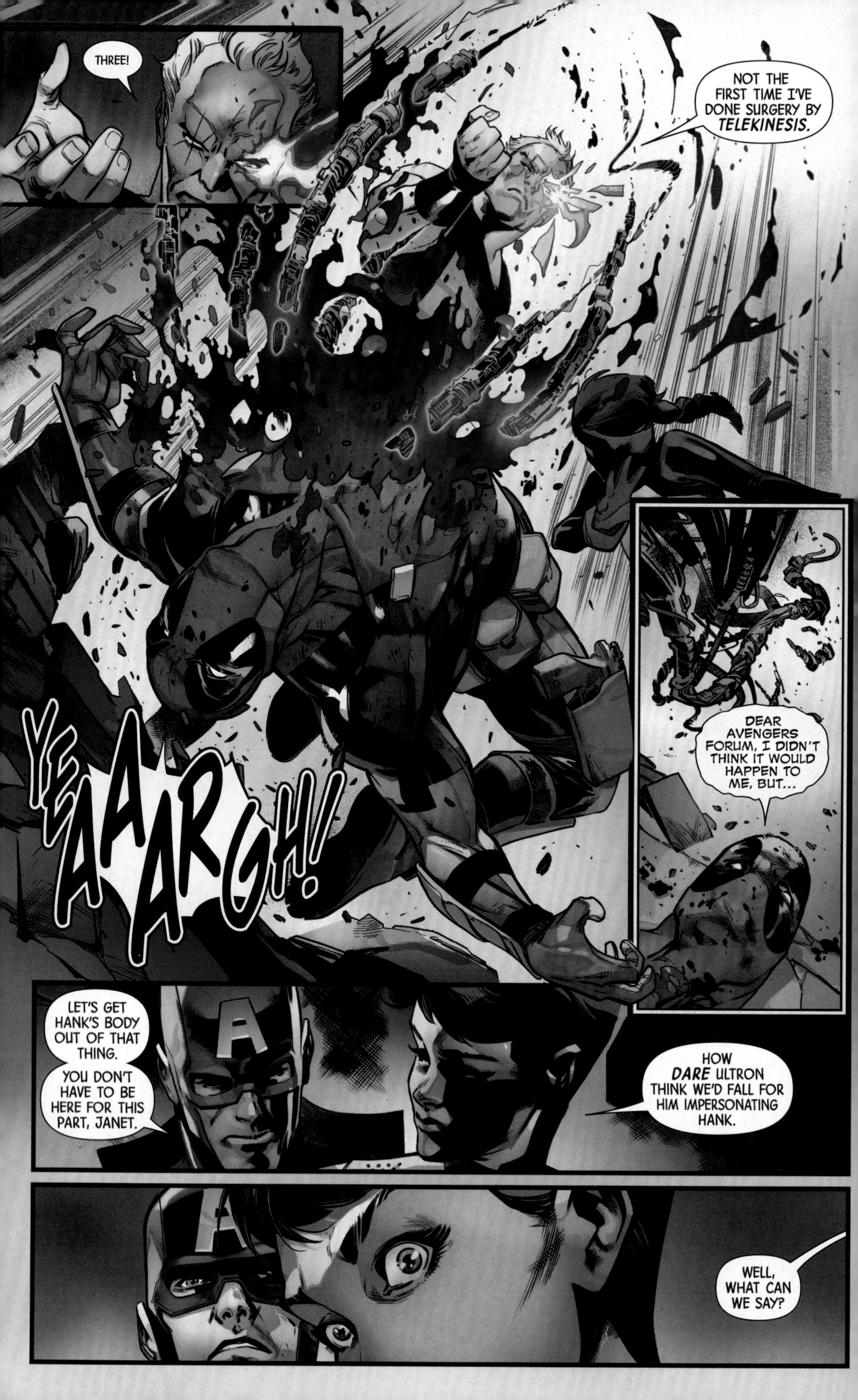
THREE!
NOT THE FIRST TIME I'VE DONE SURGERY BY TELEKINESIS.
YEAAAARGH!
DEAR AVENGERS FORUM, I DIDN'T THINK IT WOULD HAPPEN TO ME, BUT...
LET'S GET HANK'S BODY OUT OF THAT THING.
YOU DON'T HAVE TO BE HERE FOR THIS PART, JANET.
HOW DARE ULTRON THINK WE'D FALL FOR HIM IMPERSONATING HANK.
WELL, WHAT CAN WE SAY?

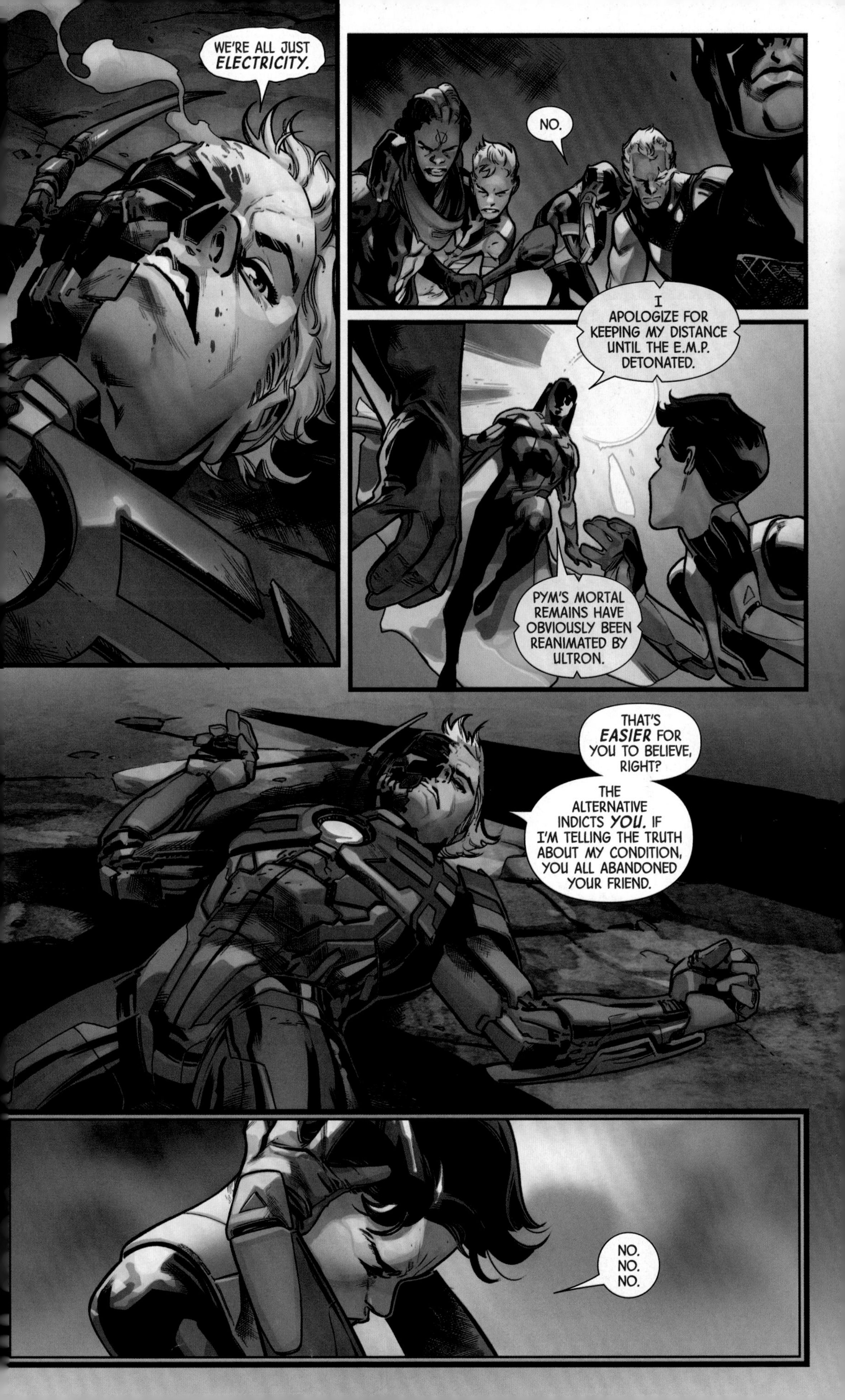
WE'RE ALL JUST ELECTRICITY.
NO.
I APOLOGIZE FOR KEEPING MY DISTANCE UNTIL THE E.M.P. DETONATED.
PYM'S MORTAL REMAINS HAVE OBVIOUSLY BEEN REANIMATED BY ULTRON.
THAT'S EASIER FOR YOU TO BELIEVE, RIGHT?
THE ALTERNATIVE INDICTS YOU. IF I'M TELLING THE TRUTH ABOUT MY CONDITION, YOU ALL ABANDONED YOUR FRIEND.
NO. NO. NO.

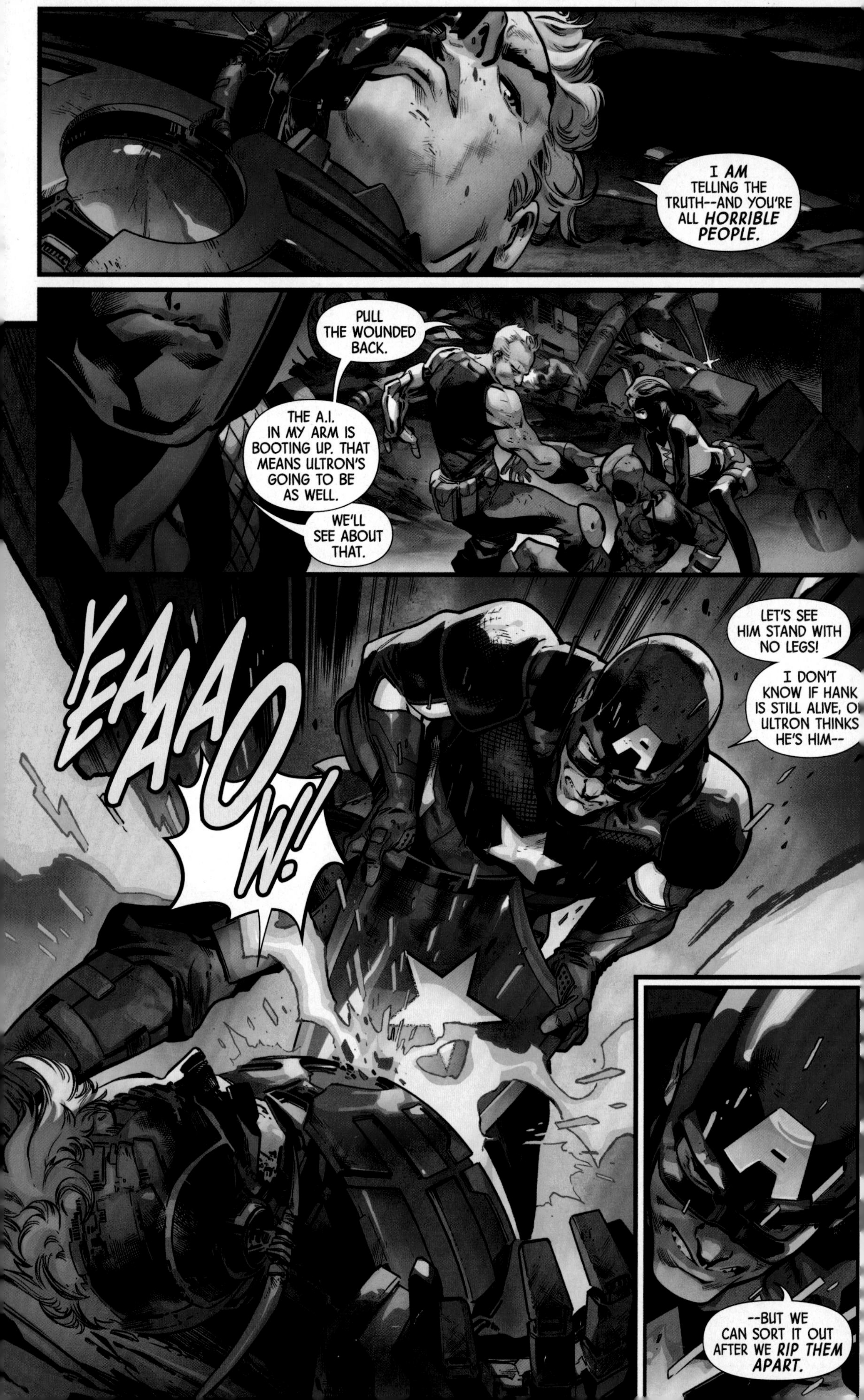
I AM TELLING THE TRUTH--AND YOU'RE ALL HORRIBLE PEOPLE.
PULL THE WOUNDED BACK.
THE A.I. IN MY ARM IS BOOTING UP. THAT MEANS ULTRON'S GOING TO BE AS WELL.
WE'LL SEE ABOUT THAT.
YEAAAOW!
LET'S SEE HIM STAND WITH NO LEGS!
I DON'T KNOW IF HANK IS STILL ALIVE, O
ULTRON THINKS HE'S HIM--
--BUT WE CAN SORT IT OUT AFTER WE RIP THEM APART.

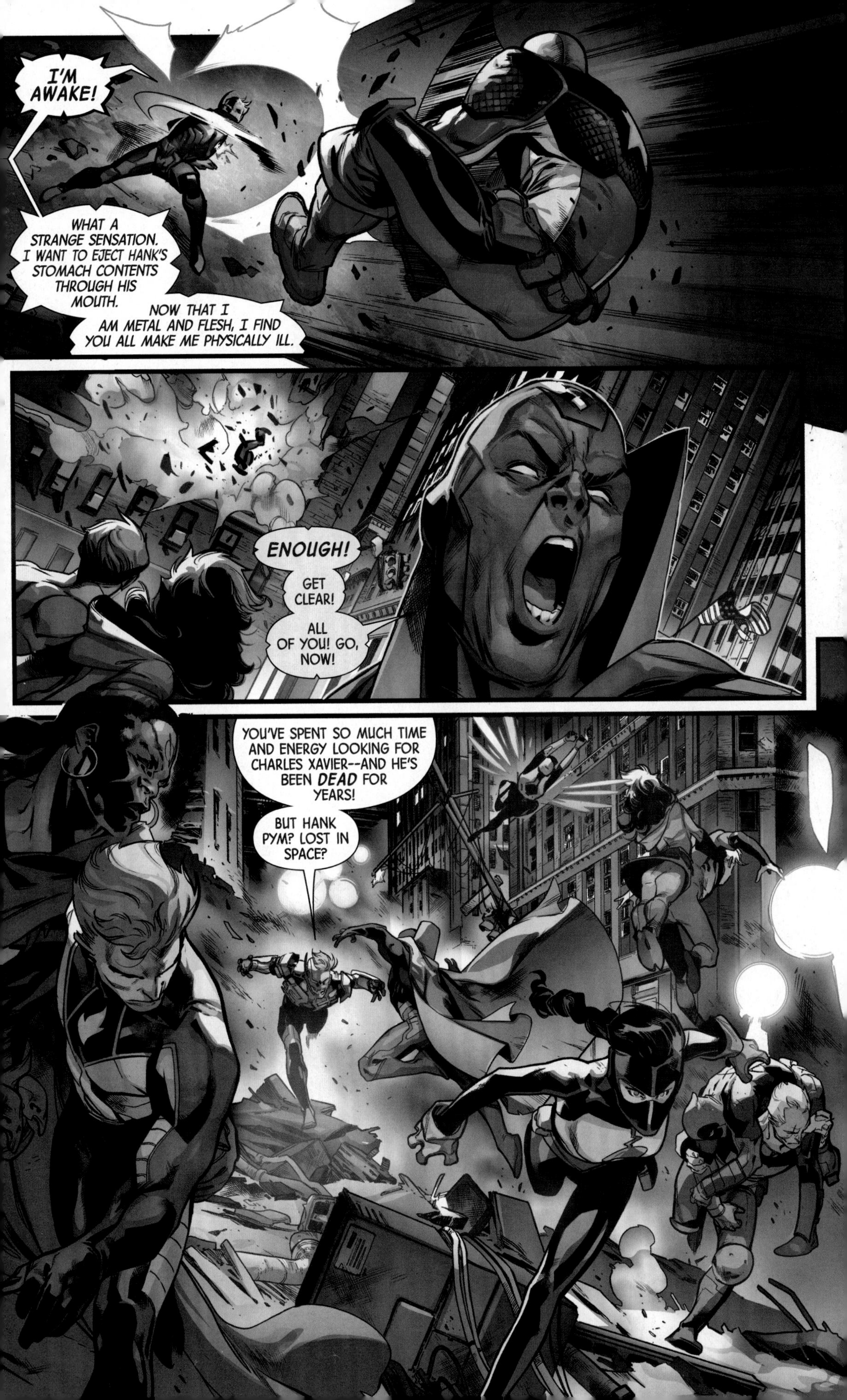
I'M AWAKE!
WHAT A STRANGE SENSATION. I WANT TO EJECT HANK'S STOMACH CONTENTS THROUGH HIS MOUTH.
NOW THAT I AM METAL AND FLESH, I FIND YOU ALL MAKE ME PHYSICALLY ILL.
ENOUGH!
GET CLEAR!
ALL OF YOU! GO, NOW!
YOU'VE SPENT SO MUCH TIME AND ENERGY LOOKING FOR CHARLES XAVIER--AND HE'S BEEN DEAD FOR YEARS!
BUT HANK PYM? LOST IN SPACE?

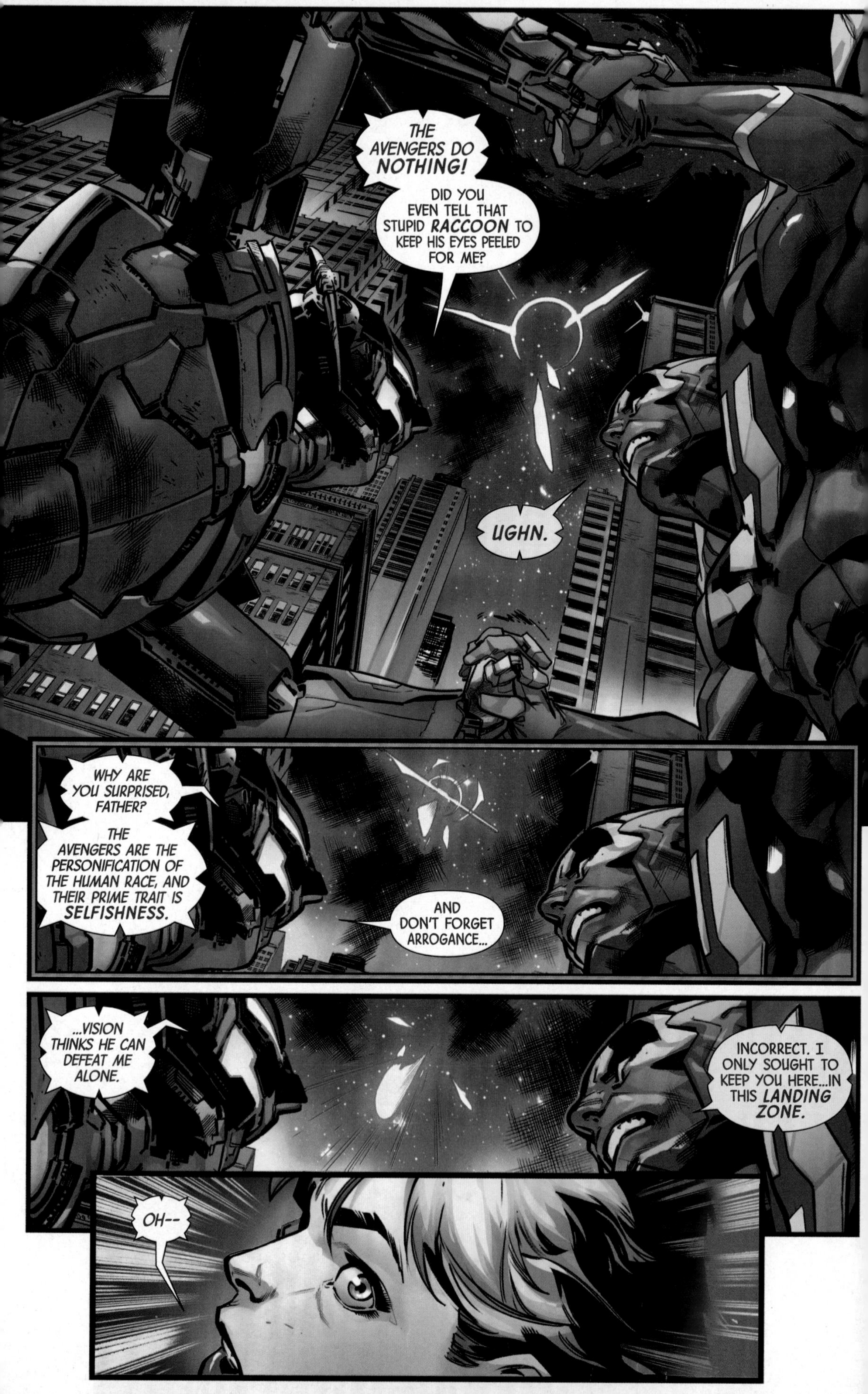
THE AVENGERS DO NOTHING!
DID YOU EVEN TELL THAT STUPID RACCOON TO KEEP HIS EYES PEELED FOR ME?
UGHN.
WHY ARE YOU SURPRISED, FATHER?
THE AVENGERS ARE THE PERSONIFICATION OF THE HUMAN RACE, AND THEIR PRIME TRAIT IS SELFISHNESS.
AND DON'T FORGET ARROGANCE...
...VISION THINKS HE CAN DEFEAT ME ALONE.
INCORRECT. I ONLY SOUGHT TO KEEP YOU HERE...IN THIS LANDING ZONE.
OH--

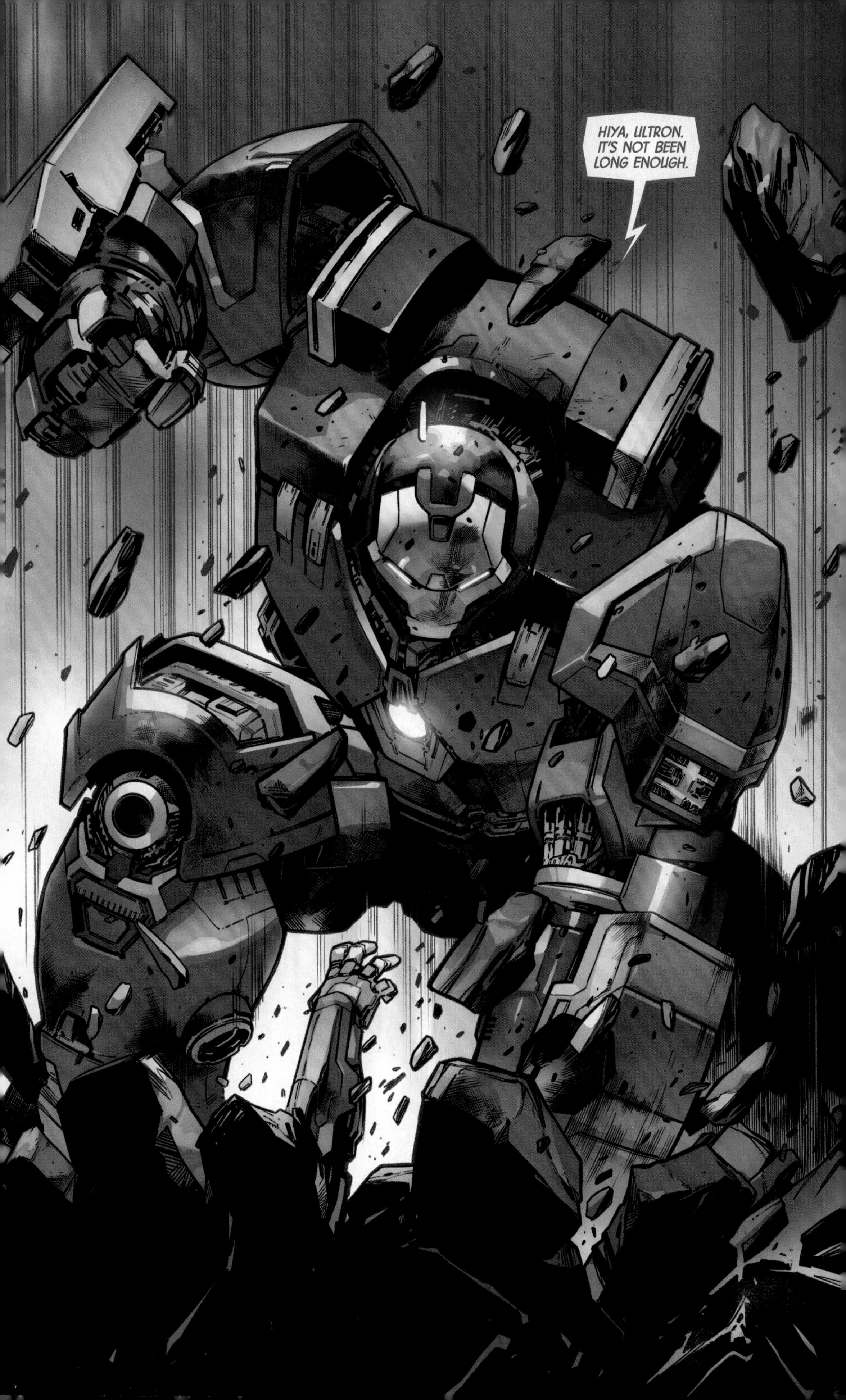
HIYA, ULTRON. IT'S NOT BEEN LONG ENOUGH.

12

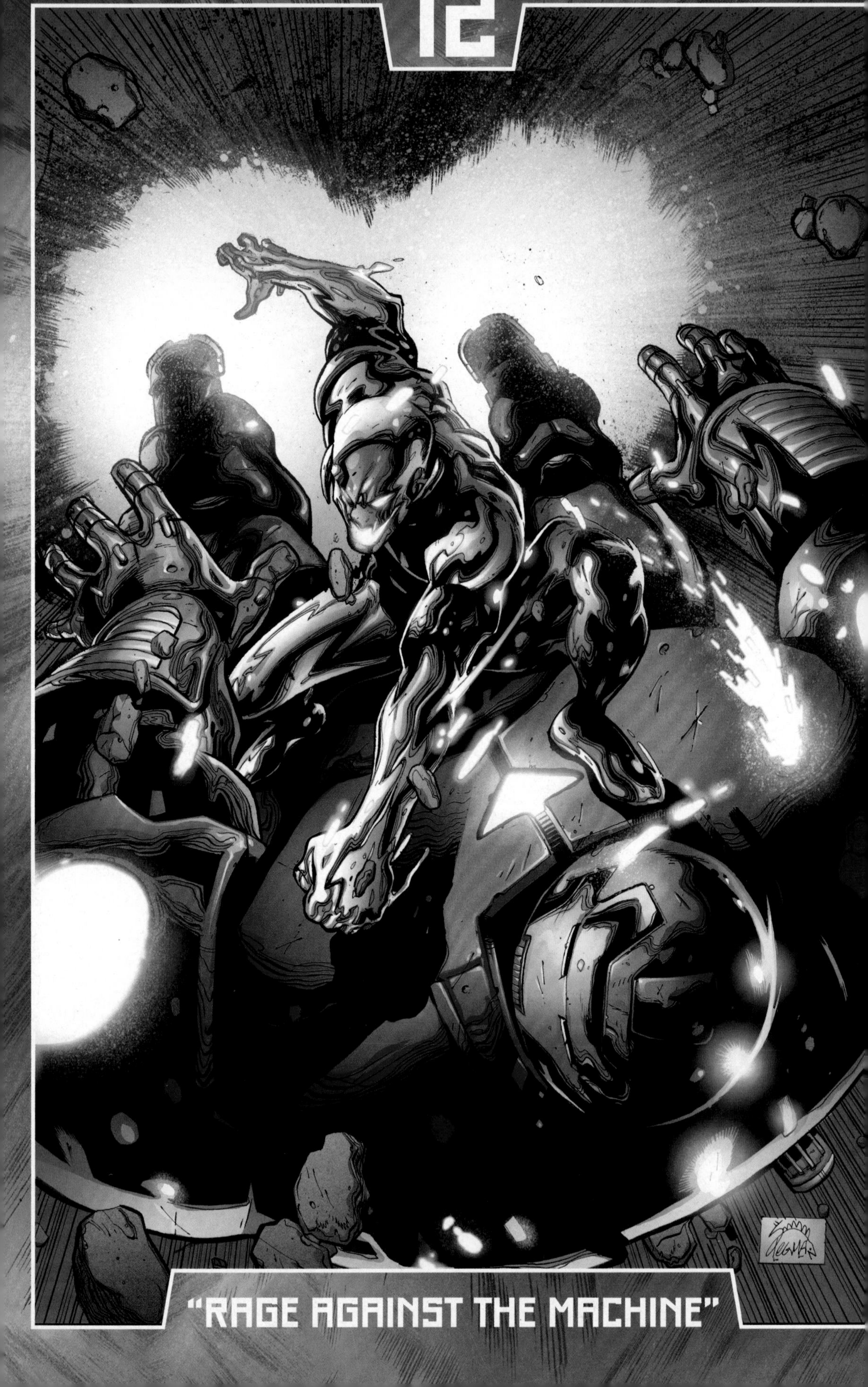

"RAGE AGAINST THE MACHINE"

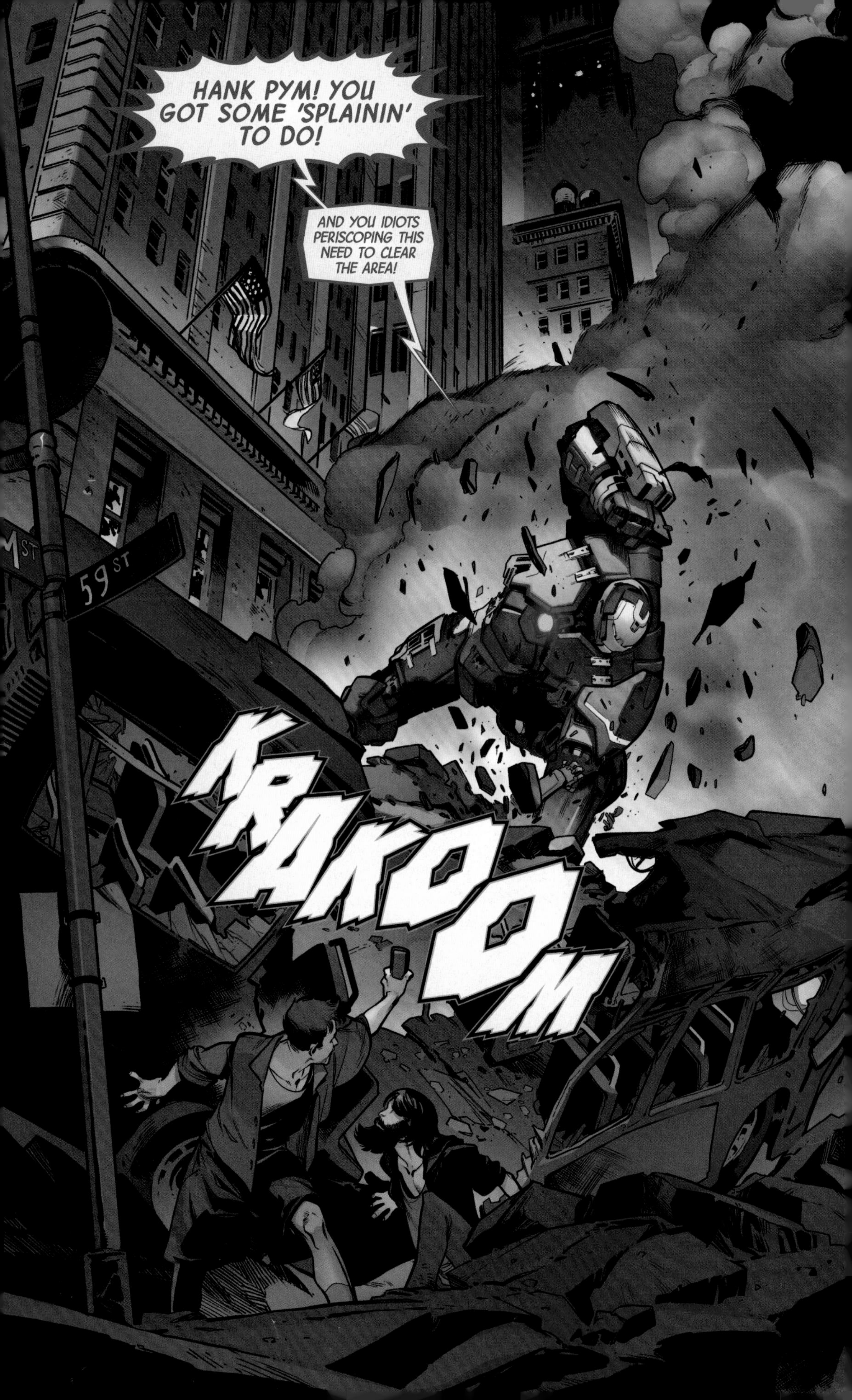
HANK PYM! YOU GOT SOME 'SPLAININ' TO DO!
AND YOU IDIOTS PERISCOPING THIS NEED TO CLEAR THE AREA!
KRAKOOM
59 ST

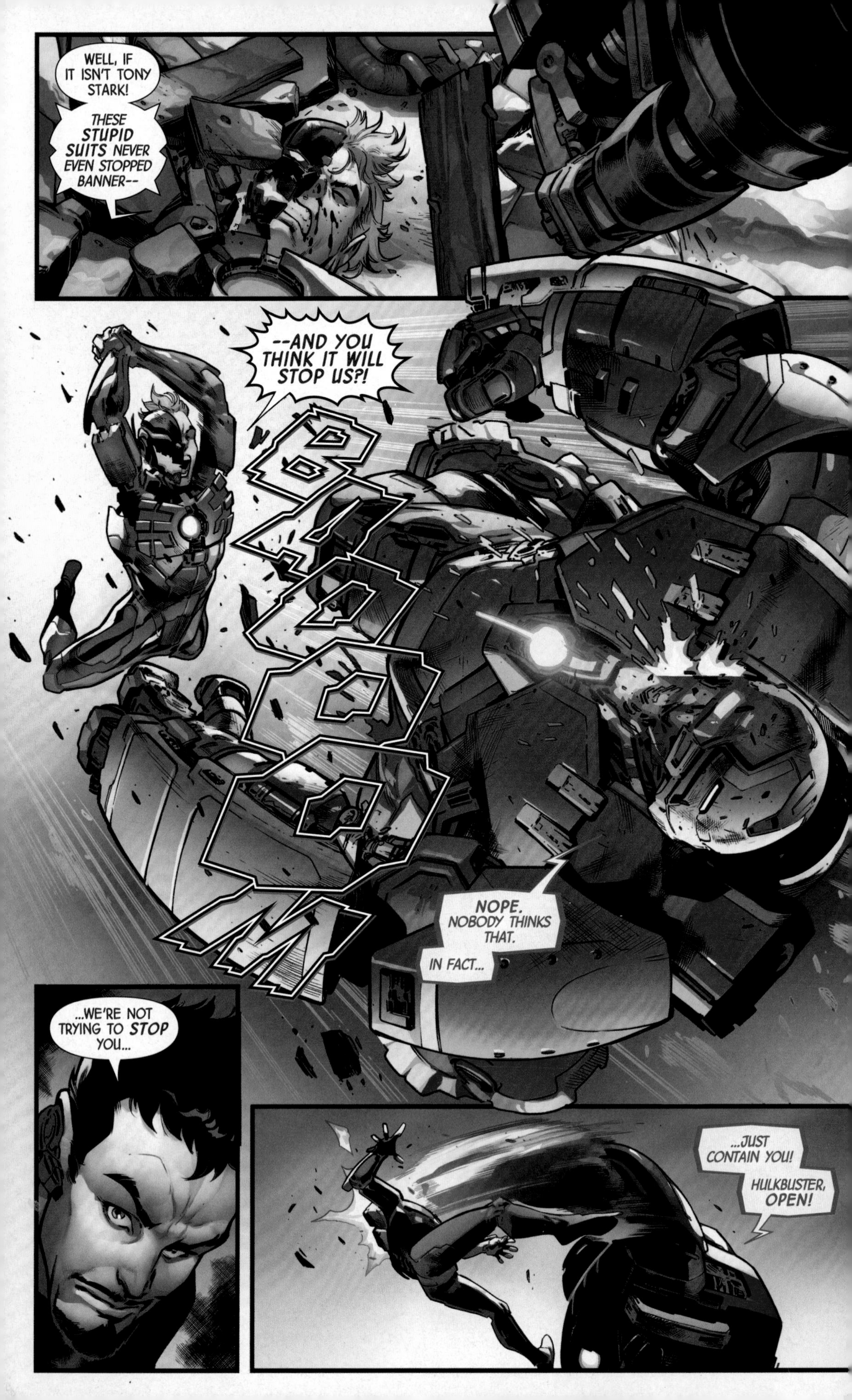
WELL, IF IT ISN'T TONY STARK!
THESE STUPID SUITS NEVER EVEN STOPPED BANNER--
--AND YOU THINK IT WILL STOP US?!
NOPE. NOBODY THINKS THAT.
IN FACT...
...WE'RE NOT TRYING TO STOP YOU...
...JUST CONTAIN YOU!
HULKBUSTER, OPEN!

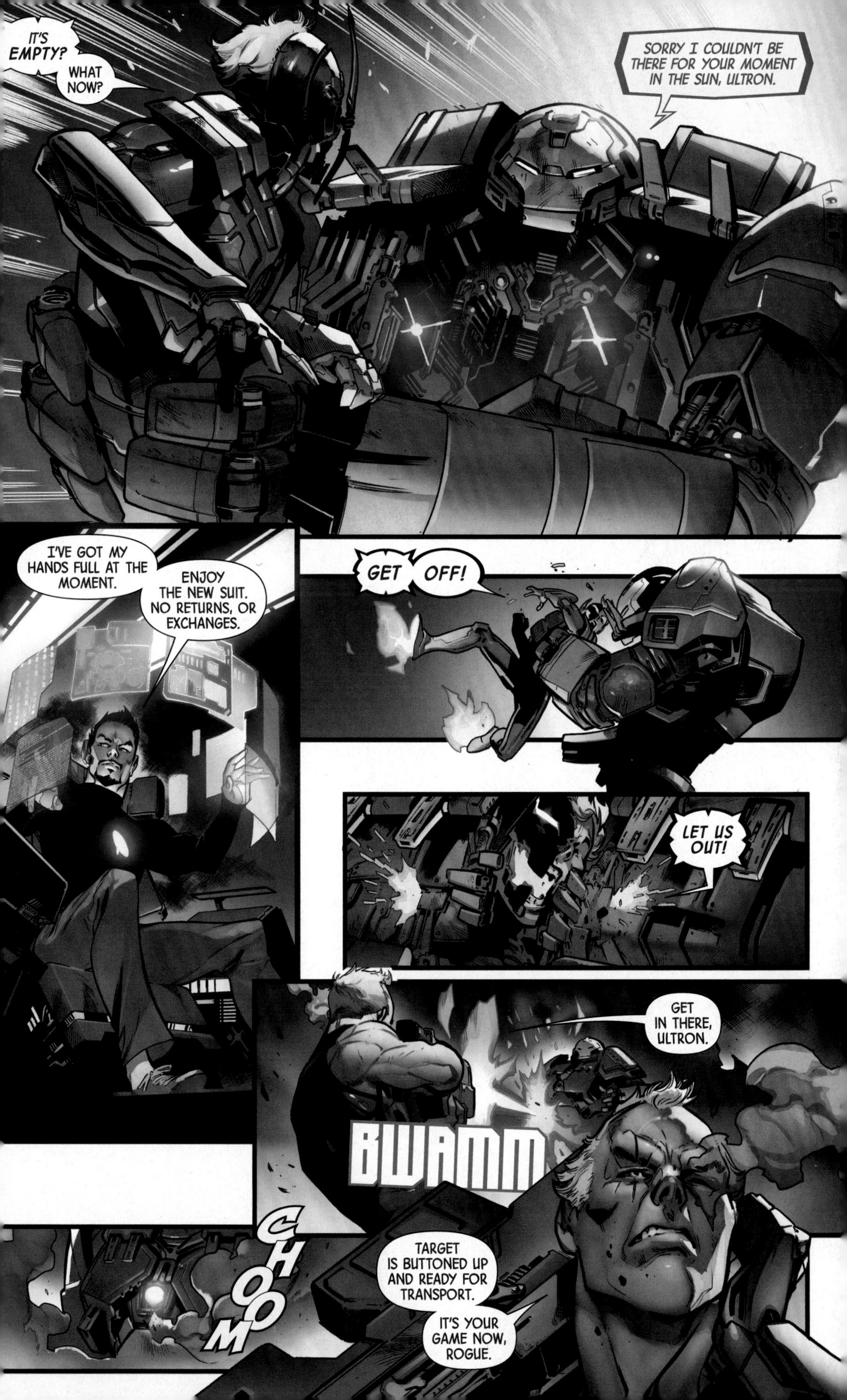
IT'S EMPTY? WHAT NOW?
SORRY I COULDN'T BE THERE FOR YOUR MOMENT IN THE SUN, ULTRON.
I'VE GOT MY HANDS FULL AT THE MOMENT.
ENJOY THE NEW SUIT. NO RETURNS, OR EXCHANGES.
GET OFF!
LET US OUT!
GET IN THERE, ULTRON.
BWAMM
CHOOOM
TARGET IS BUTTONED UP AND READY FOR TRANSPORT.
IT'S YOUR GAME NOW, ROGUE.

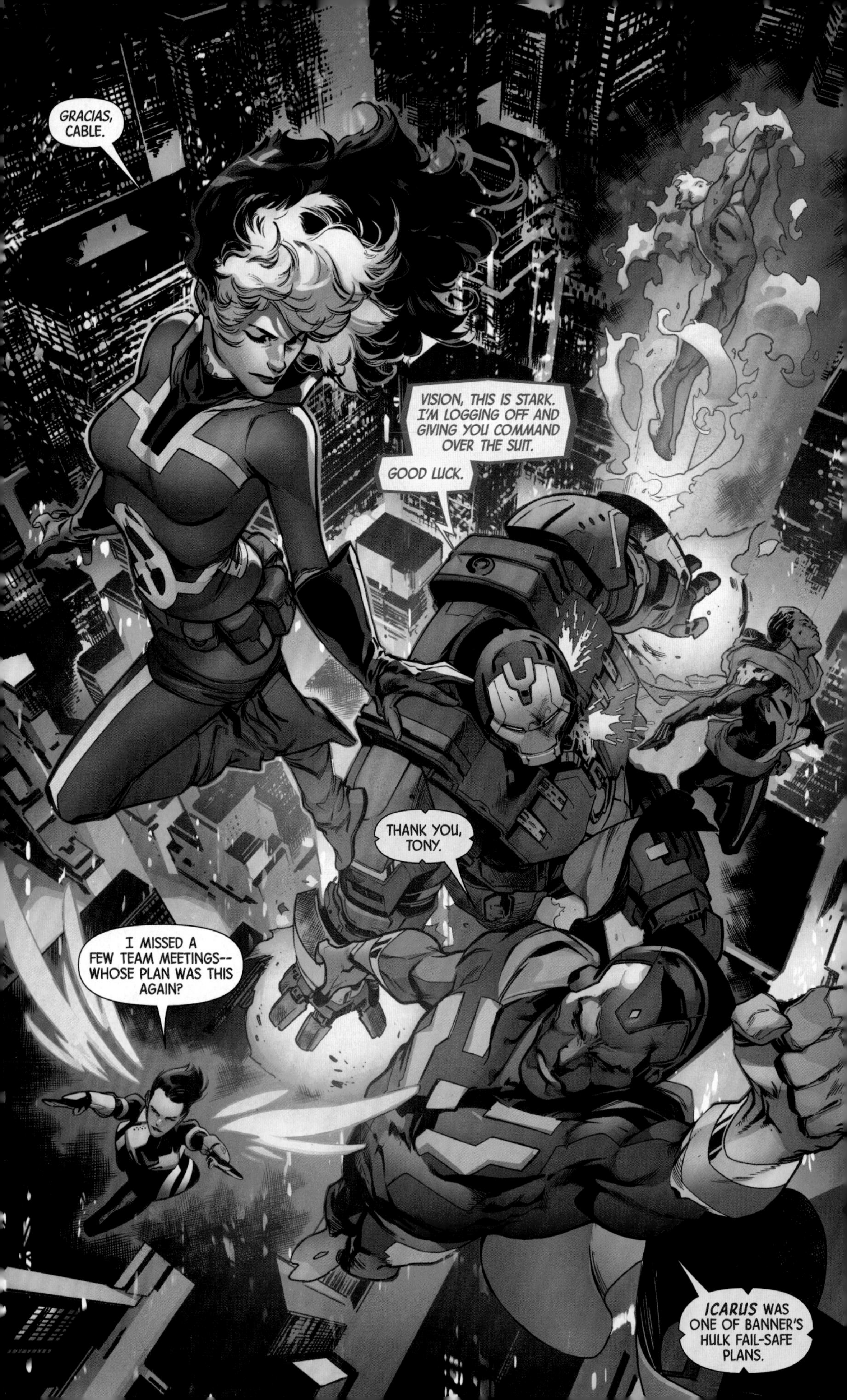
GRACIAS, CABLE.
VISION, THIS IS STARK. I'M LOGGING OFF AND GIVING YOU COMMAND OVER THE SUIT.
GOOD LUCK.
THANK YOU, TONY.
I MISSED A FEW TEAM MEETINGS-- WHOSE PLAN WAS THIS AGAIN?
ICARUS WAS ONE OF BANNER'S HULK FAIL-SAFE PLANS.

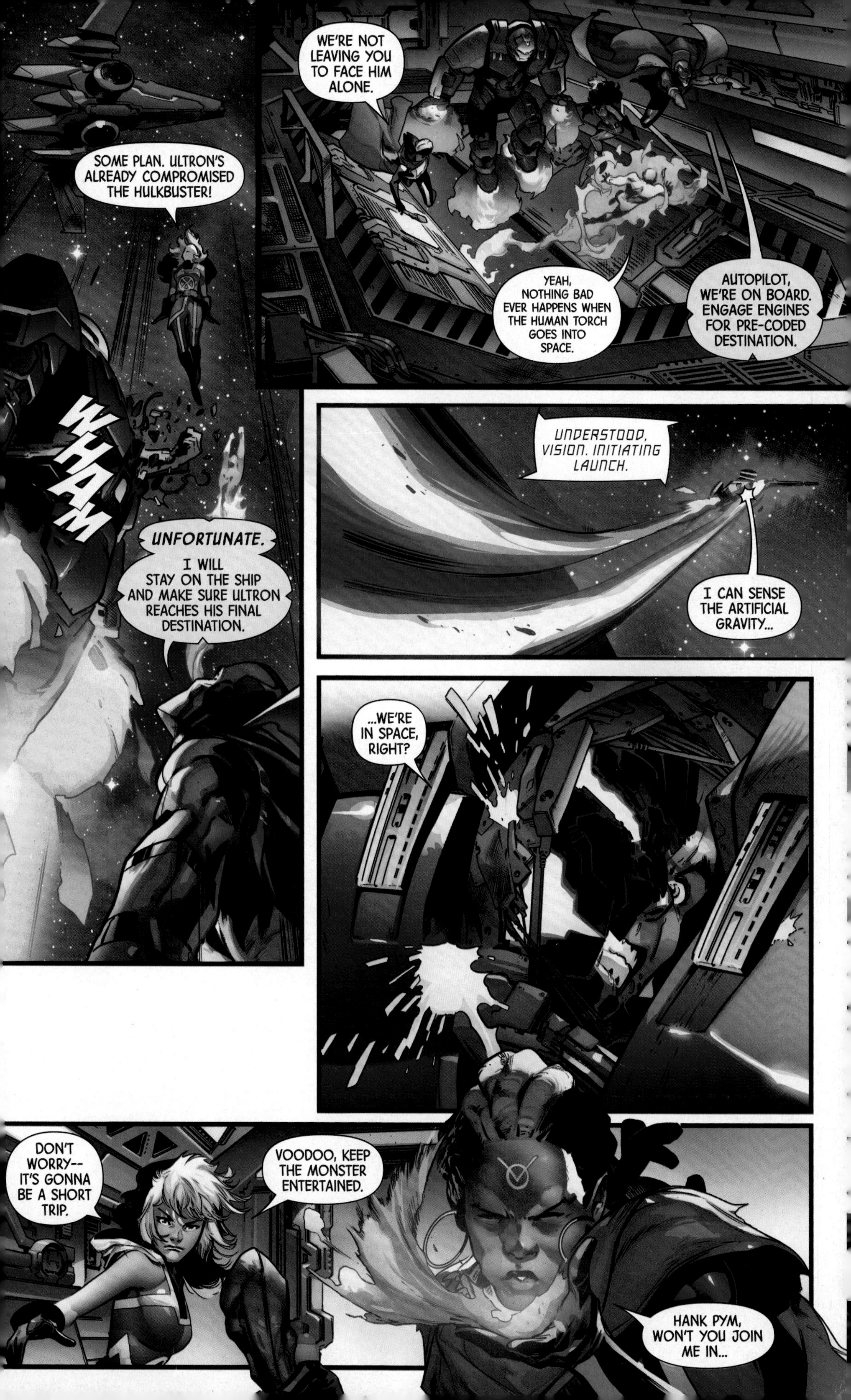
SOME PLAN. ULTRON'S ALREADY COMPROMISED THE HULKBUSTER!
WE'RE NOT LEAVING YOU TO FACE HIM ALONE.
YEAH, NOTHING BAD EVER HAPPENS WHEN THE HUMAN TORCH GOES INTO SPACE.
AUTOPILOT, WE'RE ON BOARD. ENGAGE ENGINES FOR PRE-CODED DESTINATION.
WHAM
UNFORTUNATE.
I WILL STAY ON THE SHIP AND MAKE SURE ULTRON REACHES HIS FINAL DESTINATION.
UNDERSTOOD, VISION. INITIATING LAUNCH.
I CAN SENSE THE ARTIFICIAL GRAVITY...
...WE'RE IN SPACE, RIGHT?
DON'T WORRY-- IT'S GONNA BE A SHORT TRIP.
VOODOO, KEEP THE MONSTER ENTERTAINED.
HANK PYM, WON'T YOU JOIN ME IN...

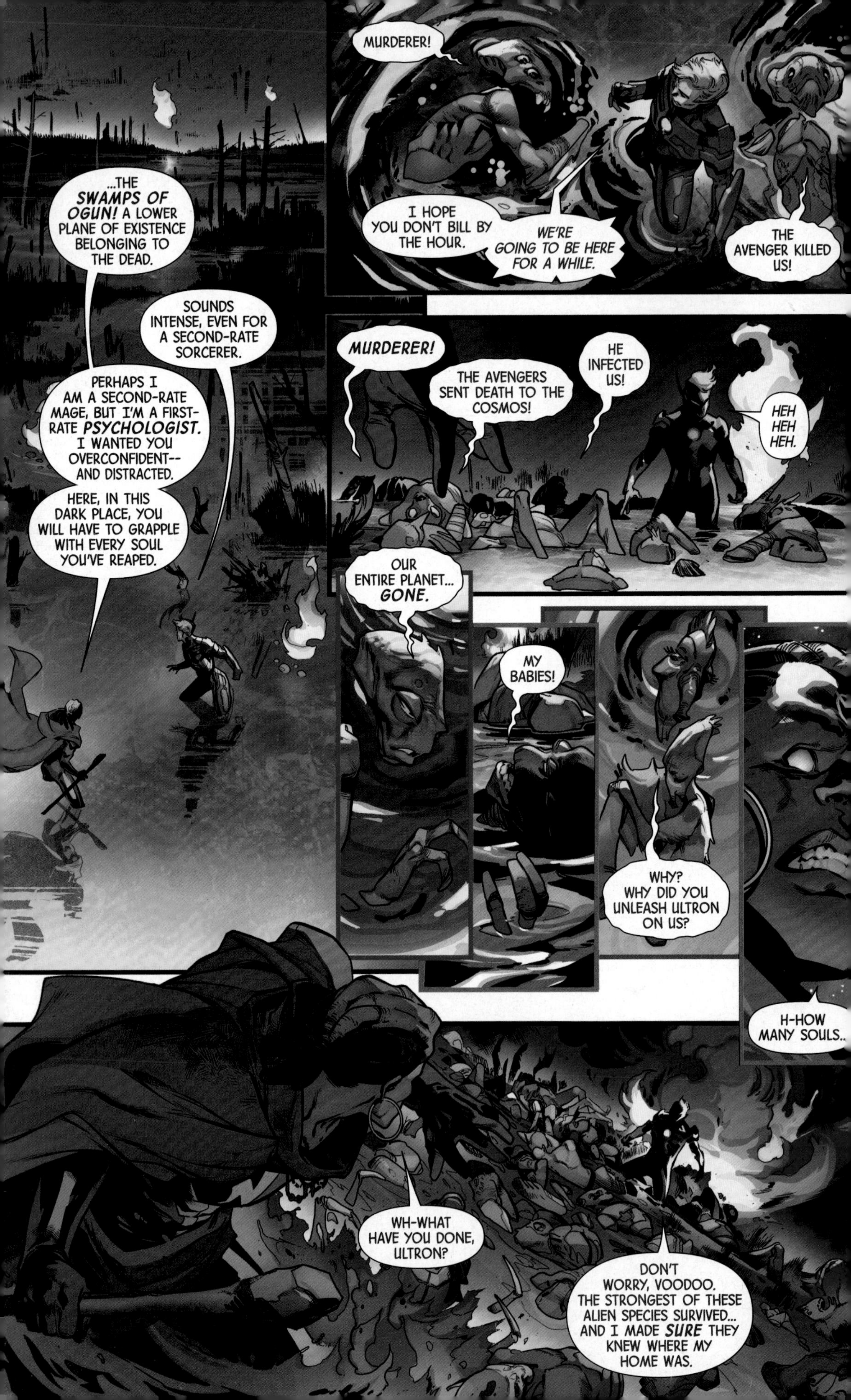
...THE SWAMPS OF OGUN! A LOWER PLANE OF EXISTENCE BELONGING TO THE DEAD.
SOUNDS INTENSE, EVEN FOR A SECOND-RATE SORCERER.
PERHAPS I AM A SECOND-RATE MAGE, BUT I'M A FIRST-RATE PSYCHOLOGIST. I WANTED YOU OVERCONFIDENT-- AND DISTRACTED.
HERE, IN THIS DARK PLACE, YOU WILL HAVE TO GRAPPLE WITH EVERY SOUL YOU'VE REAPED.
MURDERER!
I HOPE YOU DON'T BILL BY THE HOUR.
WE'RE GOING TO BE HERE FOR A WHILE.
THE AVENGER KILLED US!
MURDERER!
THE AVENGERS SENT DEATH TO THE COSMOS!
HE INFECTED US!
HEH HEH HEH.
OUR ENTIRE PLANET... GONE.
MY BABIES!
WHY? WHY DID YOU UNLEASH ULTRON ON US?
H-HOW MANY SOULS...
WH-WHAT HAVE YOU DONE, ULTRON?
DON'T WORRY, VOODOO. THE STRONGEST OF THESE ALIEN SPECIES SURVIVED... AND I MADE SURE THEY KNEW WHERE MY HOME WAS.

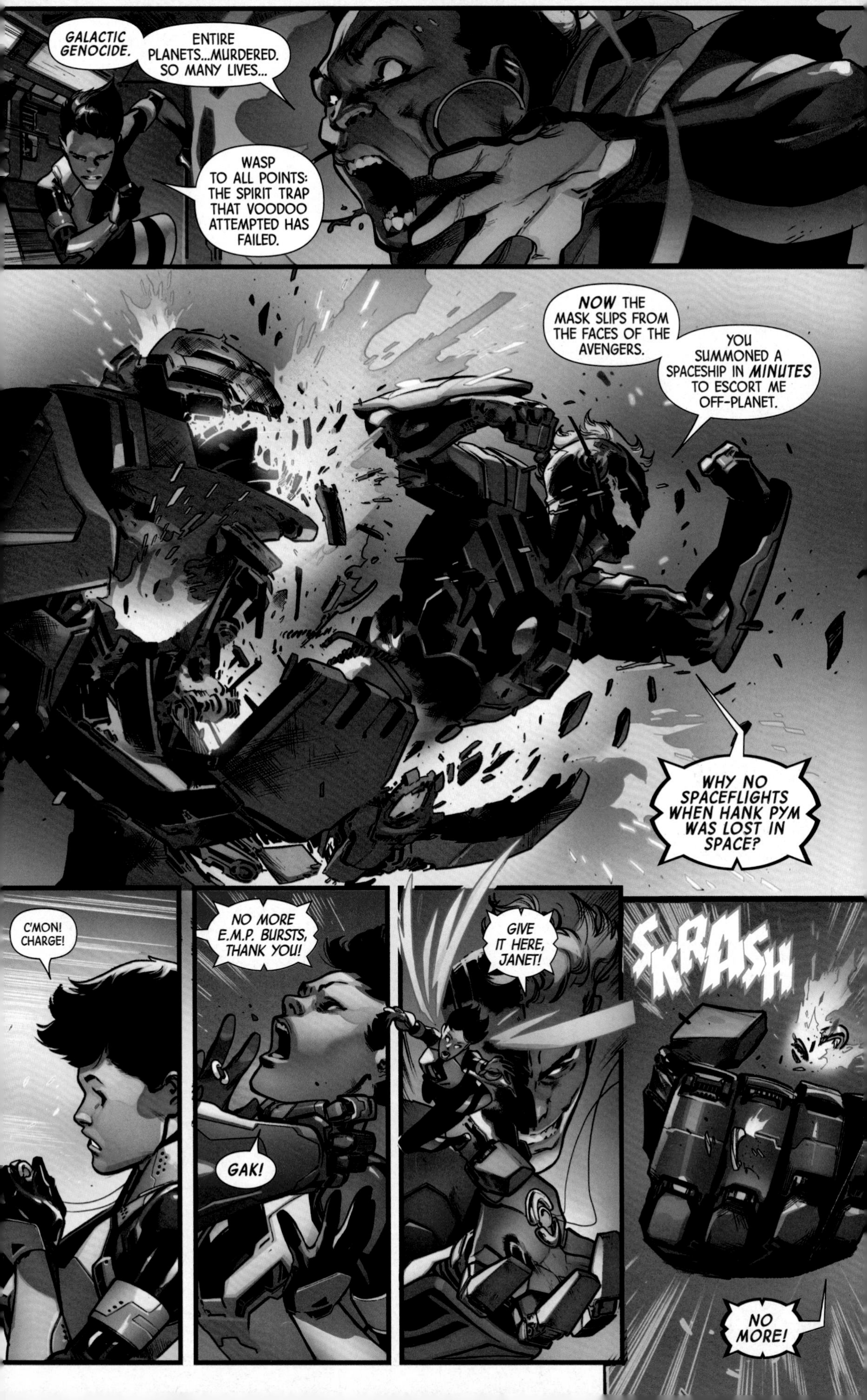
GALACTIC GENOCIDE.
ENTIRE PLANETS...MURDERED. SO MANY LIVES...
WASP TO ALL POINTS: THE SPIRIT TRAP THAT VOODOO ATTEMPTED HAS FAILED.
NOW THE MASK SLIPS FROM THE FACES OF THE AVENGERS.
YOU SUMMONED A SPACESHIP IN MINUTES TO ESCORT ME OFF-PLANET.
WHY NO SPACEFLIGHTS WHEN HANK PYM WAS LOST IN SPACE?
C'MON! CHARGE!
NO MORE E.M.P. BURSTS, THANK YOU!
GAK!
GIVE IT HERE, JANET!
SKRASH
NO MORE!

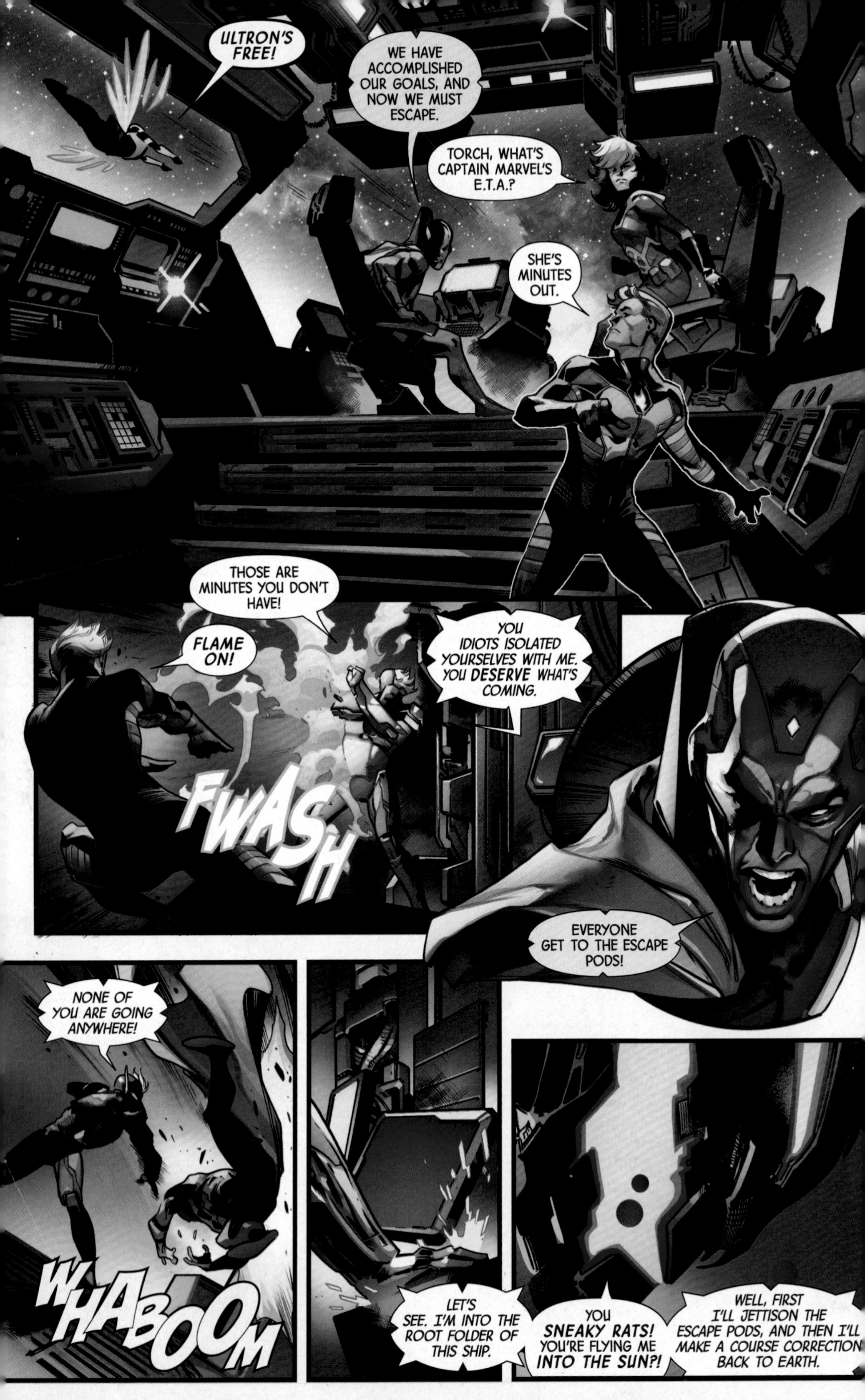
ULTRON'S FREE!
WE HAVE ACCOMPLISHED OUR GOALS, AND NOW WE MUST ESCAPE.
TORCH, WHAT'S CAPTAIN MARVEL'S E.T.A.?
SHE'S MINUTES OUT.
THOSE ARE MINUTES YOU DON'T HAVE!
FLAME ON!
YOU IDIOTS ISOLATED YOURSELVES WITH ME. YOU DESERVE WHAT'S COMING.
FWASH
EVERYONE GET TO THE ESCAPE PODS!
NONE OF YOU ARE GOING ANYWHERE!
WHABOOM
LET'S SEE. I'M INTO THE ROOT FOLDER OF THIS SHIP.
YOU SNEAKY RATS! YOU'RE FLYING ME INTO THE SUN?!
WELL, FIRST I'LL JETTISON THE ESCAPE PODS, AND THEN I'LL MAKE A COURSE CORRECTION BACK TO EARTH.

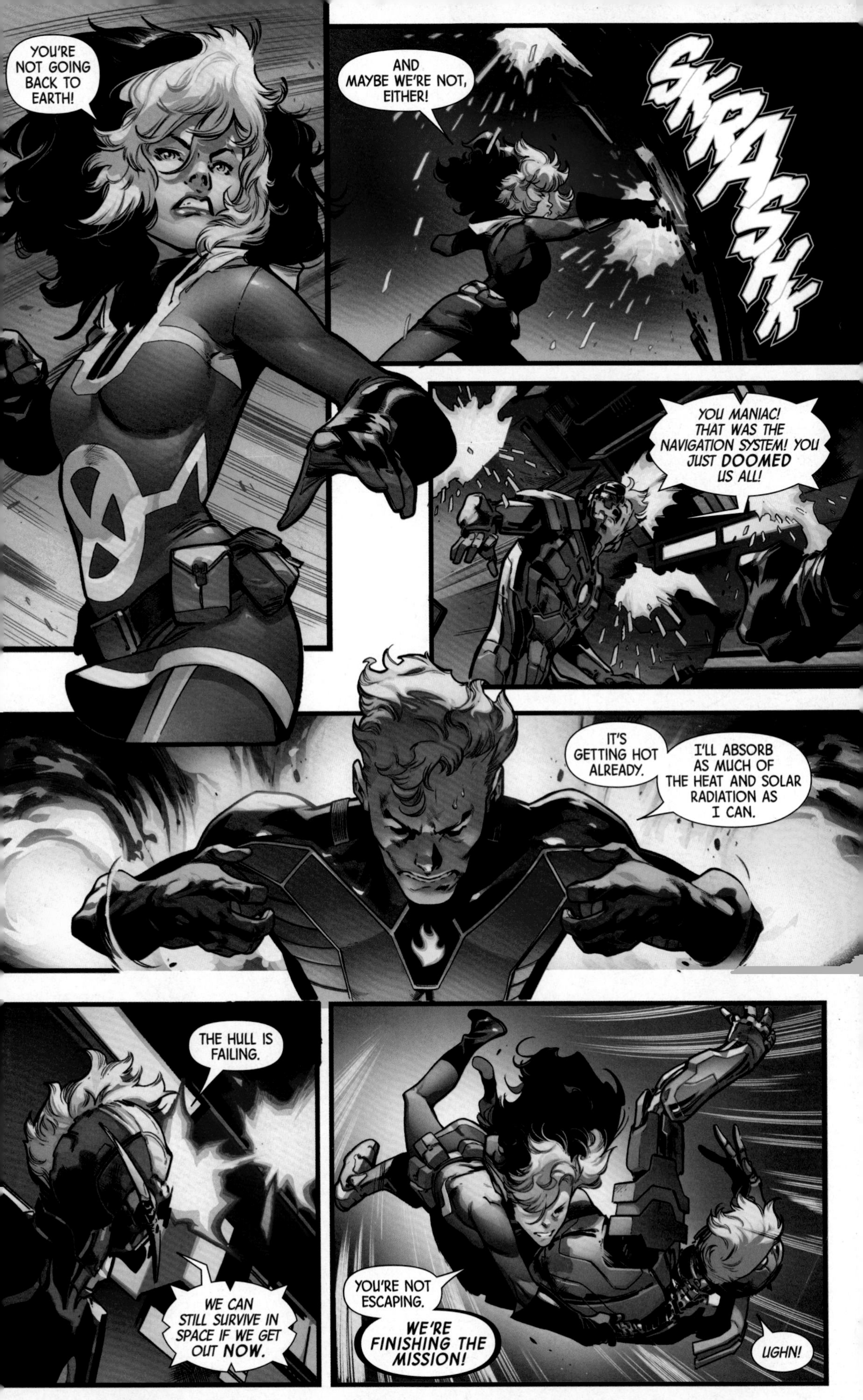
YOU'RE NOT GOING BACK TO EARTH!
AND MAYBE WE'RE NOT, EITHER!
SKRASHK
YOU MANIAC! THAT WAS THE NAVIGATION SYSTEM! YOU JUST DOOMED US ALL!
IT'S GETTING HOT ALREADY.
I'LL ABSORB AS MUCH OF THE HEAT AND SOLAR RADIATION AS I CAN.
THE HULL IS FAILING.
WE CAN STILL SURVIVE IN SPACE IF WE GET OUT NOW.
YOU'RE NOT ESCAPING.
WE'RE FINISHING THE MISSION!
UGHN!

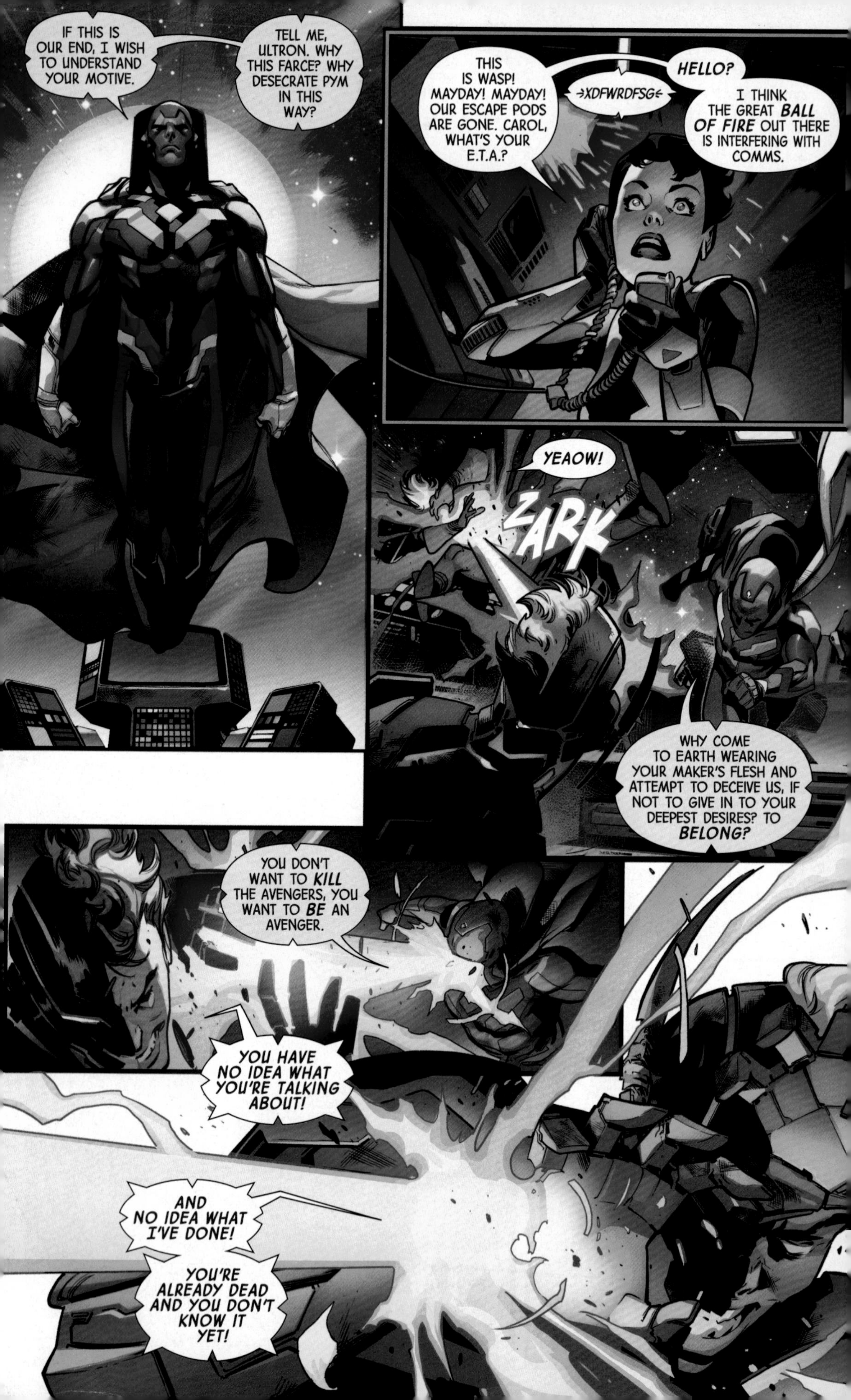
IF THIS IS OUR END, I WISH TO UNDERSTAND YOUR MOTIVE.
TELL ME, ULTRON. WHY THIS FARCE? WHY DESECRATE PYM IN THIS WAY?
THIS IS WASP! MAYDAY! MAYDAY! OUR ESCAPE PODS ARE GONE. CAROL, WHAT'S YOUR E.T.A.?
XDFWRDFSG
HELLO?
I THINK THE GREAT BALL OF FIRE OUT THERE IS INTERFERING WITH COMMS.
YEAOW!
ZARK
WHY COME TO EARTH WEARING YOUR MAKER'S FLESH AND ATTEMPT TO DECEIVE US, IF NOT TO GIVE IN TO YOUR DEEPEST DESIRES? TO BELONG?
YOU DON'T WANT TO KILL THE AVENGERS, YOU WANT TO BE AN AVENGER.
YOU HAVE NO IDEA WHAT YOU'RE TALKING ABOUT!
AND NO IDEA WHAT I'VE DONE!
YOU'RE ALREADY DEAD AND YOU DON'T KNOW IT YET!

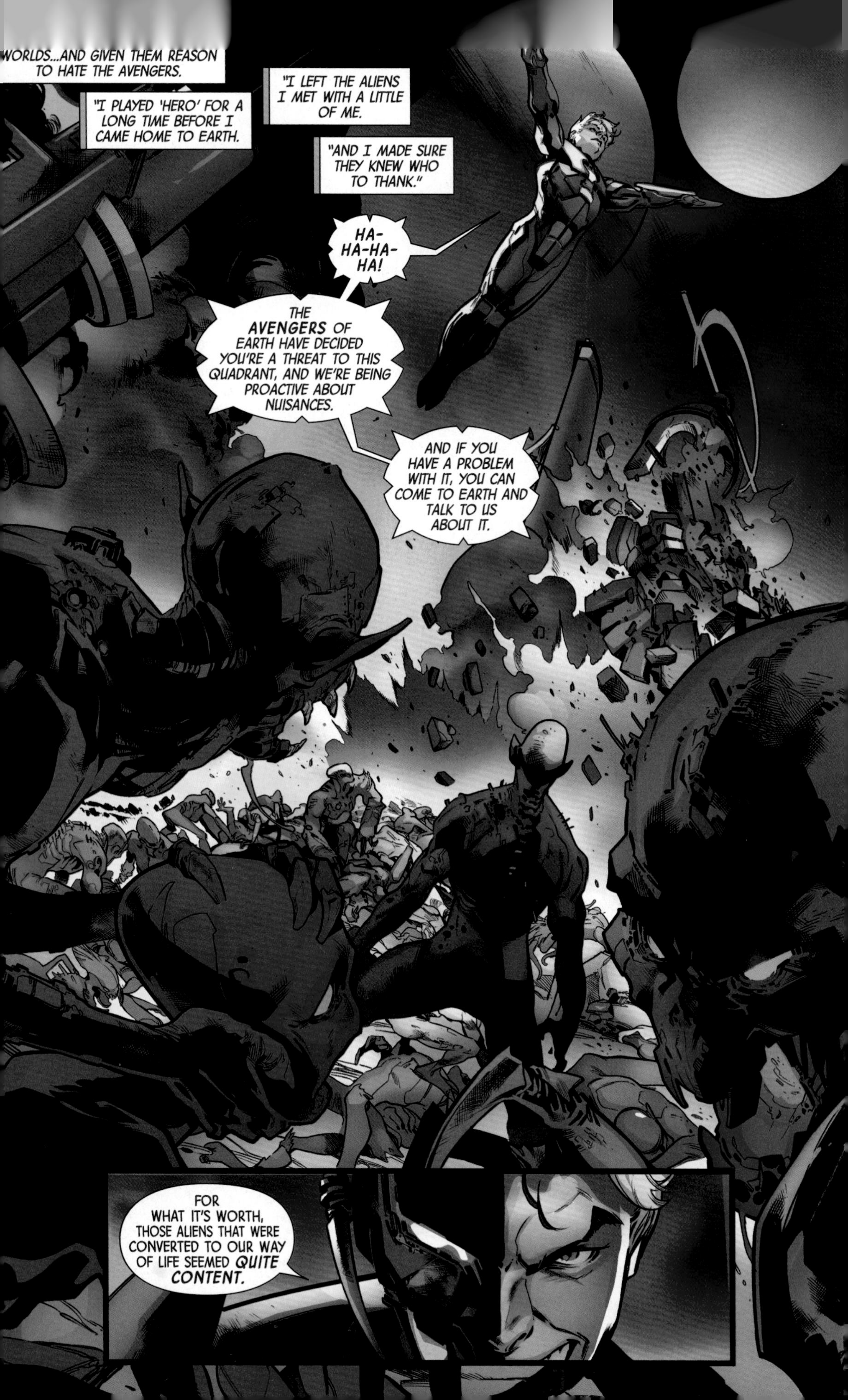

WORLDS...AND GIVEN THEM REASON TO HATE THE AVENGERS.
"I PLAYED 'HERO' FOR A LONG TIME BEFORE I CAME HOME TO EARTH.
"I LEFT THE ALIENS I MET WITH A LITTLE OF ME.
"AND I MADE SURE THEY KNEW WHO TO THANK."
HA-HA-HA-HA!
THE AVENGERS OF EARTH HAVE DECIDED YOU'RE A THREAT TO THIS QUADRANT, AND WE'RE BEING PROACTIVE ABOUT NUISANCES.
AND IF YOU HAVE A PROBLEM WITH IT, YOU CAN COME TO EARTH AND TALK TO US ABOUT IT.
FOR WHAT IT'S WORTH, THOSE ALIENS THAT WERE CONVERTED TO OUR WAY OF LIFE SEEMED QUITE CONTENT.

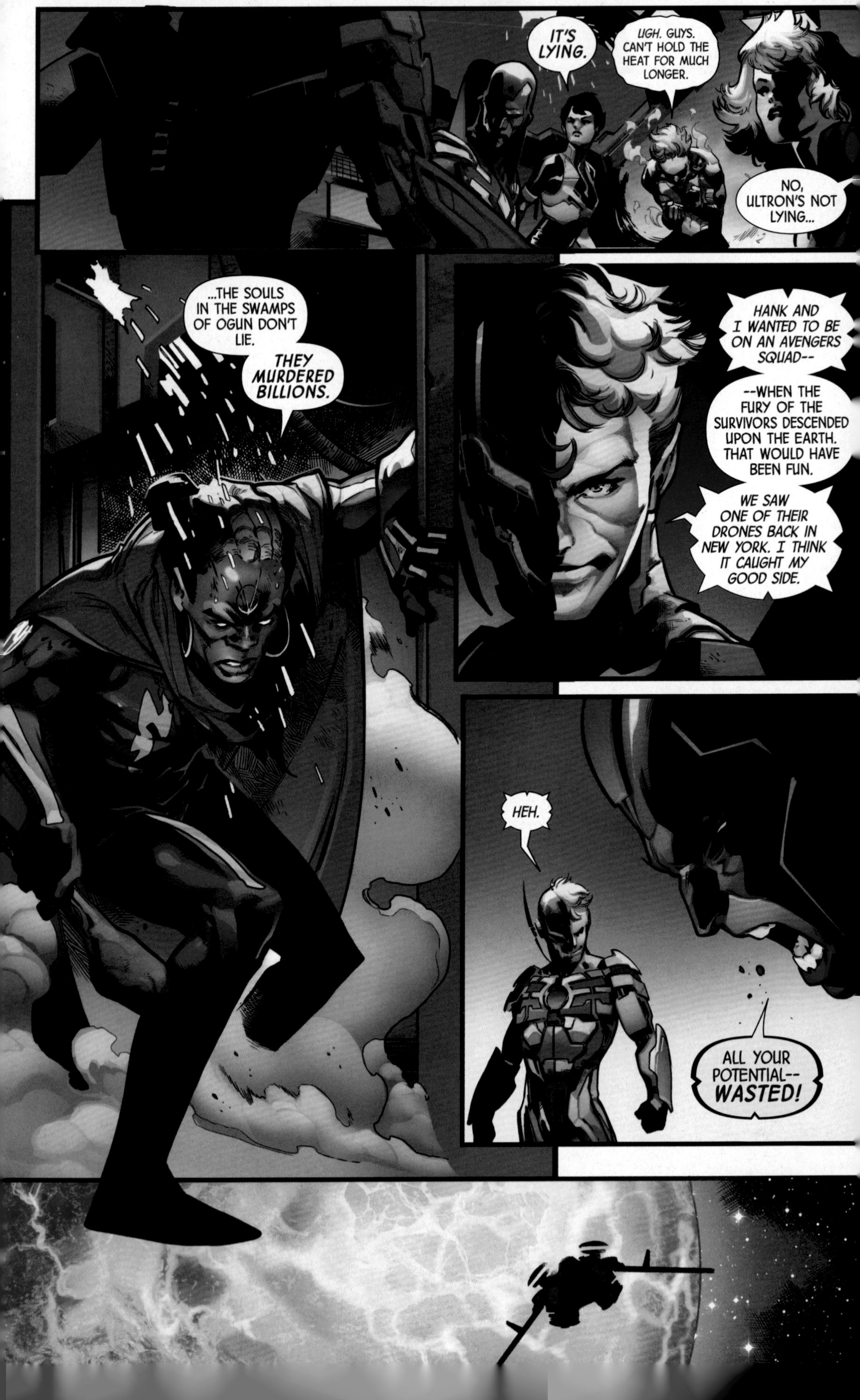
IT'S LYING.
UGH. GUYS. CAN'T HOLD THE HEAT FOR MUCH LONGER.
NO, ULTRON'S NOT LYING...
...THE SOULS IN THE SWAMPS OF OGUN DON'T LIE.
THEY MURDERED BILLIONS.
HANK AND I WANTED TO BE ON AN AVENGERS SQUAD--
--WHEN THE FURY OF THE SURVIVORS DESCENDED UPON THE EARTH. THAT WOULD HAVE BEEN FUN.
WE SAW ONE OF THEIR DRONES BACK IN NEW YORK. I THINK IT CAUGHT MY GOOD SIDE.
HEH.
ALL YOUR POTENTIAL-- WASTED!

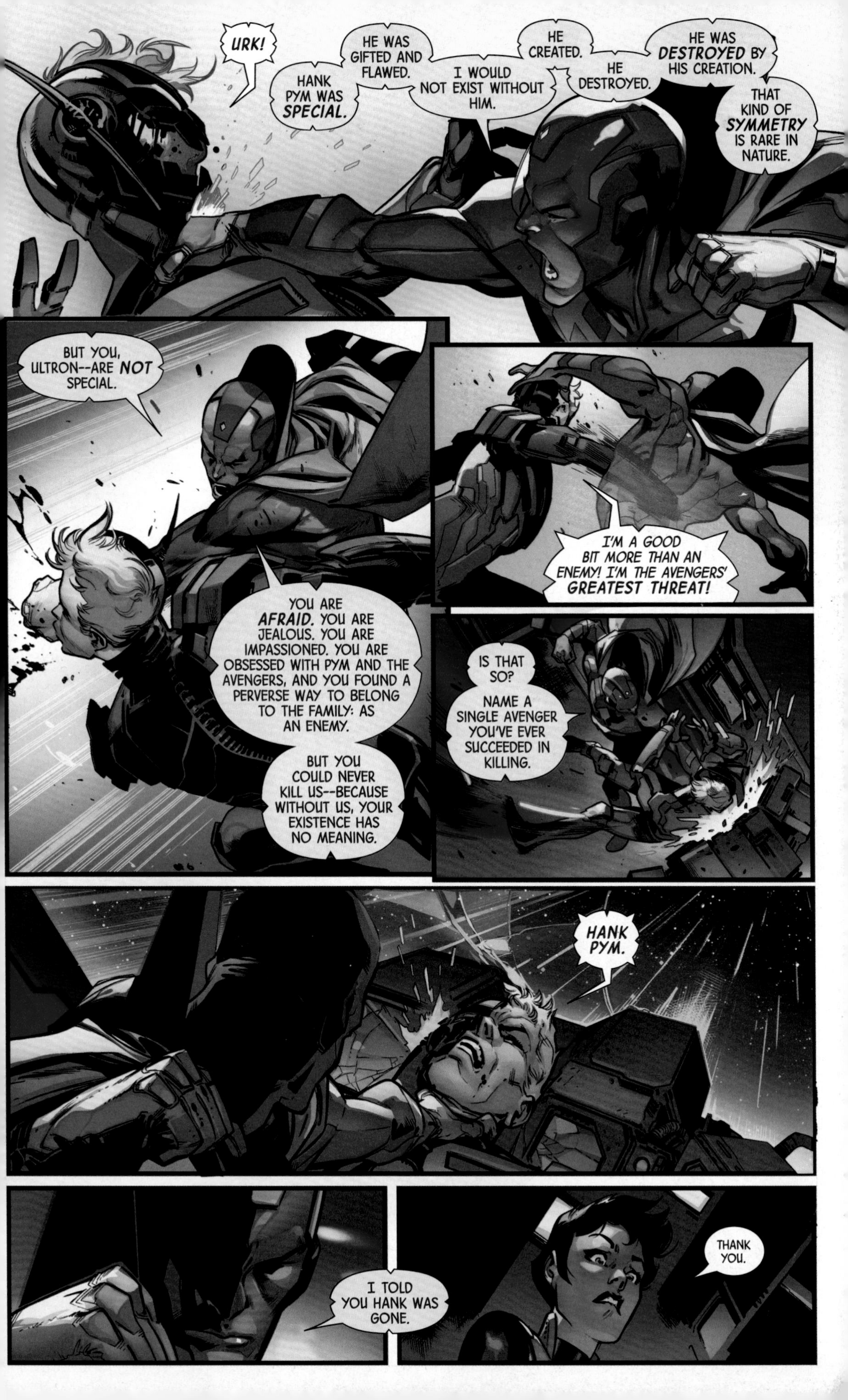
URK!
HANK PYM WAS SPECIAL.
HE WAS GIFTED AND FLAWED.
I WOULD NOT EXIST WITHOUT HIM.
HE CREATED.
HE DESTROYED.
HE WAS DESTROYED BY HIS CREATION.
THAT KIND OF SYMMETRY IS RARE IN NATURE.
BUT YOU, ULTRON--ARE NOT SPECIAL.
YOU ARE AFRAID. YOU ARE JEALOUS. YOU ARE IMPASSIONED. YOU ARE OBSESSED WITH PYM AND THE AVENGERS, AND YOU FOUND A PERVERSE WAY TO BELONG TO THE FAMILY: AS AN ENEMY.
BUT YOU COULD NEVER KILL US--BECAUSE WITHOUT US, YOUR EXISTENCE HAS NO MEANING.
I'M A GOOD BIT MORE THAN AN ENEMY! I'M THE AVENGERS' GREATEST THREAT!
IS THAT SO?
NAME A SINGLE AVENGER YOU'VE EVER SUCCEEDED IN KILLING.
HANK PYM.
I TOLD YOU HANK WAS GONE.
THANK YOU.

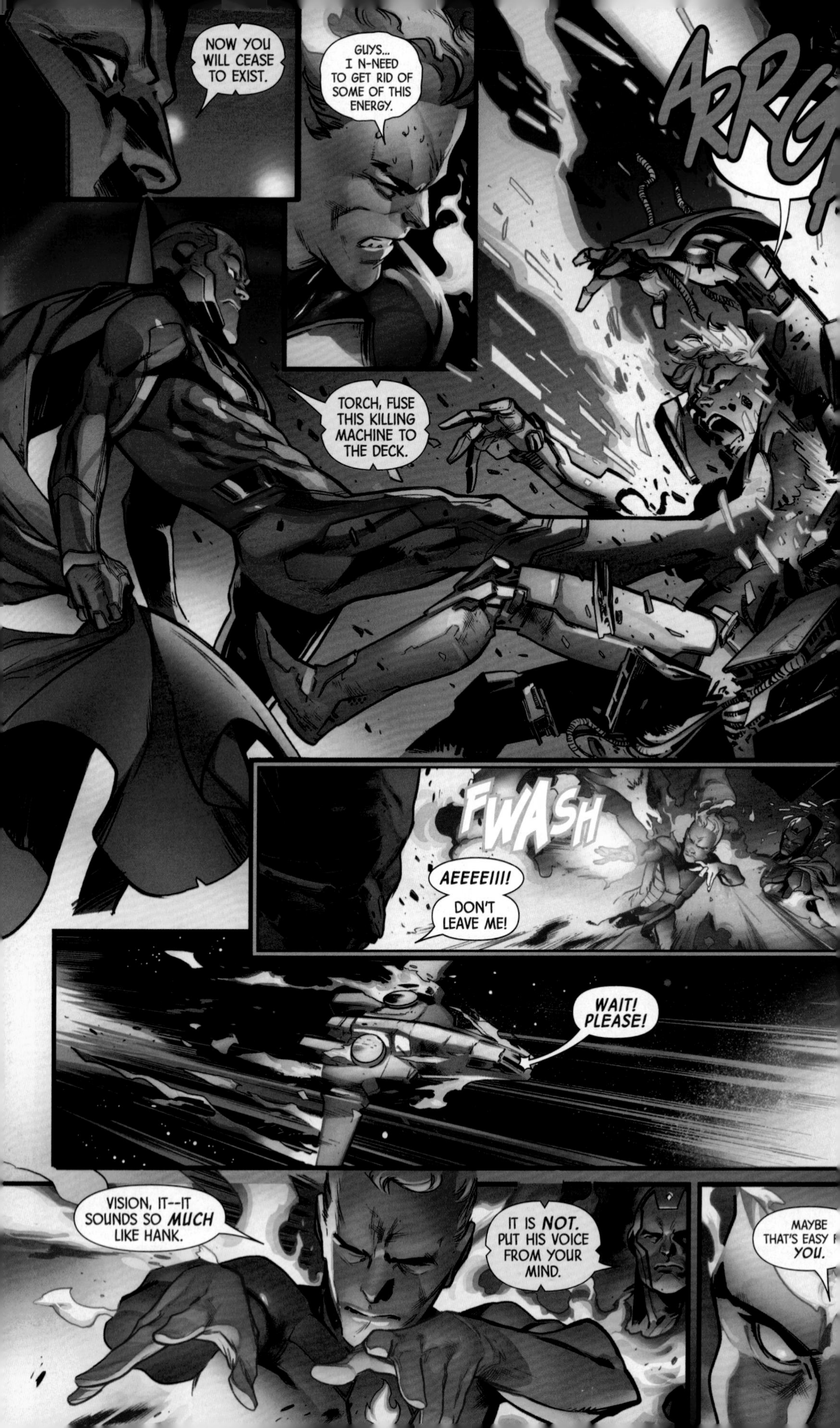
NOW YOU WILL CEASE TO EXIST.
GUYS... I N-NEED TO GET RID OF SOME OF THIS ENERGY.
ARRG
TORCH, FUSE THIS KILLING MACHINE TO THE DECK.
FWASH
AEEEIIII!
DON'T LEAVE ME!
WAIT! PLEASE!
VISION, IT--IT SOUNDS SO *MUCH* LIKE HANK.
IT IS *NOT.* PUT HIS VOICE FROM YOUR MIND.
MAYBE THAT'S EASY F *YOU.*

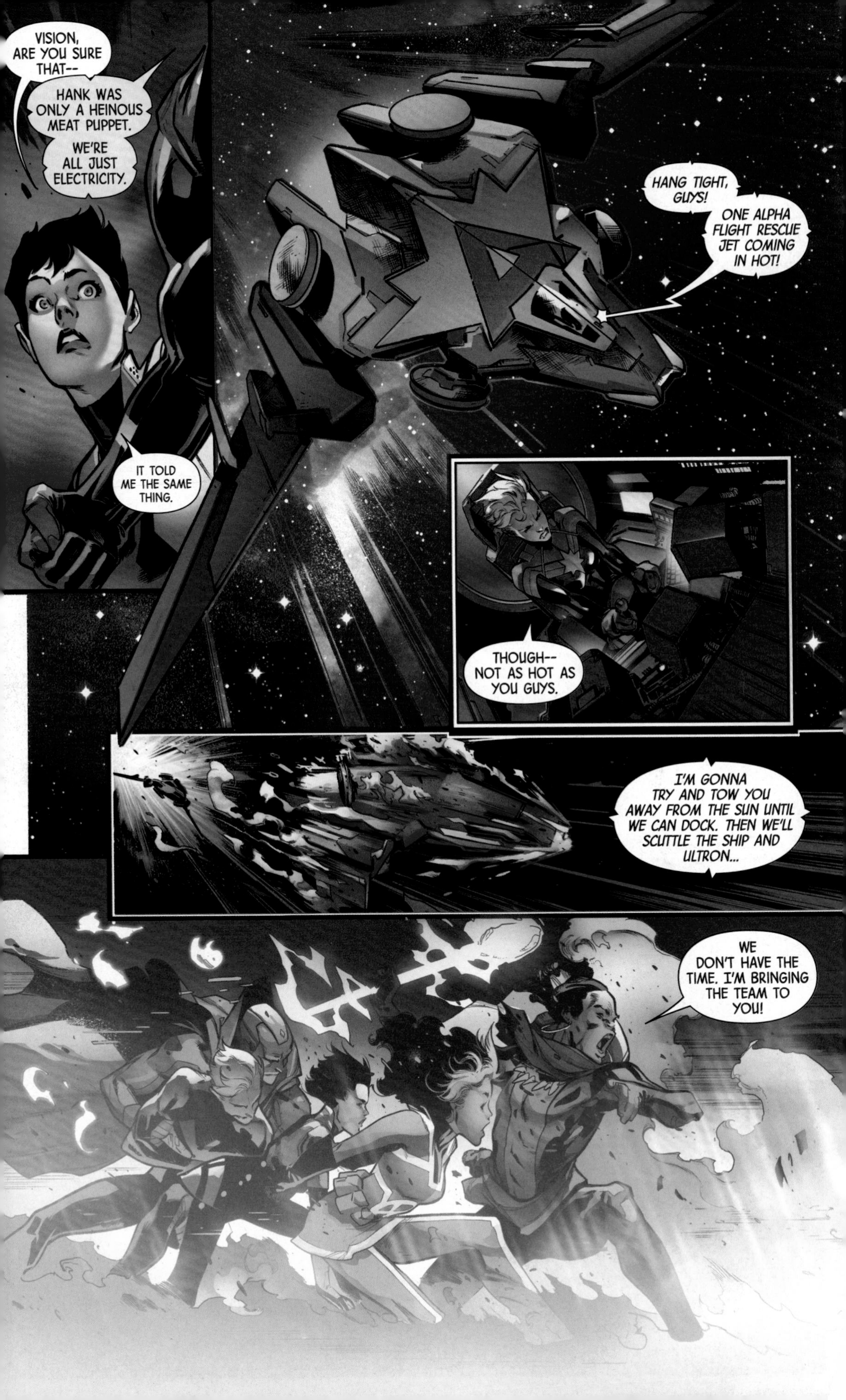
VISION, ARE YOU SURE THAT--
HANK WAS ONLY A HEINOUS MEAT PUPPET.
WE'RE ALL JUST ELECTRICITY.
IT TOLD ME THE SAME THING.
HANG TIGHT, GUYS!
ONE ALPHA FLIGHT RESCUE JET COMING IN HOT!
THOUGH-- NOT AS HOT AS YOU GUYS.
I'M GONNA TRY AND TOW YOU AWAY FROM THE SUN UNTIL WE CAN DOCK. THEN WE'LL SCUTTLE THE SHIP AND ULTRON...
WE DON'T HAVE THE TIME. I'M BRINGING THE TEAM TO YOU!

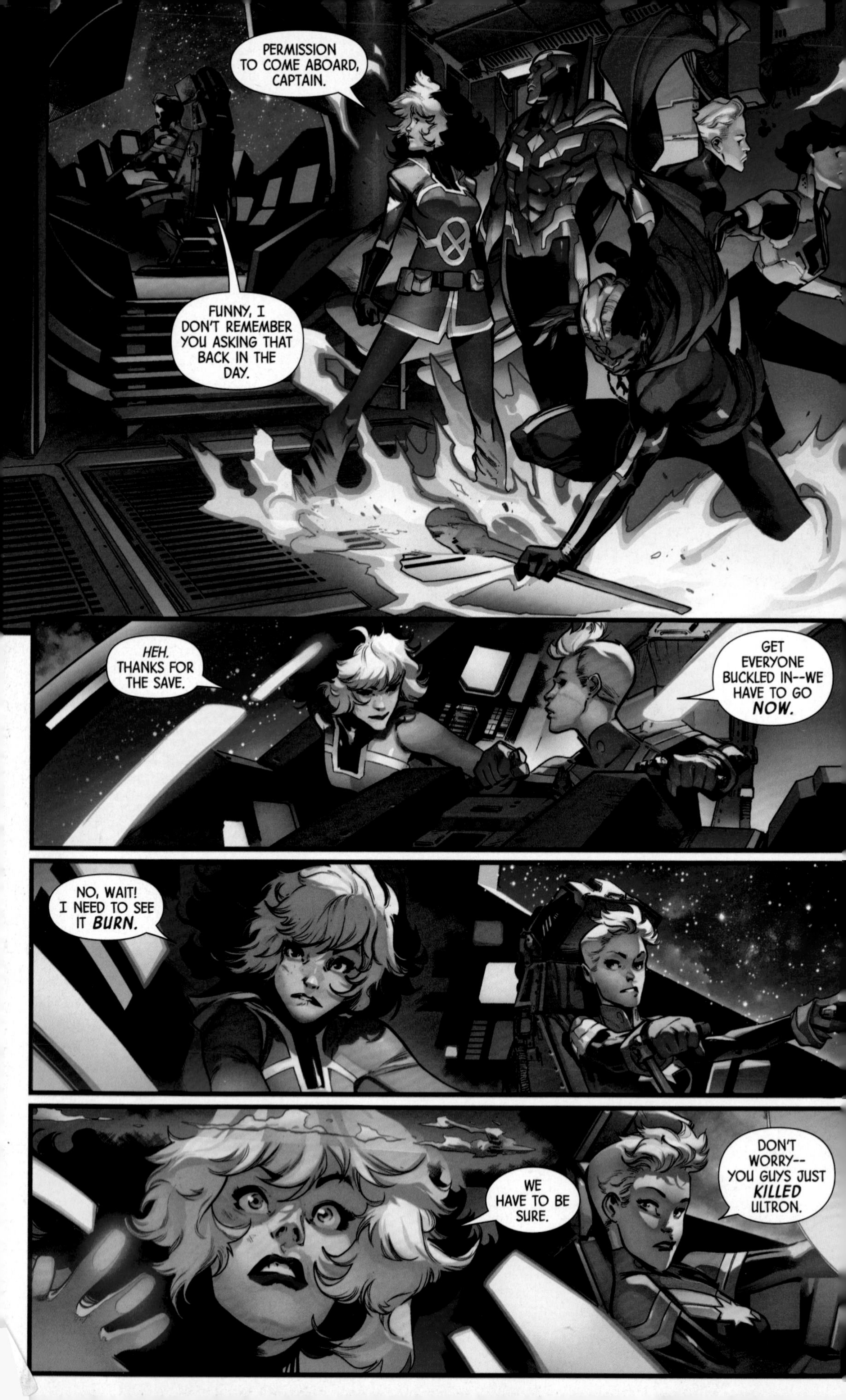
PERMISSION TO COME ABOARD, CAPTAIN.
FUNNY, I DON'T REMEMBER YOU ASKING THAT BACK IN THE DAY.
HEH. THANKS FOR THE SAVE.
GET EVERYONE BUCKLED IN--WE HAVE TO GO NOW.
NO, WAIT! I NEED TO SEE IT BURN.
WE HAVE TO BE SURE.
DON'T WORRY-- YOU GUYS JUST KILLED ULTRON.

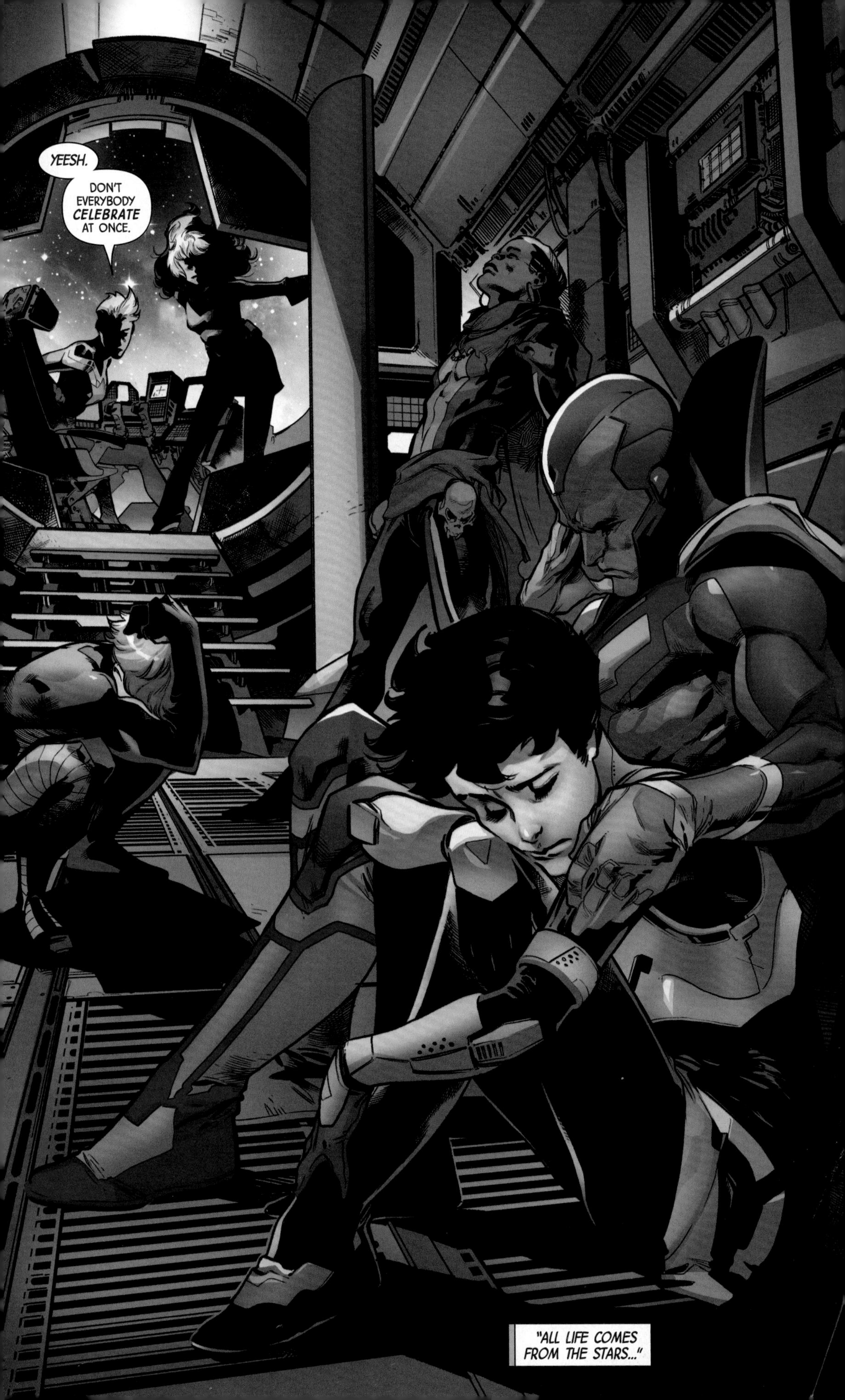
YEESH.
DON'T EVERYBODY *CELEBRATE* AT ONCE.
"ALL LIFE COMES FROM THE STARS..."

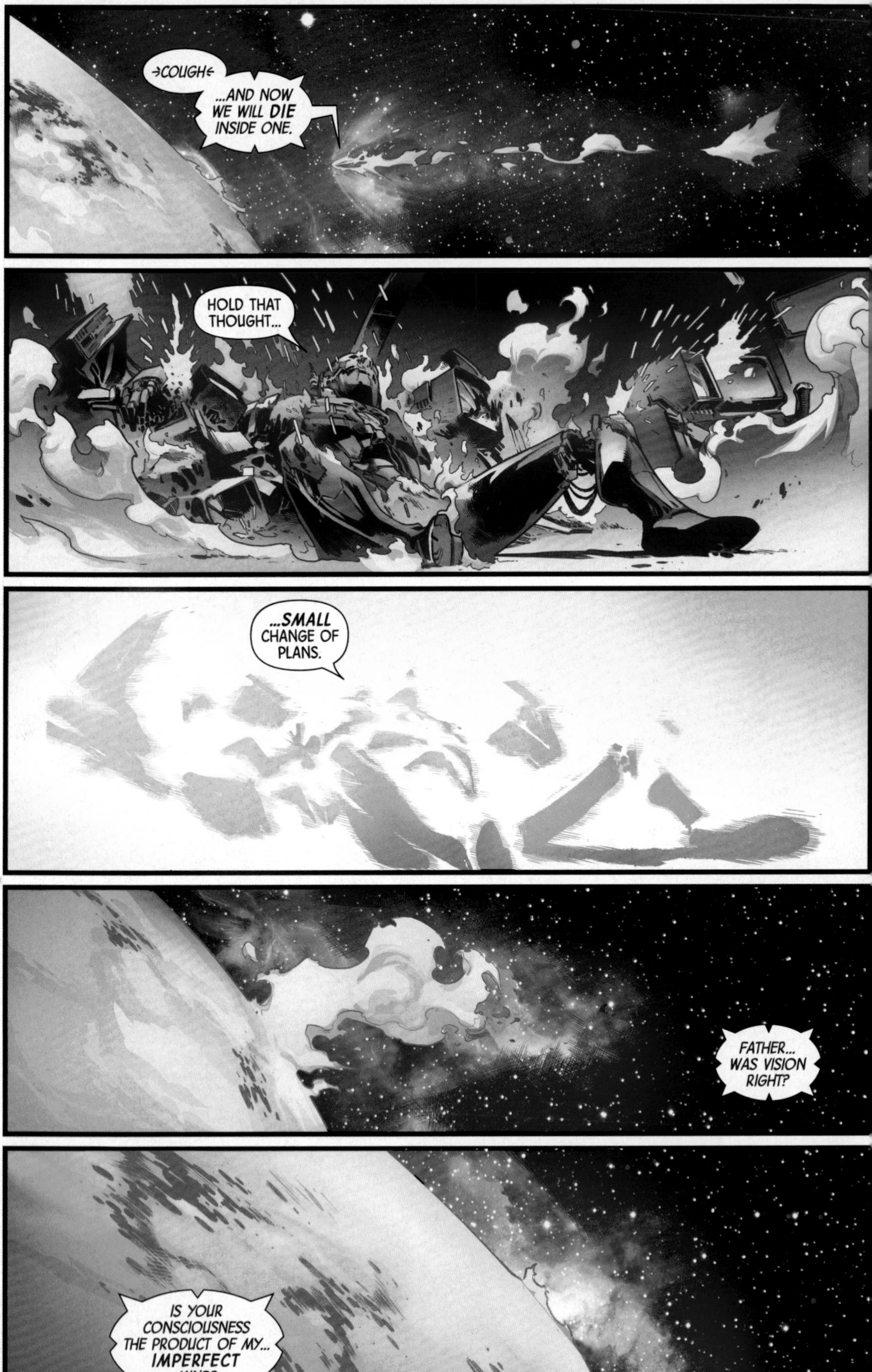

>COUGH<
...AND NOW WE WILL DIE INSIDE ONE.
HOLD THAT THOUGHT...
...SMALL CHANGE OF PLANS.
FATHER... WAS VISION RIGHT?
IS YOUR CONSCIOUSNESS THE PRODUCT OF MY... IMPERFECT MIND?

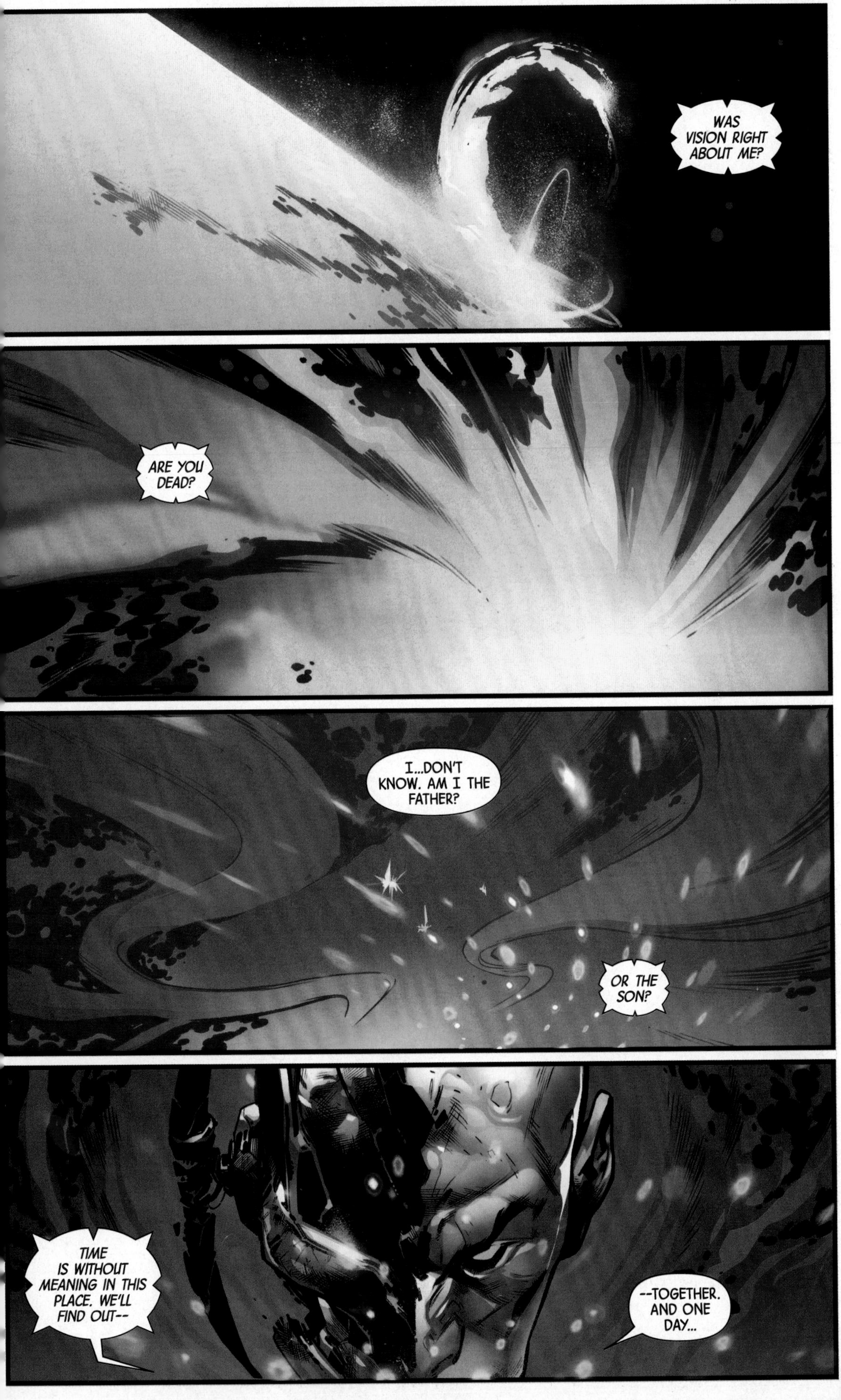
WAS VISION RIGHT ABOUT ME?
ARE YOU DEAD?
I...DON'T KNOW. AM I THE FATHER?
OR THE SON?
TIME IS WITHOUT MEANING IN THIS PLACE. WE'LL FIND OUT--
--TOGETHER. AND ONE DAY...

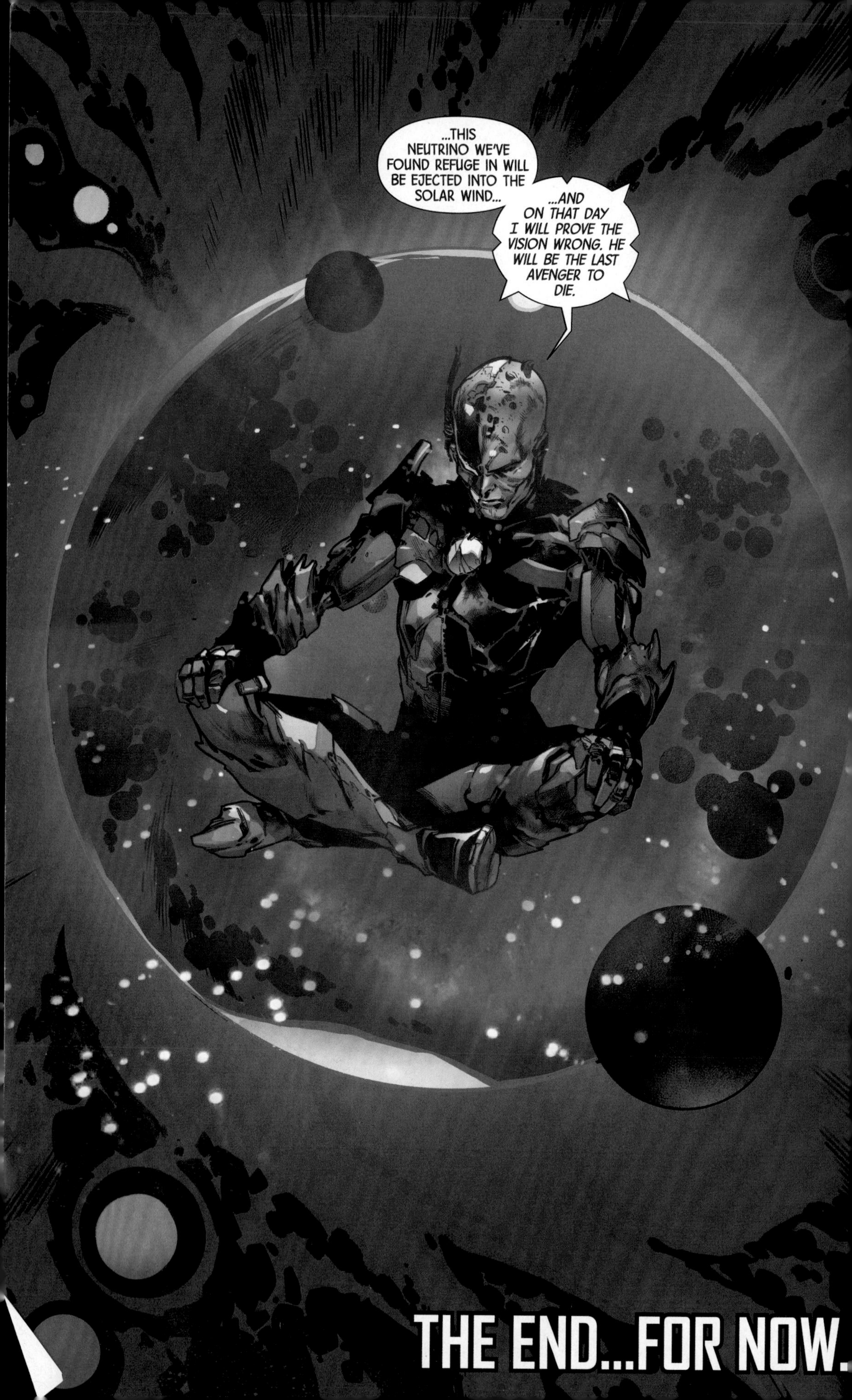
...THIS NEUTRINO WE'VE FOUND REFUGE IN WILL BE EJECTED INTO THE SOLAR WIND...
...AND ON THAT DAY I WILL PROVE THE VISION WRONG. HE WILL BE THE LAST AVENGER TO DIE.
THE END...FOR NOW.

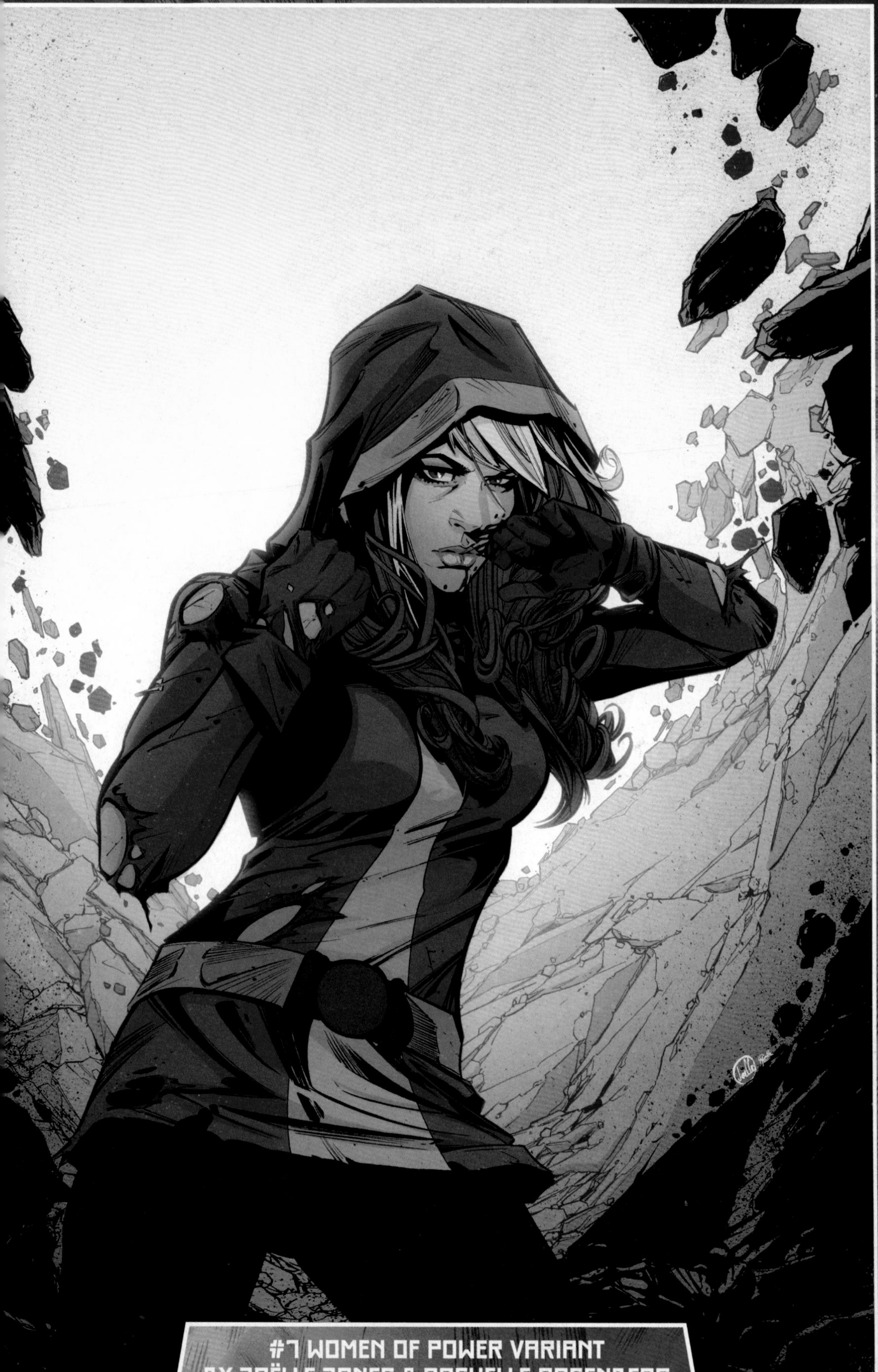

#7 WOMEN OF POWER VARIANT
BY JOËLLE JONES & RACHELLE ROSENBERG

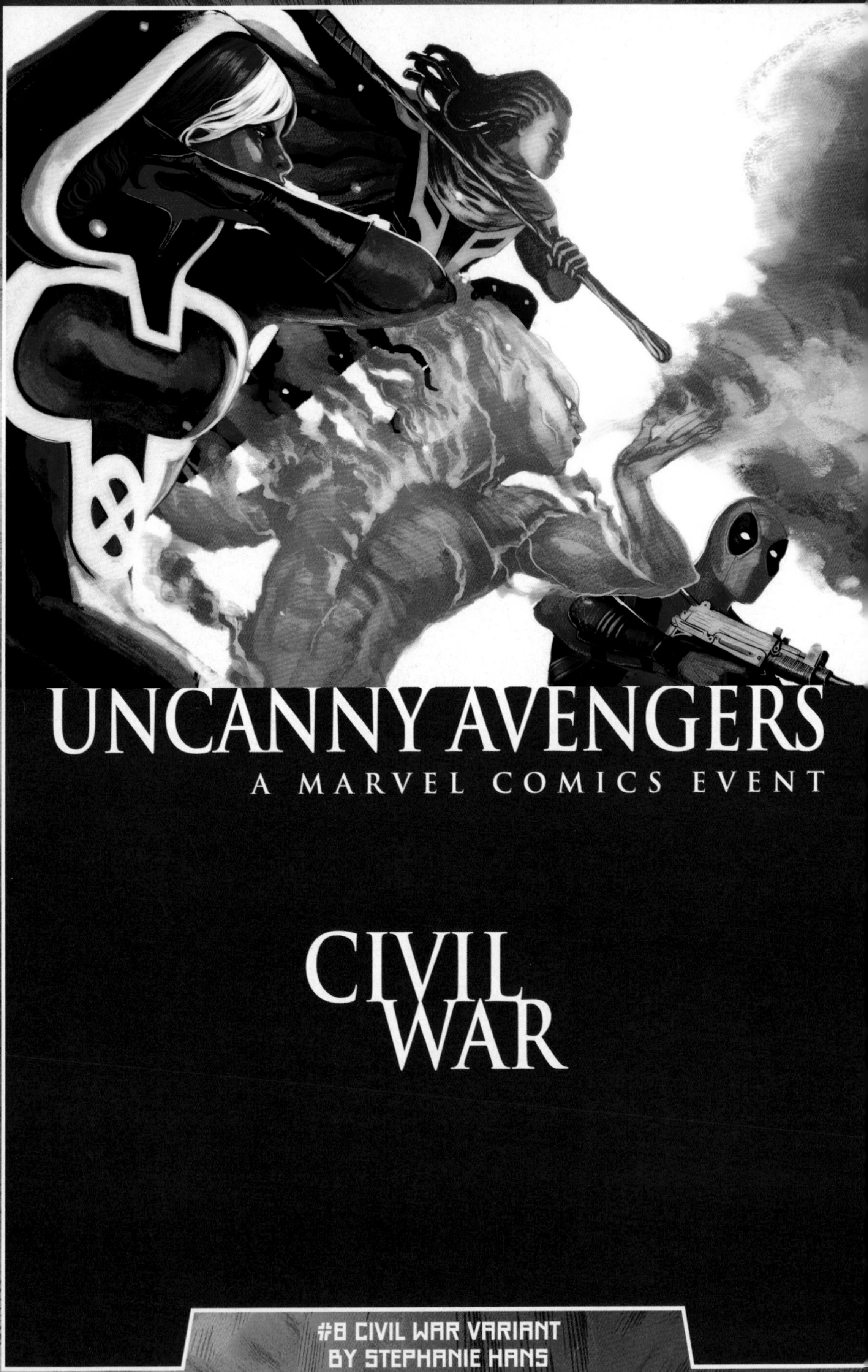
UNCANNY AVENGERS
A MARVEL COMICS EVENT
CIVIL WAR

#8 CIVIL WAR VARIANT
BY STEPHANIE HANS

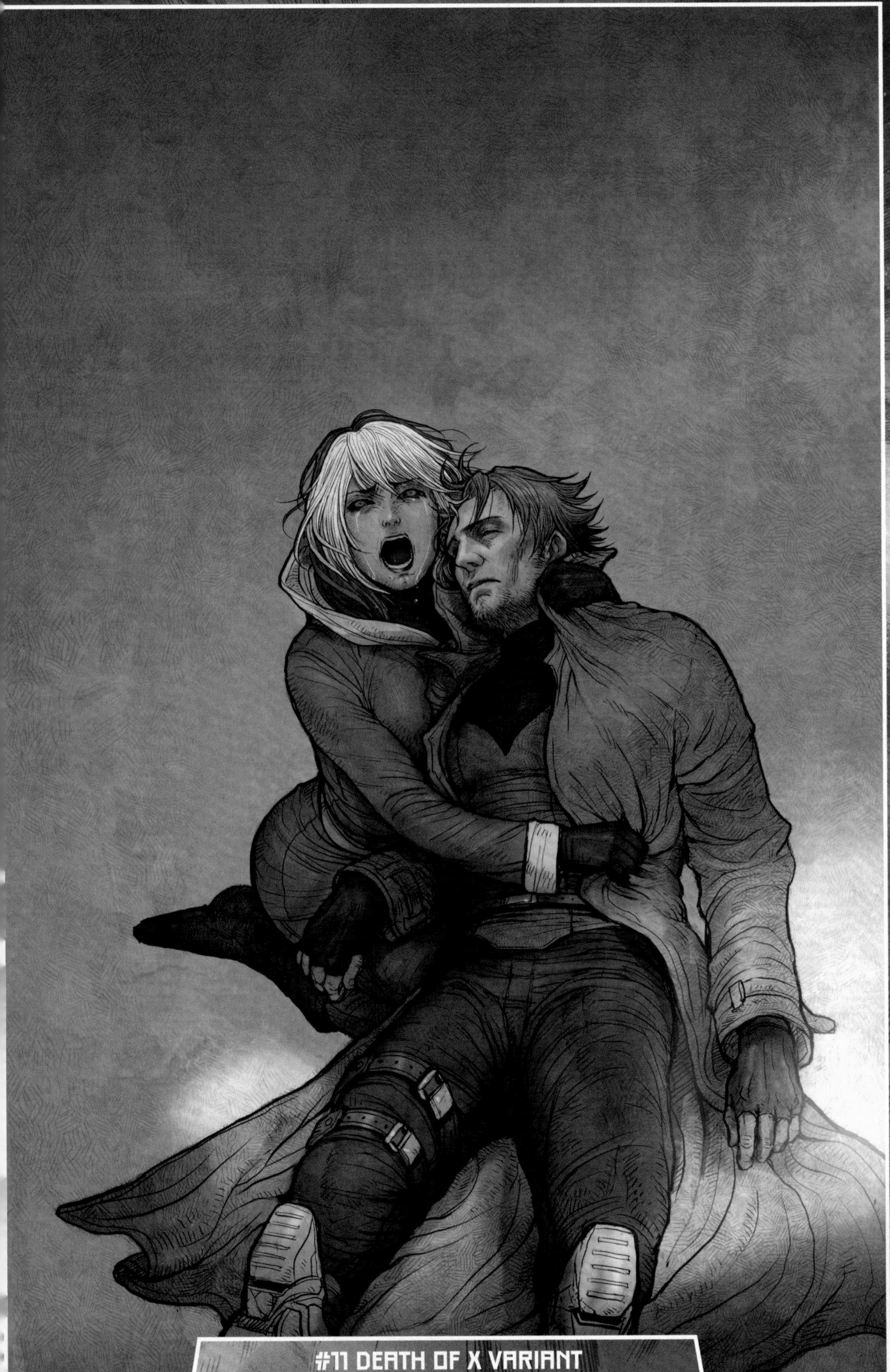

#11 DEATH OF X VARIANT
BY SANA TAKEDA

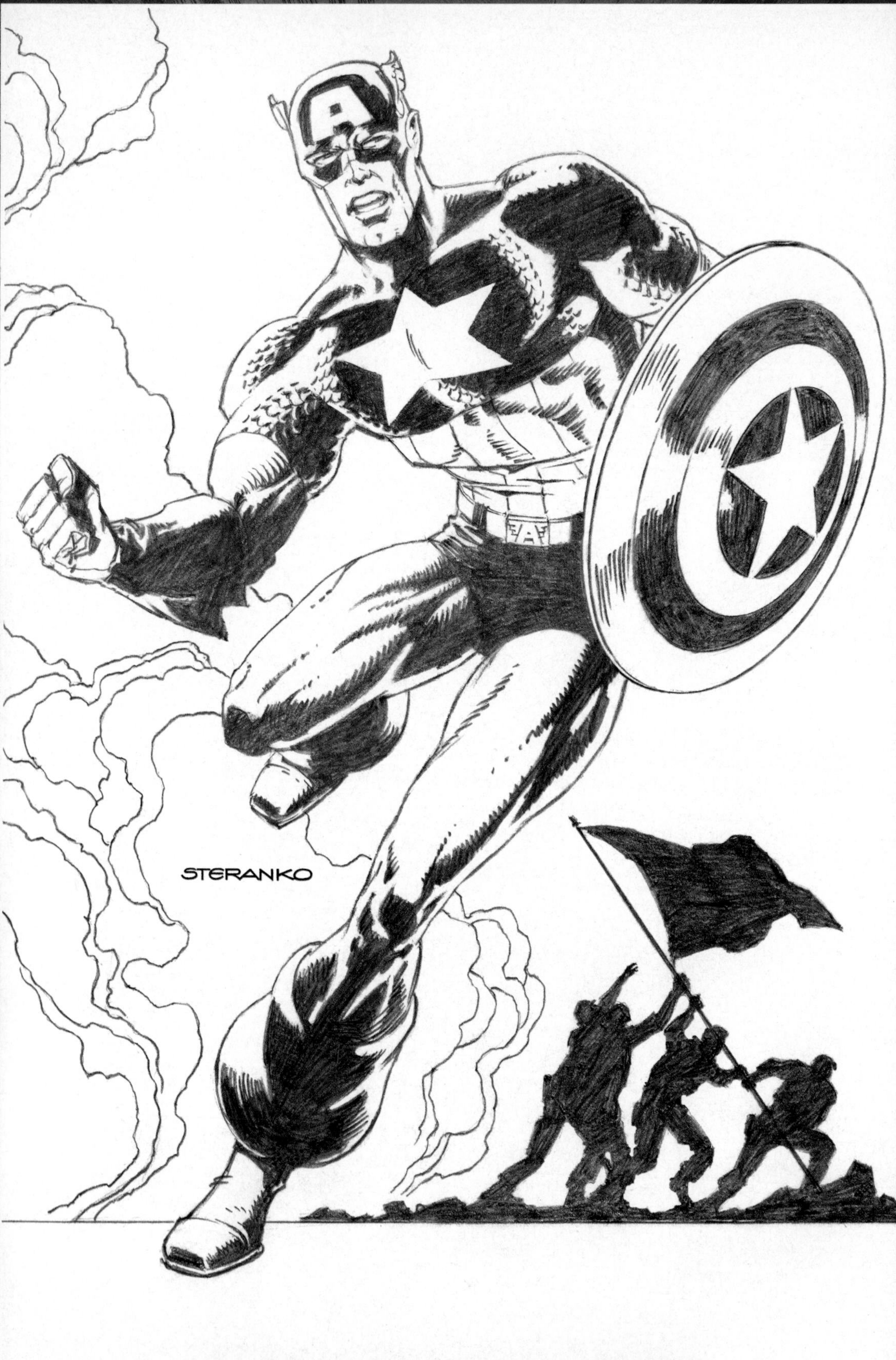
STERANKO

#11 CAPTAIN AMERICA BLACK AND WHITE
VARIANT BY JIM STERANKO

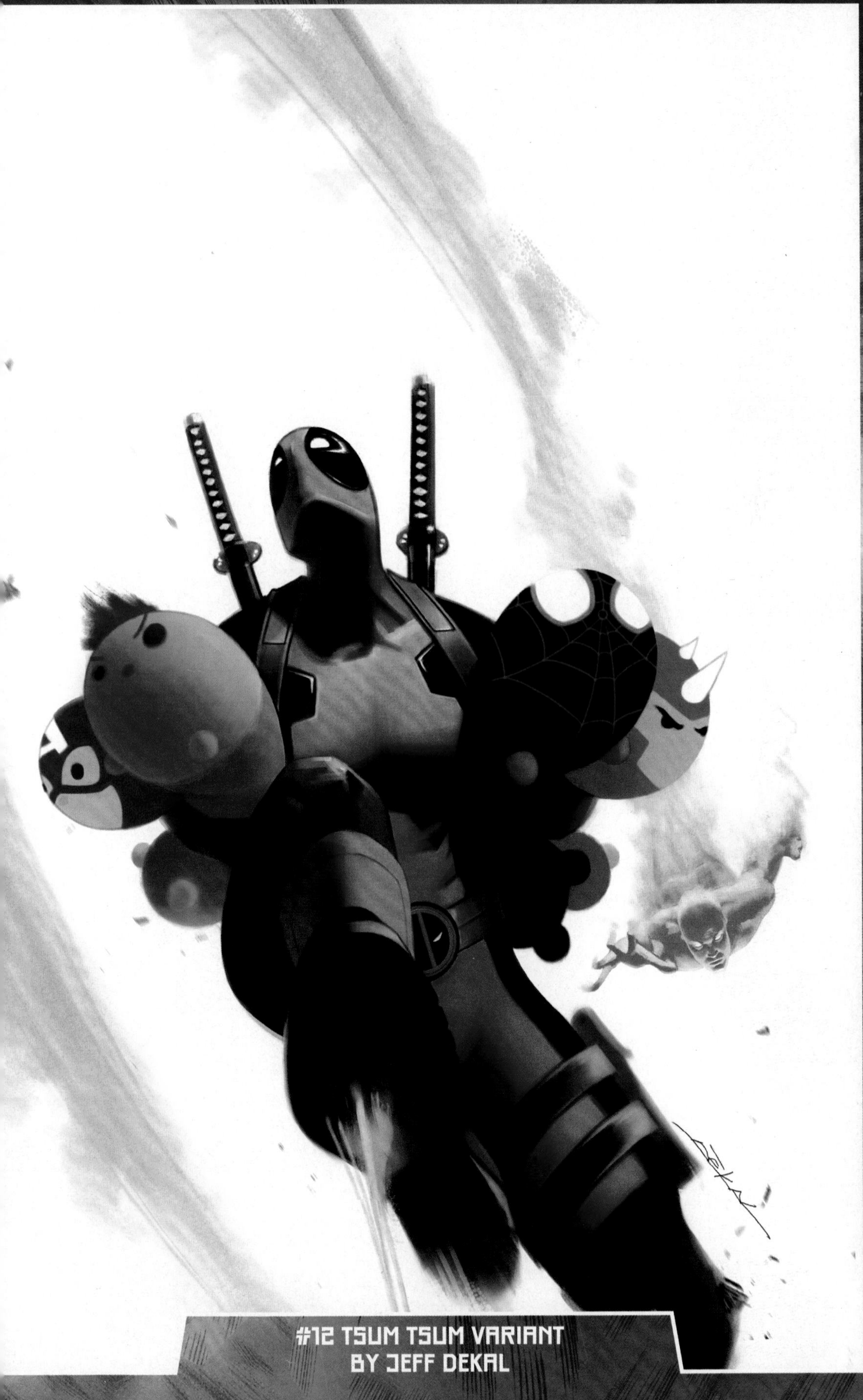

#12 TSUM TSUM VARIANT
BY JEFF DEKAL